SAVING INTERNATIONAL ADOPTION

SAVING
INTERNATIONAL
ADOPTION

AN ARGUMENT FROM ECONOMICS AND PERSONAL EXPERIENCE

MARK MONTGOMERY
and
IRENE POWELL

Vanderbilt University Press
Nashville

© 2018 by Vanderbilt University Press
Nashville, Tennessee 37235
All rights reserved
First printing 2018

This book is printed on acid-free paper.
Manufactured in the United States of America

Library of Congress Cataloging-in-Publication Data on file
LC control number 2017005438 (print) | 2017037251 (ebook)
LC classification number HV875.5 .M66 2017
Dewey classification number 362.734—dc23
LC record available at *lccn.loc.gov/2017005438*

ISBN 978-0-8265-2172-9 (hardcover)
ISBN 978-0-8265-2174-3 (ebook)

For Kurt, Gibrila, and Isata.

CONTENTS

PREFACE

Isata

In 2001, seven-year-old Isata was placed in an orphanage in Freetown, Sierra Leone, by the people she thought were her parents—although later she would be told otherwise.[1] One day, after about a year in the orphanage, Director Diane called Isata into her office to explain that Isata would be going to America. Another little girl, three-year-old Sia, would go with her and would now be her sister. Isata burst into tears. "I already have a sister," she told Diane. A few days later, the staff dressed Isata up and did her hair. She first took a scary helicopter ride to the Freetown airport, then a plane to Senegal. Near midnight in the air terminal in Dakar, the two exhausted girls met the white man, Jason Sibley, who would be their new father. Later that day, they had lunch with Jason, who "seemed pretty nice." The next day, the two girls left with this man on a long, long plane ride. Isata was suffering from typhoid fever and slept almost the entire way from Senegal to Portland, Oregon.

Eventually they got off the plane in America, where their new father told them they would now meet their new mother. Their mother was a tall woman with pale skin and reddish hair, and as soon as she saw the two little girls she started crying. "She doesn't like us," Isata thought.

Isata and Sia spoke Krio, a pidgin of English that is the lingua franca of Sierra Leone. During the first few days in Redmond, Oregon, where Jason and Beckie Sibley lived with their two new daughters and an adopted American son, Isata absorbed as much as she could of the language she heard. After a week or so she knew enough to tell her adopted parents the thing she most desperately wanted to say to them. She looked at the adoption papers with Beckie and pointed to the name written right after "Isata."

"That not my name," she said. The adoption papers gave the wrong last name she told them.

As Isata's Krio gave way to English, she told Beckie and Jason that she already had a mother and a father, plus three brothers and a sister in Sierra Leone. She could not understand why she'd been "given away." But the orphanage had told Beckie that Isata's parents were killed in the war and that the child had been placed in the orphanage by relatives. No honey, Beckie told Isata, those people you remember were your aunt and uncle, not your mom and dad. Isata insisted that this wasn't true. She still had a mother and father. It broke Beckie's heart that her daughter was so traumatized by loss that she'd had to reconstruct her own memories to make them bearable. In an interview years later, Isata told us that "at some point I even began to believe they were my aunt and uncle."

Until she found out she had been right all along—ten years later when her birth family found her on Facebook. So, what was the true story of Isata's placement in the Freetown orphanage?

BETWEEN CHAPTERS THROUGHOUT this book we will use the story of Isata Sibley to illustrate some of the problems with, as well as the benefits of, international adoption. In telling this story, we are able to get the viewpoints of the child herself, the adoptive family, the birth family, and even the adoption facilitators who arranged her placement with the Sibleys. Some names have been modified to protect people's privacy. The problems illustrated by Isata's story, among other factors, are contributing to a steep decline in the number of orphaned and vulnerable children who find permanent homes with American and European families. Between 2004 and 2013, the number of children adopted internationally fell from more than forty-five thousand to twenty thousand.[2] This book is an attempt to explain why this has happened and whether anything can be done about it. Isata's story will help illustrate our view that the issues causing the implosion of international adoption are not inevitable. Instead, they are largely artifacts of the way the international adoption system is organized and regulated. As we shall argue, a different type of system—and an example of such a system exists—could avoid many of these difficulties.

How We Came to Write about International Adoption

We did not intend to write this book; it kind of slipped out, you might say. In fact, it feels strange to have written any book, as our careers have been mostly about crunching numbers. In any case, we set out to write a different book, not a book about international adoption, but a book that explored our family's links to Africa. The connections were several. In 1963, when Irene—hereafter called Tinker, as she has been since birth—was eight years old, her family spent time at Cuttington College in Liberia, at that time the only liberal arts college on the continent.[3] Her father went to Cuttington on a Ford Foundation grant to help the college develop its business and economics program. Tinker, her mother, and two older brothers had to return home mid-year when it appeared that her mother was pregnant. (Tragically, the pregnancy was misdiagnosed—she died from colon cancer within a year.) The first Liberian Civil War (1989–1996) mostly destroyed Cuttington's campus and spread into Sierra Leone in 1991, ostensibly making the boy who would become our youngest son, Gibrila—everyone calls him GB—an orphan. And these disparate African connections drew our oldest child, birth daughter Mary, to Rwanda after she graduated from college in 2007. She first taught at a girls' middle school run by an American foundation, then was employed by the Akela Foundation to help train women to enter the tourist industry, and now teaches school in Kigali.

As economists, we were aware, of course, that development in sub-Saharan Africa seemed to have utterly stalled. In Iowa, Tinker taught her Economics of Developing Countries students that many African countries are as poor today as when the colonials finally left, over half a century ago. Year after year, Mark showed his environmental economics students graphs of rising per-capita GDP, rising per-capita food consumption, rising per-capita sanitation, rising per-capita nearly everything. But while living standards were rising all around the world, Africa seemed to be stuck.

When we decided in 2000 to adopt for the second time—having had Mary in 1985 and then adopting an African American infant, Kurt, in 1991—Africa seemed a good place to find a child in need of a home. Besides the poverty and lack of development, it was then at the peak of the AIDS epidemic. We were astounded to discover that of some fifty sub-Saharan African countries, only three regularly released children for international adoption: Sierra Leone, Ethiopia, and Liberia. News stories abounded of African children losing both parents to AIDS, of grandmothers raising a dozen orphaned grandchildren, of young children living on the streets. Why weren't more of these kids coming to America? Everybody knows a family with an adopted Korean or Chinese child; where were the Africans? In the crass language of economics, the continent was bulging with excess "supply" of needy children; American couples were "demanding" adoptees from China and Guatemala to the tune of thousands of dollars per kid. Why weren't more children coming out of Africa? Pride and prejudice? That is, African pride about caring for its children, American prejudice against people with black skin? Surely both played some role. But how could adoption, even if it could only save a tiny fraction of them, bypass an entire continent overrun with orphans?[4] We began trying to sort out the riddle of African adoption—that is, the riddle of African *non*-adoption.

Our Own Journey to Adoption

For brevity, this preface presents a somewhat smooth and streamlined version of our two adoptions; Chapter 9 describes a road that was considerably bumpier logistically, morally, and emotionally. How did we construct our family? Mary was born to us in 1985. If there was some moment when we decided that our second child would be adopted, we don't remember when that was. We were brought to that decision gradually by a combination of factors. Mark was teaching environmental economics and had entered his (short-lived) neo-Malthusian period; he felt squeamish about expanding the world population. Tinker's pregnancy with Mary was grueling. In any case, we wanted more children and many children need homes; this seemed an excellent coincidence of self-interest with very small-scale social justice.

We opted for an infant because we had already raised one; Mary was almost six, so we felt that a baby wouldn't test us beyond our limits as parents. We had no interest in a white infant. Most healthy white infants, like the baby in the movie *Juno*, have middle-class white couples clamoring to adopt them almost from the moment of conception, so a kid like that didn't need us to join the queue. Moreover, we could presumably have produced another one of those white babies on our own. But there is a loophole in the Law of Demand for Healthy Infants: black and biracial babies, especially boys, are not so highly prized by white couples. At the time, we were working with the Holt Agency, which suggested we consider an African American or biracial baby, and (in this streamlined version of our story) we simply agreed. We had a referral almost immediately.

The director of a children's home in Rwanda told us in an interview that transracial adoption is ultimately a form of self-promotion: white people showing the world how enlightened they are by embracing children of other races. And some critics of international adoption (IA) say that couples who adopt children from poor countries are merely indulging a "savior complex." In any case, whatever delusions of minor sainthood we may have entertained at the beginning of the adoption process, the search for a child quickly crushed them. Instead it made us feel guilty and selfish. We had to choose not to adopt so many children, and to choose one needy child over another—choices that were emotionally difficult.

At the end of the process, we traveled to another state to get Kurt. The night before we picked him up, we both lay awake in a hotel room, each having anxious thoughts that we did not share with the other until much later.

> **Mark:** I was wondering what this kid would even look like. I tried to picture myself in twenty years, standing next to a tall black man, my son, smiling into a camera at some family event. Would I love my new son as intensely as I loved Mary? Of course I would. Wouldn't I?

Tinker's thoughts on this subject were deeper and more complex.

> **Tinker:** First, I was thinking that we had really gotten ourselves into something this time. We were now really entering the world of black people in America. I imagined that whatever hardships black people endured, our son would endure them, and so would we, vicariously through him. This was absurdly naïve, of course—white parents of black children don't "enter the world of black people" in anything like the way their kids do. Some academic race theorists would say that I was suddenly having to acknowledge my "white privilege" and confront my own implicit racism. And I must admit that they'd be right.
>
> My second fear was that I wouldn't love my new son as much as I loved my daughter. This had nothing to do with race, just genetics, or "blood." Everybody seems to privilege genetic kinship over other relationships. In our society, it seems axiomatic that the bond between "birth mother" and "birth child" is primal, indissoluble, an inherent part of human physiology. The adoption literature, for example, is rife with this sentiment. By extension, therefore, the bond between an adoptive mother and her child is not like that. Presumably, it can't be—biology won't permit it. I had the experience to know what parenting requires—it certainly requires a lot of love—and I knew I would have enough love for my son. But might there always be some tiny, lingering gap between what I felt for my new son and what I felt for Mary?

Any adoptive parent will tell you that the fear of not loving your child enough is normal, and that it lasts exactly as long as it takes for your new child to be placed in your arms. And when we held Kurt for the first time the next morning, we felt exactly as we had the first time we held Mary. So that was that. We brought Kurt

TABLE 1. Children of Mark Montgomery and Tinker Powell, Grinnell, Iowa

	Born	Birthplace	Adopted
Mary Montgomery Powell	1985	Massachusetts	
Kurt Powell Montgomery	1991	Texas	1991
Gibrila (GB) Kamara Montgomery *Half-brother of Sia Sibley*	1995	Sierra Leone	2002

home the following night. Coming in from the car, we saw the Iowa sky flashing and shimmering with all sorts of colors. The aurora borealis was visible for the first time that anyone around here could remember, and we felt it marked something, even though we don't attach spiritual meaning to things.

Kurt was about nine when we considered a second adoption, and his demographic preferences were unambiguous: "I want a brown brother." This was entirely compatible with our parental goal to get an African boy who wasn't an infant. Older children are harder to place in adoption than infants, and we felt more confident now about handling an older child. We wanted a boy eight or younger, because our research warned us not to alter the birth order in our family. (Unfortunately, the research did *not* warn us about altering the birth order from the adopted child's family of *origin*. GB was the oldest in his birth family, and this caused a power struggle between the boys that we hadn't anticipated.)

At the time, one of the few African countries releasing children for adoption was Sierra Leone, on the continent's west coast. In 2001, the country was just emerging from a civil war fought over "blood diamonds." Online we located an American organization based in Freetown, The Children's Home (TCH, as we shall call it).[5] As we were told, six-year-old GB and a younger cousin, Sia (the aforementioned Isata's new sister), had been placed in their custody by his aunt, who had an infant and could no longer support the two older children, especially as her current husband was not genetically related to either child. Court documents said GB's aunt had taken him in after his parents, fleeing south from Makeni, had been caught en route and killed by the rebels. (We would discover while researching this book in 2014 that this aunt was actually his birth mother.) The "aunt," the current husband, and the three children had been living in an unfinished house with other homeless people in Freetown. A few years later, our daughter visited that house in search of the "aunt," but she was no longer there.

It took about a year to get GB to America. Among other complications, the consular officer at the US embassy in Dakar, Senegal, processed visa applications quite slowly, if at all, because, we were told, she was deeply suspicious of international adoption. This was our first illustration of the power of a single bureaucrat, for good or ill, to disrupt all adoptions from a given country. It would not be our last.

Economics and Adoption

This book applies a market perspective to something you should *never* apply a market perspective to: the adoption of vulnerable children. At least, according to the conventional view. As Ethan B. Kapstein writes in *Foreign Affairs*, "A free market for babies is out of the question: while infants can fetch a high price, they are not, and should never be treated as, commodities."[6] So, arguably, the focus on markets that our PhDs in economics have given us as authors makes us not merely *un*qualified to talk about adoption, but positively *dis*qualified.

But even critics of international adoption recognize that the forces of supply and demand are effectively turning the system into a (for them) much-dreaded market for children.[7] Because such a market is so repugnant, sometimes their general impulse is to shut it down. Better to regulate international adoption out of existence than to permit the surreptitious buying and selling of children. One of the main arguments of this book, however, is that this view denies very poor families the opportunity to remove their children from a life of poverty and to obtain resources that would mitigate their own poverty. Doesn't it make more sense to acknowledge the influence of market forces, that some children (or their parental rights) are, in effect, bought and sold and to accept this—thereby, incidentally, permitting more effective regulation—than to axiomatically reject the idea? We propose that the market forces in adoption should be acknowledged, accepted, and monitored, rather than suppressed.

We have no illusions that this book can alter international adoption policy, especially with a viewpoint so orthogonal to the mainstream. Our hope is merely that it might challenge some of the regulation-focused, anti-market orthodoxy that is almost universal among adoption professionals.

ACKNOWLEDGMENTS

We are grateful to so many people for help and support in writing this book. First and foremost, we thank our friend and colleague Ralph Savarese. As an English professor, author, and teacher of nonfiction writing, he was the godfather of this effort. He read multiple drafts and made valuable suggestions about style, tone, content, organization, and publishing.

Donna Vinter, Kevin Montgomery, and Heather Lobban-Viravong read early parts of the manuscript and provided valuable help and encouragement. We thank Grinnell College for its generous financial support of our research. Kesho Scott, colleague and friend, was unusually generous in providing us with information, suggestions, and contacts in Ethiopia. We are grateful to Michael Ames of Vanderbilt University Press for believing in this project and to two anonymous reviewers whose suggestions greatly improved this book.

A number of experts helped us become more familiar with the world of adoption. These include Elizabeth Bartholet, professor of law at Harvard University; Marijke Bruening, professor of political science at the University of North Texas; Thomas DeFilipo, then-president of the Joint Council on International Children's Services; author Melissa Faye Greene; Dr. Dana E. Johnson, professor of Pediatric Neonatology and cofounder of the International Adoption Clinic at the University of Minnesota; Diane B. Kunz, executive director of the Center for Adoption Policy; Dan Lauer of Holt International; John Lowell, former general consul at the US embassy in Guatemala City, Guatemala; Peter Selman, Visiting Fellow, School of Geography, Politics & Sociology, Newcastle University; David M. Smolin, professor, Cumberland School of Law, Samford University; and Kathleen Strottman, Congressional Coalition on Adoption Institute.

We want to thank the directors and other personnel of numerous orphanages in Sierra Leone, Rwanda, Uganda, and Ethiopia for allowing us to tour their facilities and for answering our many questions. Most of these facilities are not now placing children for adoption, some have never done so, but all are doing a difficult, much-needed service for poor and vulnerable children in Africa.

Most importantly, we are grateful to those individuals, birth parents, adoptees, and adoptive parents, who graciously allowed us to tell their personal stories in print. We are profoundly thankful to the M. family, especially Shaun, for telling us the story of Isata's adoption. We thank Diane of The Children's Home for answering our e-mail queries about Isata's history. This book would have been much poorer without the generosity of Isata Sibley and her parents, Jason and Beckie, in relating the tale of Isata's journey.

Please forgive us for any omissions. All remaining errors are ours.

Finally, much love and gratitude to our beloved sons Kurt Powell Montgomery and Gibrila Kamara Montgomery for letting us relate their experiences of growing up in our family and for continuing to let us share their lives. Special thanks to S., Gibrila's first mom, and to Kurt's birth parents for sending these precious boys to us.

Why Is International Adoption Collapsing?

Child trafficking is the fastest growing organized crime in the globe and so the use of the word of inter country adoption was just a false piece of sticky plaster over a very evil thing indeed.

Baroness Emma Nicholson, Rapporteur for
Romanian Accession to EU Membership[1]

The compound of the Office of the Prime Minister of Rwanda was a tidy arrangement of low brick buildings surrounded by a high wall and guarded by soldiers in navy blue fatigues. In fact, the whole city of Kigali is noticeably tidy. Rwanda has a tradition, called *umuganda* in Kinyarwandan, that on one Saturday each month citizens pitch in on public service tasks like cleaning streets of trash and tending flower beds in parks.[2] This tradition of neighborhood work teams, which dates back in various forms to precolonial times, helps foster a sense of community in a country still recovering from horrific interethnic violence. Sadly, however, *umuganda* may have also indirectly facilitated that violence. When the plane of President Juvénal Habyarimana, an ethnic Hutu, was shot down on April 6, 1994, the (mostly Hutu) government launched the systematic massacre of more than eight hundred thousand of its (mostly Tutsi) citizens over a period of three months.[3] Machetes had been previously stockpiled. It was merely a matter of distributing them to the local work teams and setting the Hutus to killing their Tutsi neighbors and moderate Hutus who wouldn't cooperate. Partly because of such efficiency, in some parts of Rwanda the massacre had the highest killing rate, in deaths per day, of any genocide in recorded history.[4]

The meeting between Mark and Mr. Nzaramba, the assistant to the minister of Gender and Family Promotion, in the summer of 2011 was granted as a favor to our daughter who lives in Kigali and happened to be acquainted with the minister, Aloisea Inyumba.[5] (Though it has a million people, Kigali can feel like a small midwestern town.)

Mr. Nzaramba was a slight man, wearing a jacket, no tie, with his shirt buttoned all the way up. Nothing in his diffident, soft-spoken manner would make you suspect that this person could write, read, and speak six languages, including English, French, and Latin (as we found out later). He came into his office with an armful of black, three-ring binders full of dossiers of foreign families wanting to adopt. He placed them on his desk, as if to demonstrate that his ministry did indeed consider such applications. From what we had heard from our daughter about the attitude of his boss, the minister, Mark was doubtful. Mr. Nzaramba proceeded to explain politely that adoption by foreigners would be considered only after all other options for placing a Rwandan child in Rwanda had failed. First, the ministry would try to reunite a child with her birth family, next it would try to place her permanently with a Rwandan family, and third, it would try to place her temporarily in a Rwandan foster home. Only failing all these options would international adoption be considered.

This struck Mark as very strange. Why, he wanted to ask Mr. Nzaramba, would Rwanda not welcome international adoption? It's true that after the genocide the Rwandan government called upon its citizens to take in parentless children—many responded. But Rwanda remained a poor country, with thousands of orphaned children, and caring for orphans is a burden on the government. American families could relieve some of that burden. More importantly, hundreds of these children were currently stuck in institutions, and institutionalization is widely understood to be bad for child development.[6] Why would keeping them in Rwanda matter more than getting them as quickly as possible into a permanent family? Perhaps the mystification reflected our mainstream economists' theoretical bias—that is, our tendency to expect economically rational agents to make decisions based on simple comparisons of costs and benefits. In any case, Mark decided not to press Mr. Nzaramba. In describing this hierarchy of priorities for placing orphaned children, he was likely espousing the ministry's boilerplate adoption policy and was unlikely to be more forthcoming. So, after a very few minutes Mark stood up, shook his hand, and thanked him for his time. Before Mark reached the door, Mr. Nzaramba stopped him.

"Let me ask you something," he said. "Why do Americans want to adopt these children?" Mark had to stop and think. *How am I going to answer that question?*

"Foreign Adoptions Hit Three-Decade Low"
Wall Street Journal, April 1, 2015

On December 21, 2001, the then US Immigration and Naturalization Service (INS) stopped processing all visa applications for children being adopted from Cambodia. Commissioner James W. Ziglar declared that INS would never sanction "any action that results in the exploitation of innocent children by separating them from their biological families as a result of fraud, trafficking in human beings or other criminal activity."[7] Within two years of the closing of Cambodia as a source of children, adoption exploded in Guatemala. By one estimate, in 2007, one out of every one hundred babies born alive in Guatemala was placed for adoption.[8] But the frenzy was short-lived. In January of 2008 the *New York Times* reported that "4,000 Americans... found themselves stuck in limbo when Guatemala shut down its international adoption program... amid mounting evidence of corruption and child trafficking."[9] Three months later, Vietnam also suspended adoptions by Americans after a US embassy report accused local officials and orphanages of "bargain[ing] among US adoption agencies to gain the highest price for their babies" and claiming that some babies were taken without the mother's consent.[10]

With Vietnam and Guatemala out of the picture, adoption fever swept into Ethiopia. The number of adoption agencies in Ethiopia increased from a handful in the 1990s to more than seventy in 2011.[11] The number of orphans coming to America from that country "skyrocketed from fewer than 900 in 2003 to 4,564 in 2009."[12] Then history re-repeated itself. The government (and UNICEF) announced a 90 percent slowdown in the number of adoptions being processed.[13] In December 2013, the Speaker of Ethiopia's House of Peoples' Representatives and the minister of Women, Children and Youth urged "the public to undertake integrated work to totally stop adoption of Ethiopian children by foreign families."[14] Most recently, a suspension of all adoptions was announced at the beginning of May 2017.[15]

As Kathryn Joyce, author of *The Child Catchers: Rescue, Trafficking, and the New Gospel of Adoption*, puts it, "International adoption tends to work in this boom-bust cycle... one country closes, and another country becomes this popular hotspot."[16] Typically, when a country grants American and European

FIGURE 1. Adoptions to U.S. from selected countries 1999–2014

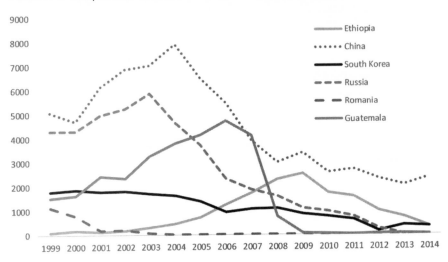

Source: Author calculations from U.S. Department of State data

families access to its "orphans"—which prospective adoptees often are not—placement for adoption expands rapidly until, within a couple of years, the press starts getting reports of scandals, often called child trafficking, and the system implodes.

It takes only a few minutes of research to discover that international adoption, from pretty much everywhere in the world, is in a state of collapse. As mentioned, according to Peter Selman international adoptions fell from a peak of more than forty-five thousand in 2004 to fewer than twenty thousand in 2013.[17] The graph in Figure 1 shows that adoption to the United States from the leading sending countries is currently falling, in some cases quite sharply. Why is this happening? In researching this book, we were surprised to find that the whole concept of adoption across cultures, and especially across races, has quite vigorous opponents. To see how much animosity adoption provokes, we suggest an easily implemented, if profoundly unscientific, research methodology: type "anti-adoption" into a search engine. Google gives more than seventy-two million hits. Not all of those are about international adoption—we admitted it was unscientific—but seventy-two million websites is a lot of "anti" anything.

The antagonists come from many walks of international adoption, so to speak. There are vocal opponents like some adult adoptees, some birth mothers, even some adoptive parents, and of course many academics.[18] These people write books and articles, talk at conferences, and write blog entries reporting the hurt and anguish caused by transnational adoption and the corruption they see as endemic to it. There are also quiet opponents, like UNICEF. In 2003, a report from UNICEF stated, "Today, over 11 million children under the age of 15 living in sub-Saharan Africa have been robbed of one or both parents by HIV/AIDS. Seven years from now, the number is expected to have grown to 20 million."[19] It would seem to follow, therefore, that over the ensuing seven years UNICEF would have been an avid supporter of international adoption. Quite the opposite, however. International adoption advocate Elizabeth Bartholet states that "UNICEF has over recent years been a major force driving down the numbers of international adoptions worldwide."[20] Officially, UNICEF approves of international adoption, but virtually every adoption professional we have asked confirms that the organization consistently acts to undermine it.[21] Then there are government officials who won't publically denounce adoption, but who can disrupt the process in the course of their work, whether deliberately or not. There are several places along the adoption pipeline where a single bureaucrat can close a single valve and put a potentially adoptable child in limbo temporarily or forever. For example, in 2002, while we waited for our son Gibrila to come from Sierra Leone, we were told that one official in Dakar, Senegal, where visa applications were processed, was simply opposed to international adoption, so our adoption might have to wait until she was reposted elsewhere.

That intercountry adoption is a lightning rod for criticism is illustrated by the cases of two women whose privacy we will protect by using only their first names: Madonna and Angelina. Their adoptions of African children caused a huge uproar primarily because each child had a living parent, though this parent had left the child in an orphanage. These adoptions got lambasted in the press, criticized by some adoption experts, and were even accused of "ripping the heart out of Africa," by supermodel Tasha de Vasconcelos.[22]

Why such hostility to what seem to be acts of compassion? Law professor David Smolin, a well-known critic of IA, explained the problem to the *New York Times*: "Celebrity adoptions highlight in extreme form the problems of the international adoption system: 'orphans' often turn out to have immediate and extended families, laws are circumvented, money corrupts, facts are elusive, powerful adoptive parents and their agents overwhelm vulnerable birth families and the desire of comparatively wealthy Western people for children drives adoptions."[23] That does indeed sound bad. But isn't the ultimate issue whether someone is actually being harmed by an international adoption? Sometimes innocent people are truly hurt: the Smolin family was shocked to discover that their adopted daughters were "basically" stolen from their birth mother in India.[24] But other times the victims are less obvious, as when very poor families in Romania relinquished their children in exchange for payment. Are these both cases of "child trafficking," as they are often called? Does either justify shutting down international adoption?

Having adopted twice ourselves—domestically, internationally and (both times) transracially—we disagree with the critics of international adoption. But we understand and respect much of their critique. We believe, however, that IA can save the lives of hundreds of children and improve the lives of thousands more. Moreover, it can help America, even if only a little bit. In malls and in restaurants and just out on the street, the multiracial, international family visually demonstrates the possibility of loving someone of another race and culture. Our society has finally come to accept interracial love of the romantic sort, but adoption shows a love that resides on another plane: the desire of a parent to care for a child.[25]

In its current form, there are some serious deficiencies in international adoption that should be addressed, and we will propose some simple and possibly counterintuitive ways to address them. But our main problem with international adoption is this: there isn't enough of it. By UNICEF estimates, in 2010 more than fifty million children in sub-Saharan Africa had lost at least one parent, over ten million had lost both.[26] This was before the Ebola crisis. According to NPR, by December of 2014, that virus had created two thousand orphans in Liberia alone.[27] And while not all orphaned children need adoption, because often extended family can care for them, there can be little doubt that many would have a better chance at life with adopted parents than with no parents at all. Some critics point out that adoption can only help tens of thousands of children, but that's still a lot of lives.

The Benefits of International Adoption

Economists tend to look at things by comparing the costs with the benefits. We argue, for example, that before we outlaw, or impose strict regulations upon, some economic activity (e.g., international adoption) we should carefully consider the benefits and costs of that activity. We cannot do this for international adoption using formal and quantitative methods. But even a cursory review of the literature about international adoption shows that it makes much more of its costs than its benefits. For example, the anti-adoption literature directs disapproval at the supposed self-congratulation of affluent, white, Western adopters who think they're "rescuing" orphans from a horrible fate.[28] Fair enough—that rescue/horrible fate scenario should not be accepted without close examination of the *costs* to these children from adoption and the Western bias of the "horrible fate" assumption. But then must we not also acknowledge what adoption can so obviously do for vulnerable children?

The movement to oppose or limit international adoption also tends to focus on the pain and bereavement of families whose children are taken by westerners. E. J. Graff of Brandeis University has said that "Madonna is showing exactly what *shouldn't* be done: airlifting one or two pretty children into the comparative wealth of the West, leaving behind bereft families who want—but can't afford—to bring that child home."[29] Implicit in this statement is the assumption that families only lose when their children are adopted abroad. But many families are eager to have their children grow up in a developed country, even when that requires emotional sacrifice on their part. We once got a letter addressed to "Muhammad's American Family" from a mother in Sierra Leone whose twelve-year-old son we had been sponsoring.[30] "He's ready to come to you whenever you can take him." We didn't bring Muhammad to America. As we will discuss later, we feel significant guilt and moral discomfort over some adoption decisions we have made, but the feelings are about the children we *didn't* adopt, not the two that we did.

Objection 1: International Adoption Deprives Children of Their Birth Culture

What Mr. Nzaramba, assistant to the minister of Gender and Family Promotion, had said to Mark at the ministry in Kigali, that international adoption is only considered after other options had been exhausted, was an informal statement of what is called the "Subsidiarity Principle." We would see this repeated in countless books, articles, and news accounts about international adoption. In fact, it's the central concept of adoption expressed in the United Nation's 1990 Convention on the Rights of the Child (CRC). Simply put, the principle says this: giving a child to a foreign family is acceptable only as a *last resort*. In other words, every option for caring for a child in her own country must be exhausted before she can be adopted abroad. In the language of the CRC, therefore, a home country may decide an orphanage is better than a foreign family. The 1993 Hague Convention on the Protection of Children and Co-operation in Respect of Intercountry Adoption (Hague Convention) would later temper this preference, saying foreign families are better than institutions. But in *practice* this still leaves many a child waiting in an orphanage for a local placement instead of being declared eligible for foreign adoption.

The Subsidiarity Principle is affirmed time and again. At a meeting in Addis Ababa, Ethiopia, in May of 2012, for example, the African Child Policy Forum (AFPC) decided that international adoption of African children "must at all costs be discouraged." In a press statement, AFPC executive director David Mugawe said, "It should be a last resort and an exception rather than the normal recourse.... Every child should have an inalienable right to be nurtured and reared in the country and culture in which they are born."[31]

Some opposition to international adoption is based on this assertion: that IA denies children their right to a "birth culture." In this view, there is something congenital, even genetic, about culture; therefore, transnational adoption alienates a child from his or hers. In this view, a child raised outside her own culture (or her own race) will always feel peripheral in some way.

Our book does not dismiss the problem of adopted children feeling alienated—we have observed it in our own living room. But we challenge it as a reason to oppose intercountry adoption. We have two points to make. First, we argue that complaints about children losing their culture are more complaints about cultures losing their children. That is to say, when children are adopted out of a country or out of an ethnic group, it's the *adults* who feel harmed, more than the kids. Sometimes this is explicit and reasonable, as when small Native American tribes face the genuine risk of cultural extinction. But other times it seems more a matter of national embarrassment. Several examples demonstrate countries' willingness to promote a national political agenda using international adoption, without considering children's well-being. In Chapter 2 we will discuss several examples wherein an apparent attempt to protect children's well-being was in fact a stalking horse for some other national political agenda.

Objection 2: Transracial Adoption Is Bad for Children

Our second point about the "birth culture" argument against international adoption is that it isn't really about culture at all. Researching this book suggested that when antagonists of international adoption discuss "culture" they usually mean "race." For example, in *Culture Keeping*, her book about how American adoptive parents try to maintain their children's ethnic heritage, Heather Jacobson reports that culture keeping is much more common among adopters of Chinese children than of Russian children because the latter visually appear to be part of the adoptive family while the former clearly do not.[32] Few commentators complain that Russian children will lose touch with their Slavic roots.[33] But much more is written about what a Korean, Guatemalan, or Ethiopian child will experience about differences between herself and her white family and/or community based on appearance. This is a serious issue. Moreover, the history of intercountry adoption cannot be understood without reference to race.

The historical relationship between race and adoption is always troubling, and sometimes tragic. For example, the first large-scale international adoption program was a brutal effort to bolster the Aryan "race." Nazi doctors scoured the conquered areas of Eastern Europe for racially acceptable children, often kidnapping them from their parents so they could be adopted back in Germany.[34] Or consider the prevailing practice in early postwar America to make adoption "invisible," matching physical appearance between child and family so closely that the adoptive placement would "erase itself." It was boldly innovative, therefore, when in the 1950s the US government launched the first-ever attempt to deliberately create interracial families via the Indian Adoption Project.[35] Yet by the 1970s, that program would trigger an angry backlash that precipitated congressional action.[36] The growth of the adoption of black children by whites led to a similar reaction in the 1970s by the National Association of Black Social Workers that placing black children in white families was a form of "cultural genocide."[37] Thus, the historical interaction between race and adoption explains the long and continuing battle fought by interracial adoption to gain social acceptance—even within the adoption community.

For the authors, race is not an academic issue, but one we *had* to consider in expanding our family through adoption.[38] We live in Iowa, a state not noted for its ethnic diversity. Because it has a liberal arts college, the small town we live in is far more racially diverse than might be expected, as we have students and others from all over the world. Nevertheless, our two adopted sons composed a significant fraction of the African Americans in the local school system. Growing up, they have been quite limited in the number of people of color, especially black people, they might have in their circle of friends. Was it fair of us to raise them in the Caucasian heartland of this country? We had considered this question before we adopted, but now this book takes a closer look.

Ultimately, however, the question of whether interracial adoption harms children must be settled empirically. And here there remains great controversy. For example, the editors of *Outsiders Within: Writing on Transracial Adoption*, say that "our experiences of racism, isolation, and abuse and our struggles with depression, addiction, and alienation indicate that adoption across boundaries of race, nation, culture does indeed exact a very real emotional and spiritual cost."[39] Contrast this with *The Case for Transracial Adoption*, by Simon, Altstein, and Melli, who state that while statistical evidence supports transracial adoption, "the case *against* transracial adoption is built primarily on rhetoric... There is no empirical or scientific evidence that transracial adoption works against the best interests of the child."[40] The statistical analysis often conflicts with the self-reported emotional difficulties of some transracial adoptees. To reach a conclusion on this issue, we must review both the statistical analysis and the qualitative studies (personal stories, interviews, etc.) that represent the primary discourse on this subject and reconcile the two types of evidence.

Objection 3: International Adoption Is Too Commercial

Consider just a handful of recent news stories: "Buy, Sell, Adopt: Child Trafficking in China" (*New York Times*, December 26, 2012); "Mexico Adoption Bust Reveals Vast Child Trafficking Ring" (*Huffington Post*, February 29, 2012); "Ethiopia: US Adoption Agency Involved in Child Trafficking" (CBS News online, February 10, 2011). We could easily fill several pages with these headlines.[41] David Smolin has said that "the [intercountry] adoption system has become so intertwined with market behavior as to, in theory and practice, frequently permit child selling as a form of adoption."[42]

Money, markets, profit-seeking: these are the reasons that adoption was shut down in countries like Romania, Cambodia, Vietnam, and Guatemala. E. J. Graff writes, "Everyone but the prospective adoptive parents knew... that [Guatemala's] international adoption system was a cesspool of corruption and crime, and motivated by money."[43] In the *Harvard Political Review*, Gina Kim says, "With this enormous market, many opportunities exist for profit seekers. Promises of astronomical adoption fees... [cause] orphanages to resort to drastic measures, even occasionally paying kidnappers directly."[44] Most discussions of improper practices in adoption do not distinguish between types of, and harm created by, various forms of fraudulent actions. Often these discussions group all of these transgressions under the rubric "child trafficking for the purposes of international adoption." It is important to distinguish between types of irregular IA practices and analyze their causes and consequences to develop good public policy.

But is market behavior really the problem? Everyone thinks international adoption has become too commercial, but what if international adoption is *not commercial enough*? What if international adoption functioned *more* like an actual market, not less? Policy makers need to address that question.

The Best Interest of the Child: A Cautionary Tale

The Hague Convention on International Adoption states as its first object "to establish safeguards to ensure that intercountry adoptions take place in the *best interests of the child*" (emphasis added).[45] In a UNICEF research report titled *The Best Interests of the Child in Intercountry Adoption*, Nigel Cantwell states,

"Not only might it seem evident that this 'best interests' condition should be fulfilled, but there is also now an absolute obligation, anchored firmly in international human rights law, for the best interests of the child to be the 'paramount consideration'—the decisive factor—where adoption is concerned."[46] Nearly everything written about adoption—every law, every policy, every court decision, every op-ed piece—claims to be guided by this single principle: the best interest of the child. It is universally invoked in discussions of adoption.

But those who are deciding what is in a child's best interest, the policy makers, the judges, and the pundits, are not, of course, the children themselves. They are making pronouncements on someone else's behalf. It is worth pausing to consider a famous historical example of the danger in this type of thinking, that is, of deciding how best to protect someone else. In 1854, Virginian George Fitzhugh wrote that "Political Economy... is at war with all kinds of slavery, for [economists] in fact assert that individuals prosper when governed least."[47] His pamphlet, *The Sociology of the South; or, The Failure of Free Society*, was a notorious apology for Southern slavery.

His argument was not made on behalf of the white plantation owners, rather he specifically based his argument on concern that doing away with slavery would harm slaves. According to Fitzhugh, emancipation would bring about free competition, which "is quite as destructive to the weak, simple and guileless as the war of the sword."[48] Among the simple and guileless, of course, Fitzhugh counted those poor enslaved black people. "The negro race is inferior to the white race and living in their midst they would be far outstripped or outwitted in the chase of free competition. Gradual but certain extermination would be their fate."[49] So, said Fitzhugh, the simple-minded slave must be protected from the competition to which economists would like to expose them.

We mention Fitzhugh because in his piece one sees prototypes of arguments that still echo down into current discussions of international adoption. As we saw, for example, Fitzhugh made no attempt to defend slavery on behalf of the slaveholder. Quite the opposite; he supported slavery because, he argued, it was in the best interest of the *slave*.[50] And, as in Fitzhugh's pamphlet, in all arguments about adoption, the speaker is asserting what is in the best interest of *someone else*, namely the child. And because that someone *is* a child (or as Fitzhugh saw it, child*like*) she cannot be, or need not be, consulted. Fitzhugh's pamphlet reminds us that humans have a positive genius for persuading ourselves that we are, in fact, helping others even if those others don't quite see it that way. The makers of international adoption policy are generally not held accountable by their constituents, the children, any more than slave owners were held accountable by their slaves. We will argue that some of the rules touted to be in the best interest of the child, and of their birth families, are actually in the best interest of the people making the rules.

A second way in which Fitzhugh's treatise is relevant to international adoption is his insistence that people like illiterate slaves are incapable of succeeding in a free-market economy because, he asserts, they will be outwitted. No educated person would make that claim today, yet one still hears a similar sentiment in the regulations controlling international adoption. The primary international standard for regulating international adoption, the United Nation's Hague Convention, explicitly rules out compensating birth families for children adopted abroad. It directly states that placement must not be "induced by payment of any kind." Why? For one, it is argued that payment puts undue pressure on birth families, tempting them into transactions that will ultimately harm them. Johanna Oreskovic and Trish Maskew, for example, warn against "excessive reimbursement" for prenatal expenses (meaning payments beyond the actual expense) because "such payments can ... have substantial coercive effects; indeed, it is difficult analytically to view them as anything other than a legalized way to pay indigent families for their children."[51] Extremely poor birth families, presumably, may not be able to resist offers of compensation, that is, they will be outwitted by the rich, educated westerners who want to adopt their children. Hence offers of payment can actually harm them.

Economists generally regard this kind of view, that people must be protected from their own decisions, to reflect the paternalism that Fitzhugh showed toward slaves. *Why* must we ensure that payment doesn't persuade parents to relinquish a child with whom they would otherwise not have parted? If it does, should we assume they have been "outwitted" in the adoption market? Have they been swindled by carpet-bagging adopting parents? Is it immoral if they have been pressured by circumstances? On what moral grounds do we deny them the right to negotiate all aspects of the adoption exchange? We must address these questions.

A third and final way in which Fitzhugh's treatise is relevant to our book is his prediction about what social scientists call the "counterfactual" to slavery. The counterfactual is the situation that does not currently obtain, the "what if" outcome. For Fitzhugh that's the circumstance of the slave after emancipation, for an adoptee it's what would have happened had she remained in the birth family, or at least in the birth culture. But counterfactuals are unobservable by definition. Fitzhugh said that "at all events [slavery] is better than the tender mercies of an American mob [of angry whites] or an African cannibal, the Scylla and Charybdis which now threaten [the slave]."[52] We now know that he was simply wrong. Emancipation did not worsen the status of the slaves, much less exterminate them (though neither did it make their lives a bed of roses). How much better or worse off does transnational/transracial adoption make the adoptee? The answer must incorporate the appropriate counterfactuals, which much of the literature critiquing international adoption often fails to do.

We are not the first to draw a parallel between intercountry adoption and slavery, and we use this opportunity to address that analogy head on. According to some noted critics, the two practices share a number of unsavory characteristics. Tobias Hubinette, for example, identifies "striking similarities" between international adoption and the Atlantic slave trade.[53] Both are "driven by insatiable consumer demand, private market interests, and cynical profit making." Both use a "highly advanced system of pricing where the young, the healthy, and the light-skinned are the most valued." Finally, both the adopted and the enslaved are separated from their families and "stripped of their original cultures and languages; reborn at harbors and airports; Christianized, rebaptized, and bestowed with the names of their masters." In discussing Madonna's adoption of a boy from Malawi, Karen Finley wrote in the *Huffington Post* (October 13, 2006) that "the image of a white, powerful, rich woman and her entourage landing in Africa and selecting a black boy brings America's history of slavery and the middle passage to mind."

The comments of Hubinette and Finley show how extreme the rhetoric about international adoption can become and how powerful but misleading false analogies can be. Can adoption really be meaningfully compared to a voyage in a slave ship? While there may be "insatiable consumer demand" and "private market interest," adoption certainly doesn't materially enrich the buyer, as slavery once did. For middle class families, it's a huge financial sacrifice. Also, child labor laws protect adoptees from being exploited for work. Indeed, a number of African orphanage directors have told us that—ironically, in light of the Subsidiarity Principle—children placed with extended or local families are more likely to end up being treated as servants. Of course, Hubinette has a point that often, in adoption, "the light-skinned are the most valued." This is an indictment of our society's racial attitudes. But international adoption *creates* interracial families, people of different color in close and loving personal relationships. Suppressing international adoption seems to be a step *backward* in race relations, not a step forward.

Where Economic Rationality Fears to Tread

The final thing we want to say by way of introduction is that although this book tries to rely on economic logic and empirical evidence, it nevertheless invokes a nonrational "value judgment." Our value judgement is that our agenda does not treat everyone equally. Our primary concern is children, the vulnerable children in poor countries, particularly in Africa. Thus, the first priority is getting children out of, or preventing them from being sent to, orphanages and similar institutions and then, second, improving the lot of other vulnerable children. Our next concern is the well-being of the desperately poor families into which many of these children are born. And note that some critics think the international adoption system has devolved from "finding families for children" to "finding children for families." Without necessarily agreeing, we understand this view. We explicitly give a lower priority to the welfare of parents like ourselves, adopters or prospective adopters. We certainly don't dismiss the frustrations and heartache that adoptive couples can suffer, but we see the problems of middle/upper-middle-class potential adopters as of a different magnitude than those of the children and birth families struggling for survival.[54]

"Let Me Ask You Something"

Back in the office of Rwanda's assistant to the minister of Gender and Family Promotion: Mr. Nzaramba had just told Mark that Rwanda would place a child for international adoption only after all local possibilities had been exhausted. Mark had thanked him and turned to leave.

"Let me ask you something," he said. Mark turned back to him. "Why do Americans want to adopt these children?" His face showed genuine curiosity. He was apparently as mystified about our position on international adoption as Mark was about his. Was the antipathy of so many African governments toward adoption just some big cultural misunderstanding? Even for a man with as much cross-cultural knowledge as Mr. Nzaramba clearly had?

Mark paused. How would he answer that? Why did Americans want to raise Rwandans? Mark acknowledged that it was partly the plunge in the number of adoptable babies born in America. He hated saying that because he was implicitly admitting that Americans were coming to adopt young black children because our country was so short of young white ones. That felt awful to say, but there was so much truth in that answer; how could it not be spoken? Mark hurried on to cheerier topics. He waxed enthusiastic about how race relations were improving in America—he should have crossed his fingers—and how adoption from Africa was an example of that. Shushing his conscience, Mark invoked the magic words, the words that could melt even the iciest of anti-American hearts in Africa: "President Obama." He told Mr. Nzaramba something we both truly believe: that international adoption was a form of foreign aid. Not the regular kind of foreign aid where rich countries help poor countries, but the reverse. Bringing African children to America would make our country a better place. Maybe only a tiny bit better, but still better. Mark told him how our little Iowa town was slightly more aware of Africans, and the difficulties some Africans face, because of the Leonean boy who was now our son. And we were proud that GB could have that slight but genuine effect.

For the first time, Mr. Nzaramba smiled. He seemed genuinely moved by Mark's appeal, and he said something to the effect that all people were children of God and that's what mattered. Mark nodded and smiled, making no mention of our lack of religion, and Mr. Nzaramba and Mark parted on what we thought was a hopeful note. Four years have passed and, for the Rwandan government, international adoption remains a last resort, a last resort that is rarely resorted to. The country, a ratifier of the Hague Convention, rigidly adheres to the Subsidiarity Principle. According to Kathryn Joyce, "The rules are so strictly enforced [that] when one California couple wanted to adopt an older girl they had met in an orphanage, they were refused because the girl's mother, despite being committed to a mental institution, was still alive, meaning the daughter might have a chance to know her."[55] Benilde Uwababyeyi, the child protection officer for international adoption at the Ministry of Gender and Family Promotion says, "We want children to remain here in Rwanda, because we want them to be Rwandan. To stay in the Rwandan culture and learn Rwandan values."[56]

How This Book Is Organized

The theme of this book is that international adoption is in a state of near collapse and this collapse is precipitated mainly by the opposition of officials who govern the way it functions. This official opposition is supported in many cases by the attitude of some commentators in the press, some academics, and even some parents and adoptees. We argue that the benefits of international adoption vastly outweigh its costs. And many of the problems that international adoption faces could be eliminated by altering the way it is regulated. Indeed, unlike many opponents of IA, we think improvements would come from less regulation, not more.

Chapter 1 discusses the often obvious, yet mysteriously overlooked, benefits of international adoption. Chapter 2 addresses the objection that IA deprives a child of her birth culture and argues that this is largely a smoke screen for protecting national pride or some other political agenda. Chapters 3 and 4 examine the history of objections to IA as a form of transracial adoption and the regulations that resulted, then consider the empirical evidence of the effects of making racially blended families. Chapter 5 describes the so-called child-trafficking problem—that is, the improprieties that occur in the adoption of children and the role of this problem in IA's collapse. Chapter 6 addresses whether international adoption would function better if it embraced market forces rather than trying to suppress them. Chapters 7 and 8 elaborate on how the use of market incentives works and discuss objections to the lessening of regulations against sales of parental rights. Chapter 9 summarizes briefly and puts our arguments into the broader perspective of the joy and sadness of international adoption.

A Tale of Moral Hazard in Adoption

About a year after GB joined our family, we got a call from a woman in Oregon named Beckie Sibley who had adopted two girls from the same orphanage from which he came. We are calling that orphanage The Children's Home (TCH).[1] Not only had the Sibleys adopted from the same center, but one of the girls, five-year-old Sia, was GB's cousin. Her mother was the aunt who had raised GB after his parents were killed in the war—or so the story went. It was this aunt who placed GB and Sia in The Children's Home and made them available for adoption. The two children had been raised as siblings. As it turned out, they were half-siblings, and the "aunt" was actually GB's mother, though a decade would pass before we would discover that. The other daughter adopted from TCH was eight-year-old Isata, who had also been placed for adoption by an aunt and uncle who cared for her after the war took her parents—or so the story went.

At the time of Sia's arrival in Oregon, the director of The Children's Home, Diane, had told Beckie that Sia had a relative in Iowa, and so Beckie called us to reconnect the two kids. We arranged for Tinker and GB to fly to Portland and drive two hours south to Redmond, the small town east of the mountains where the Sibleys lived with their three adopted children. In addition to the two African girls, the Sibleys had adopted Carlin, the child of a relative who couldn't care for him. Their two birth children were grown and out of the house. Both Sia and Isata remembered GB from The Children's Home in Freetown. The trip went smoothly; the kids enjoyed each other's company, happily playing together in the hotel pool where Tinker and GB were staying. At one point GB and Sia were walking along holding hands, each talking about "me Mom" in Sierra Leone. After this initial, pleasant reunion, however, GB resisted suggestions for a return visit.

Beckie reported to Tinker that the girls seemed to have adjusted well to their new life in Oregon. Unlike GB, however, Isata and Sia talked a lot about their African memories: soldiers pointing guns at them, their families fleeing in terror from the rebels. The girls' fear was still palpable for a long time after the adoption. Whenever visitors to the Sibley household would stand up, gather their coats and prepare to leave, Sia and Isata would go hide in a closet, afraid that the strangers would take them away. Beckie once said to her daughter, "Isata, how long will you be Mommy's girl?"

"Well... I don't know," Isata said.

"Forever and ever," Beckie told her. The child clamped her arms around her mother's waist and stayed that way for ten minutes.

As we stated in the Preface, we will use Isata's story throughout this book to illustrate the problems with international adoption that are discussed in the various chapters. Again and again, we will see situations wherein the rules governing intercountry adoption create strong incentives to deceive someone, or at least to ignore what you strongly suspect is deception. This applies to adoptive families, birth families, adoption facilitators, and even the government officials who oversee the process. That situation is an example of what social scientists call a "moral hazard," a strong incentive to "do the wrong thing." Moral hazards are strewn everywhere along the path to international adoption, or at least as that path is currently constructed. Isata's story can help illustrate this and other problems with adoption.

TABLE 2. Structure of Isata's birth family, Freetown, Sierra Leone

1	Brother 1
2	Shaun M.
3	Brother 3
4	Brother 4
5	Isata
6	Sister
7	Informally Adopted Sister

CHAPTER 1

The Obvious Benefits of International Adoption

No kid in America has to walk miles to get water.

Peter Opa, President, Rethink Africa[1]

We were warned to expect some trauma in our son's adjustment to his new life. He arrived at six and a half from Sierra Leone, a West African country torn apart by a civil war. As it happened, we got lucky. Within minutes of arriving at JFK, GB was seduced by an American cultural icon, which, though less celebrated than the Statue of Liberty, perhaps, has more meaning to six-year-olds: the Chicken McNugget. GB was obviously starved for protein. Chicken, bacon, and red meat were like ambrosia to him. By the time he boarded the plane from New York to Des Moines on his second day here, McNuggets had a heroin-like grip on the boy's appetite. Back in Iowa, his world expanded even further—it now included Kentucky Fried Chicken. His English vocabulary being somewhat limited, and his charming accent intact, he referred to McNuggets as "de leetle chicken" and KFC as "de beeg chicken." "Tonight let's get de beeg chicken," he would say. Life in America seemed pretty good to GB, and in this, as we said, we were extremely lucky.

The first store GB visited in our small Iowa town—primarily because it *is* a small Iowa town—was Wal-Mart. He found it amazing that America had so much *stuff*. GB had never had much stuff; he had never even *seen* much stuff, and now it was literally stacked all around him. Could he please have that shiny, red remote-control car? "Well, that's something you can ask for on your birthday," his mom told him. This birthday concept was unknown to him; in Sierra Leone, everyone becomes one year older on the first day of January. His new American sister chose a birthday for him, one thought to be accurate to within a month or so: September 9. As the appointed date approached, and his mom asked him what kind of cake he wanted for his birthday, GB shook his head. *No, no*, he said. He didn't want a cake; he wanted the remote-control car from Wal-Mart. Tinker sat him down to explain the American version of this ritual. On your birthday, you get a present and cake and ice cream, too. If he couldn't decide between vanilla cake and chocolate cake, he could have both, Mom said, and choose whichever he liked best for his next birthday. Next birthday? He looked up at his mom, brown eyes full of confusion.

"How many birthdays do I get?"

That question was even more poignant than we realized. At the time GB was adopted, in 2002, the life expectancy of a male in the United States was seventy-five; in Sierra Leone, where the war had just ended, it was only twenty-six. By 2013, the figures had improved somewhat: about seventy-nine years for the US, fifty-seven for Sierra Leone.[2] The latter figure also happens to apply to Ethiopia, whence most of the African adoptees have recently come. In Ethiopia in 2013, of every hundred children born, only ninety-two were expected to survive to age five. Adoption, especially adoption of infants, alters the expected number of birthdays a child gets to celebrate. This is not about cake and ice cream—international adoption keeps more children alive.

The susceptibility of adoptable children in poor countries to early death is illustrated in Erin Siegal's book *Finding Fernanda*. Siegal describes an electronic mailing list where parents hoping to adopt from Guatemala shared their triumphs and tragedies.

> "Referrals," or children, could be lost for a variety of reasons. At times, children died partway through the adoption process. According to posts made on [the email list] at least five adoptive mothers were told their sons-or-daughters-to-be had passed away. The boy that Jane G. was adopting died six months into the process as did Fara W.'s girl. Jill N. was told that her first referral, a seven-month old baby named Pablo, had choked to death in a freak accident. Another client experienced the deaths of two referrals in a row. Members of the list serve showered each other with condolences and prayers.[3]

It seems a reasonable conjecture that had those adoptions proceeded more quickly, some of those children might still be alive.

How Many Children's Lives Are Saved by Adoption?

To be slightly more precise about how many lives adoption saves, we offer some estimates of the number of adoptees from Guatemala and Ethiopia who could be statistically expected to have died before age five had they not been adopted to the United States. Our estimates, reported in Table 3, cover the years 2005 to 2011.[4] To understand these calculations, consider the example of the three bolded numbers in the second row for Ethiopia for the year 2006. The first bolded number, 58.3, is the difference between the rate of infant deaths in Ethiopia in 2006 (65 per 1,000) and the rate of infant deaths in the United States that year (6.7 per 1,000). What does this mean? Suppose we compare 1,000 live births in Ethiopia on a given day in 2006 with 1,000 births on the same day in the United States. If all of these 2,000 newborns remain with their birth families, in the ensuing year we can expect that about 58 *more* of the Ethiopian babies will have died than the American infants (65 − 6.7 = 58.3). In 2006, Ethiopia lost 58 more infants per year out of every thousand born than did the US. The second bolded number, 213, is the number of Ethiopian babies adopted in the US during the year in question. Multiplying the additional infant deaths, 58.3/1000 (or 5.8 percent), times the number of infant adoptions, 213, gives the third bolded value, 12.4, which is the expected number of Ethiopian infants whose lives were saved in 2006 through adoption to the United States. Doing this calculation for both age groups (less than one, and one to five) for all seven years, we estimate that adoption to the United States enabled approximately 180 infants and 127 young children to do something they would not have done had they remained with their birth families in Ethiopia: live to age five.

Similar calculations for Guatemala suggest that adoption saved 448 infants and 158 kids aged one to five. The total for the two countries for the seven-year period is about 607 children. Note that in 2010 and 2011 virtually no Guatemalan kids were saved because adoptions were all but shut down those years. Our calculations suggest that as a result of that shutdown, a few dozen Guatemalan children died before they turned five in those ensuing years.

Are these numbers believable? Did adoption to the United States from only two countries, Ethiopia and Guatemala, over a relatively short period, just seven years, actually save the lives of around six hundred children? That estimate is probably conservative. Our mortality figures are for the *average* child in these two countries, while adoptees come from among the poorest children, whose death rates are almost certainly higher than those listed in the table. So there can be little doubt that, even in just the last few years, moving thousands of children from very poor countries to American families has allowed several hundred more of them to celebrate a fifth birthday than had they all remained in their home countries. (Also, this counts only adoptions to the United States, not Europe or Canada.) Undeniably, some of the hundreds of children just described will face special challenges as a result of adoption: racial discrimination, identity confusion, possible alienation within their communities. But they remain quite lucky in the following sense: those are problems you can have only if you are still alive.

So far, this discussion covers mere mortality; we have said nothing of morbidity. Many of the deaths reported above for Ethiopia, for example, will have come from malaria, which killed an estimated 437,000 African children in 2013.[5] (Wen Kilama of the African Malaria Vaccine Testing Network says that malaria is equivalent to crashing seven jumbo jets filled with children every day.[6]) But even children who survive malaria will suffer lifelong problems as a result of the disease.[7] "Malaria can have a devastating effect on children's education. Repeated infections cause children to miss large periods of school and anemia, a side-effect of frequent malaria attacks, interferes with children's ability to concentrate and learn and causes chronic fatigue."[8] There is a long list of nonfatal maladies that afflict children in poor countries including worms, diarrhea, and a number of other parasites and diseases. Data from the World Health Organization suggest that more than 90 percent of children in Sierra Leone, Liberia, Rwanda, and Uganda live in areas heavily infested with hookworm, roundworm, whipworm, and schistosomiasis.[9] Having worms affects school performance. For example, randomized trials in Kenya show that deworming can increase children's school attendance by as much as 25 percent.[10]

Then there is malnutrition. During his first few weeks in America, six-year-old GB would sometimes throw up after eating a big meal—his stomach was unused to the sensation of being full. Yet in discussing international adoption it seems impolite to point out that moving to America from Sierra Leone provides such obvious benefits as the occasional full stomach. According to the World Bank, over the period 2009–2013, the percentage of the population that was undernourished was 37 percent in Ethiopia, 29 percent in Sierra Leone, 30 percent in Uganda, and 31 percent in Guatemala.[11]

TABLE 3. Children's lives saved through adoption to the United States from Ethiopia and Guatemala 2005-2011, based on differential child mortality rates

ETHIOPIA

	Deaths/1000 Ethiopia - US		Children adopted		Lives saved by adoption	
	Infant	1–5 yrs	Infant	1–5 yrs	Infant	1–5 yrs
2005	61.4	38.4	141	109	8.7	4.2
2006	58.3	35.9	213	254	12.4	9.1
2007	55.4	33.7	421	444	23.3	15.0
2008	52.4	31.3	595	658	31.2	20.6
2009	50	29.3	856	866	42.8	25.4
2010	47.5	27.5	871	1096	41.4	30.1
2011	45.1	25.5	448	879	20.2	22.4
Total by Age			3545	4306	180	126.8

GUATEMALA

	Deaths/1000 Guatemala - US		Children adopted		Lives saved by adoption	
Year	Infant	1–5 yrs	Infant	1–5 yrs	Infant	1–5 yrs
2005	23.8	7.4	2984	665	71.0	4.9
2006	22.8	6.9	3323	656	75.8	4.5
2007	21.7	6.6	3329	1203	72.2	7.9
2008	20.6	6.1	2317	1636	47.7	10.0
2009	19.6	5.9	43	637	0.8	3.8
2010	18.7	5.4	0	23	0.0	0.1
2011	17.8	5.1	0	21	0.0	0.1
Total by Age			11996	4841	267.6	31.4

BOTH COUNTRIES

Total by Age					447.5	158.1
Total					606.6	

Sources: Mortality statistics from the Millennium Development Goals database; adoption statistics from the US State Department

Institutions Are Even Worse

Bear in mind that the calculations made above use data for the average child in Ethiopia or Guatemala. We have said nothing about children living in orphanages or child-care institutions. For such children, the effect of international adoption (especially if they are adopted at a young age, or better, prevented from even entering such institutions) is enormous. Dr. Dana E. Johnson, cofounder of the International Adoption Clinic at the University of Minnesota and among the most distinguished researchers on the medical effects of international adoption, summarizes what we know about the impact on children of institutionalization.[12] Studies from various countries indicate that as a result of poor nutrition, institutionalized children are at best one standard deviation below average in height (sometimes much more) and almost as far behind in weight. The mind is affected as well as the body. In Romanian orphanages, for example, the average IQ score was 64 compared to 103 for children in families. Mental illness was almost four times as prevalent in those institutions, and attention deficit disorder four-and-a-half times more common. Institutionalized children have much higher rates of hearing and vision loss. The list goes on.

Rebecca Compton, in her 2016 book *Adoption Beyond Borders* (the only book we know of that focuses on the benefits of international adoption), discusses the research on this issue in great detail. She presents evidence from several studies that indicate that the physical and cognitive development of internationally adopted children improves dramatically by most measures relative to their birth siblings and relative to their peers left behind in their countries of origin. They catch up to their new non-adopted peers in their adoptive countries. Compton shows how important it is to get children out of institutions and into permanent families before the very earliest periods of early cognitive development.[13]

Adoption into a stable family does not always eliminate these deficits—especially if the child spent a long time in such facilities—but it helps a great deal. One study showed that six months after adoption, the height and weight gaps had fallen by half and continued to fall. To the extent that international adoption gets kids out of orphanages its effects are profound, yet keeping children out of orphanages has important effects as well.

Education

Most readers would agree that the value of education transcends a mere increase in earnings power—it also opens up a world of insight. Greater access to

TABLE 4. Literacy and education spending per capita, selected countries, 2013

	Adult literacy		Education expenditure	
	Male	**Female**	**Age 0-24**	**Age 0-14**
Guatemala	81%	71%	$258	$413
Ethiopia	49%	29%	$82	$118
Rwanda	75%	68%	$101	$145
Sierra Leone	55%	33%	$89	$129
Uganda	83%	65%	$69	$98
US	99%	99%	$8212	$13,590

Source: Authors' calculations from the CIA's *World Fact Book*

education is one more way in which those of us in rich countries lead privileged lives. Adoptees, therefore, enjoy more access to this benefit than their counterparts remaining in their home countries. Table 4 compares educational spending per capita in several adoption "sending" countries with those in the United States in the last two columns.[14] The calculations are simple and straightforward: total educational spending is divided by the number of young people. Two definitions of young people are offered, age zero to twenty-four and zero to fourteen.[15] The disparities are glaring. For every dollar the US spends educating people under twenty-four, Guatemala spends three cents, Rwanda and Ethiopia slightly more than one cent, Uganda slightly less than one cent.[16] Even these low levels of expenditure mask other deficiencies in the schools of some poor countries. In one study of six developing nations, unannounced visits by school inspectors found that on a given day an average 19 percent of teachers were absent. In Ugandan primary schools, the figure was 27 percent.[17] These inadequacies get reflected, of course, in literacy rates, especially for women. In Sierra Leone, for example, while only about half of adult men can read, for women it's only one-third. (See the first two columns of Table 4.)

Again, this is not breaking news: rich countries devote a lot more resources to education than poor ones. But needn't we consider whether the advantages to a Ugandan child of remaining in her birth culture, compared to joining a family in the United States in adoption, justifies a 99 percent reduction in expenditure on her education?

Our African son may or may not have trouble forming a racial identity, but he has already completed high school and is in his third year of college. When he arrived at six and a half, he had never been inside a classroom; he didn't know whether words were read left to right or right to left or down to up. At first, he found this new experience called "school" to be utterly dull and painfully constricting. "You have to listen all the time," he complained. Indeed, the whole concept of education made no sense to him: Americans had TV, neat toys, and wicked-cool video games to occupy their time; why would they waste it *listening* in school? Tinker tried to explain it to him. Working hard and paying attention in school, she told him, would allow him to grow up to be what he wanted to be. By the way, she asked, what *did* he want to be when he grew up? GB stared at her blankly. After some discussion, it became clear that he simply did not understand this question. The people in his life in Sierra Leone spent their time figuring out how to survive another day, not contemplating a future that might never arrive. The men in his family made some income from selling rocks and scavenged concrete blocks by the roadside; GB sometimes helped by carrying these on his head (at age four or five). It would take years before GB could imagine himself as a grown-up doing something with his life. So, we were happy with the first answer he came up with: "rapper"; happier yet when that eventually evolved into "artist" or "art teacher."

Stuff

A few months after GB arrived, Mark ran into him in the upstairs hallway when the six-year-old blurted out, apropos of nothing, "Don't clean it, *OXY-clean* it!" Beaming a bright smile, he walked downstairs. "He's quoting TV commercials," Mark thought, "this can't be good." GB's embrace of American materialism was slightly alarming even to us, and we're materialists by profession. On the night of his first Christmas, exhausted by the long day of presents and celebration and excitement, GB spent a quiet moment with Mark on the couch by the Christmas tree. "Dad," he looked up earnestly, "can Santa come again tomorrow?" It was not such an unreasonable question. After all, compared to Sierra Leone, America seemed a place of endless wealth and comfort, so why couldn't Santa bring toys and treats every single day?

Even economists are aware that life can't be just about getting stuff. Happiness doesn't work like that. Data from the late 1990s show, for example, that while the average income in the United States was 75 percent higher than in New Zealand, the two countries had approximately the same levels of self-reported happiness.[18] So even if Santa could come every day, GB's life here would likely not be much happier as a result. We absolutely get that.

Having made that point... while higher income may have a modest effect on happiness in the United States and New Zealand, the same does not apply to poor countries in Africa, for example. The data cited above confirm that when family income is below a certain level, about fifteen thousand dollars in 2002, for example, more income does indeed raise people's perceived well-being. Until basic needs are met, income matters a lot, and in countries like Ethiopia and Sierra Leone, the basic needs of many families are a long way from being met.[19]

The lifelong material advantages of being raised in the United States versus, say, Vietnam or Guatemala are profound, as pretty much everyone knows. Yet the debate about international adoption rarely seems to acknowledge this. Actually, it often seems worse than that—even mentioning the benefits of higher income and better education can be viewed as impolite, even boorish. At lunch one day in Kampala, a Ugandan lawyer who has worked on international adoption remarked that it was obviously better for a child to be raised in his or her own culture than to be raised abroad. But, Mark asked, doesn't a child in America get a better education and have more job opportunities? The conversation stopped; she gave him a look that suggested he had committed a social faux pas. Yet two months later, this same woman asked us for help in getting her daughter into an American college. (As many good parents would, and which we were happy to do.) The point is that mentioning the material advantages that international adoption conveys on children appears to be politically incorrect. It is the fifty-thousand-dollar gorilla that no one admits is sitting in the room. We became Ugly Americans for even bringing it up.

Actually, some people in China think it's more like an eighty-thousand-dollar gorilla. Not everything of value has a market price, but everything with a market price has some value to someone. We know that some people in China place a value on entering America because, according to NPR, the market price for being smuggled from Fujian Province, China, to the United States, by way of Asia, Europe, and Central America, is from sixty thousand to eighty thousand dollars. While exorbitant, this price does buy you a full-service package, including all transportation, housing, and food costs, plus whatever forged documents are needed.[20] What it cannot provide, however, is a guarantee that having paid that price you will actually make it to America alive. Or that having arrived in this country, you won't be shaken down for even more money. In the early 1990s, the *Washington Post* reported two incidents in New York that occurred within days of each other.

> Yesterday morning, in the frigid waters off the coast of Rockaway Beach, more than 200 Chinese illegal immigrants jumped for freedom off the side of a grounded freighter.... A week and a half ago, across the Hudson River in Jersey City, 57 Chinese were found locked inside an

autobody shop, held captive until they came up with tens of thousands of dollars in cash to win their release from those who smuggled them into the United States.[21]

Sneaking into America from next door, as opposed to halfway around the world, is cheaper of course, but still expensive. Anyone wanting to cross illegally into the United States from Mexico would be well advised to hire a "coyote" to guide him. According to the Department of Homeland Security, in 2008 the services of a coyote cost somewhere between $1,500 and $2,500.[22] While not a huge sum to Americans, perhaps, $2,500 is more than twice the per-capita GDP of Ethiopia, and five times that of Sierra Leone.[23] Having paid that price, of course, there is no guarantee that the coyote will succeed in getting the would-be immigrant into the country. Indeed, he may end up like one of 2,200 bodies found since 1990 in the Arizona desert by the Border Patrol.[24]

Every year, thousands of people spend small fortunes by their standards and risk their very lives to accomplish what adoption does automatically: gain entry to the United States. Just getting to America, however, does not grant an illegal immigrant access to the American dream.

The Only Card You'll Ever Need

How many things can you hold in your hand that weigh less than an ounce but are worth thousands of dollars? That is what Mark asked himself when he first picked up GB's green card, the credential that originally made Gibrila a permanent resident of the United States. Mark had never even seen a green card. He held this wafer-thin piece of plastic between two fingers and considered how the young African pictured there was utterly oblivious to its power to transform his life.

Everyone knows that people smuggled into America do not have the legal right to work here. This not only makes it harder to find jobs, but leaves them vulnerable to exploitation because there is no legal recourse against a dishonest or unethical employer. Complaints can result in deportation. And when booted out, those smuggled in don't get their money back. The right to work is another blessing conferred by the coveted green card that was automatically issued to GB when adopted. How valuable is that blessing? Again, market behavior—*black* market behavior—suggests that it is worth a great deal.

For example, a relatively quick way to get a green card is to marry an American citizen. This makes you eligible to apply for the card two years after the wedding. The usual procedure is to fall in love with an American, but some unsentimental types bypass the prenuptials of courtship and engagement and enter directly into a "green card marriage." In 2007, a twenty-four-year-old Russian woman living in Los Angeles, who apparently did not know that it was illegal, posted the following ad on Craigslist: "Green Card Marriage—Will pay $300/month. Total $15,000. This is [a] strictly platonic business offer, sex not involved."[25] Someone responded and she and her new "husband" were subsequently arrested. The penalty for engaging in marital fraud for immigration purposes is up to five years in prison, up to a $250,000 fine, and deportation of the petitioner.[26] But in 2011, nearly four thousand applications for a spousal green card (about one and a half percent) were deemed fraudulent by DHS.[27]

We are making a rather obvious point here. The coveted privilege of legally residing and working in the United States, accidentally conveyed upon most Americans at birth, is a huge blessing bestowed by international adoption upon thousands of children every year. We do not expect to win the Nobel Prize in Economics on the strength of this insight, but neither should this fact be ignored in the debate about international adoption.

Officially Ignoring the Benefits of International Adoption

So far in this chapter we have lamented that discussions of international adoption seem to ignore the huge benefits it confers on very poor children in very poor countries. But, arguably, refusal to acknowledge these advantages is codified in the two documents that set the current legal and ethical framework for international adoption. The United Nations Convention on the Rights of the Child (UNCRC), ratified by nearly every member of the United Nations, spells out the basic rights children are supposed to have, independently of adults, and the obligations of national governments in protecting those rights. These are the rights to safety and survival, to nondiscrimination, to freedom of expression, etc. The Hague Convention takes Article 21 of the UNCRC, which specifically covers adoption, and expands it into a comprehensive set of standards and procedures that adoption policies should follow. As of 2013, ninety countries, including the United States, have ratified the Hague Convention. The Hague Convention is slightly more favorable, or slightly less antagonistic, toward international adoption. Dillon says that the UNCRC "does not preclude [intercountry adoption] but unquestionably discourages it by seeming to state a preference for in-country foster care or other 'suitable' care and therefore not relegating institutional care to a last preference."[28] In other words, the UNCRC is more willing than the Hague to accept that even an institution might be a preferred placement to an intercountry adoption. Yet the scientific evidence shows that this is simply untrue. In an article in *The Handbook of Child Well-Being*, Schoenmaker, et al. review the literature on the effects of growing up in institutions, foster care, and adoption on various measures of child thriving. "In general," they report, "it can be said that placement in an adoptive family and the legal permanency of this rearing environment depict the most stable and potentially most positive type of parenting for children without permanent parents."[29] Adoption is better than foster care and much, much better than an institution.

From our perspective, the important point is that both conventions express a strong preference for placing a child with a local family, even a foster family or distant relative, over a family abroad. The acceptance of this preference in adoption discussions is so widespread and unquestioned that it seems to have become axiomatic. Even when the result is a virtual self-contradiction. A recent article in the journal *International Social Work*, for example, states, "Almost half (49%) of all Guatemalan children suffer chronic malnutrition, the second highest in the world. In indigenous populations that number increases to 70 percent."[30] A scant two pages later the article says that Guatemala's vulnerable children require "a continuum of care, and that continuum must start with family preservation, then family unification and domestic adoption, with international adoption only as a last resort after all other options have been evaluated and determined not to be in the child's best interest." But if the first two or three options involve a better than 50 percent chance of chronic malnutrition, compared to essentially zero chance with international adoption; how difficult could such a determination be? Bartholet makes a similar point. "But these subsidiarity provisions are inconsistent with the core principles endorsed in these same Conventions (Hague and UNCRC) and elsewhere in human rights law, principles making the child's best interest primary and recognizing the child's right to grow up in a nurturing family as fundamental."[31]

Having Said That...

The following is a hypothetical adoption scenario.

> **Scene:** A woman in a dark business suit knocks loudly on the door of a Victorian home on a quiet street in a small Iowa town. A bald man in late middle age answers the door.
>
> **Man:** Yes?

Woman: Mr. Montgomery, I represent a married couple in Redmond,
  Washington, who would like to adopt your daughter.
Man (*perplexed*): What? Our daughter is not available for adoption.
  Who are these people, anyway?
Woman: Their names are Bill and Melinda, that's all I can say.
Man: Well, tell this Bill and Melinda to get their own child! Goodbye.
Woman (*puts foot in door*): You're being selfish Mr. Montgomery.
Man: What? How am I being selfish?
Woman: Bill and Melinda are very, very wealthy people. Your child
  will have a better life. She'll live in a mansion.
Man: Well... this isn't a *mansion*, but we have four bedrooms—
Woman: Their house is surrounded by well-tended gardens.
Man: I'll probably trim these bushes on Saturday—
Woman: Bill and Melinda's house doesn't have a broken doorbell.
Man: Yeah, there's a guy coming to fix that—
Woman: Your daughter will travel the world; she'll fly in private jets.
Man: Well, Economy Plus has plenty of legroom—
Woman: She'll *never have to take her shoes off at an airport*!
Man: She won't? Ever? Hmmm...

This scenario was neither based upon, nor inspired by, actual events. It is placed here merely to make a point: children of the super-rich surely enjoy advantages in life that the authors' kids don't, but that doesn't make us willing to hand our children over to billionaires. Poor parents, even desperately poor parents, suffer no obligation to surrender their kids to "rich" Americans, and those Americans have no right to take away their children.

But what rights *do* poor families have in deciding the fate of their children? In their June 2012 policy brief *Intercountry Adoption*, the world-famous NGO Save the Children expressed a widely held belief on the subject of poverty and adoption: "Poverty and a lack of resources *should never* be a reason for the separation of a child from his or her family" (emphasis original).[32] A much-cited report by the Donaldson Foundation says the same thing: "Poverty should not be a reason for [intercountry adoption]."[33] But who has the right to make that pronouncement? Mightn't a birth family decide that "poverty and a lack of resources" are *excellent* reasons for separation of their child from the family? Might not that separation be in the child's best interest precisely *because* of severe poverty? Or take that reasoning one step further. Suppose poor parents place a child in a foreign family that promises her safety, health care, and a good education, and in so doing accepts compensation that will help relieve the desperate conditions facing their other children. Might that not be a rational decision? But, rational or not, does this poor family have the right to make that decision? Virtually everyone associated with adoption says, "No, the poor family does not have the right to accept compensation when relinquishing a child." Why not? And on what authority do the naysayers deny the family access to that option?

That poor families will sometimes go to great lengths to give their children a better life in a developed country is exemplified again and again. One such episode was related to us by people who had founded an orphanage we visited in Sierra Leone. They were unaware that one of the resident children made available for adoption was actually the granddaughter of a staff member. The grandmother and her son, the child's father, assumed it would be much easier to place her if the mother were dead, but she wasn't; she had just abandoned the child. So, the birth relatives falsified the mother's death certificate. All of this had to be kept secret from the Americans. When the employers found out, after the child had gone abroad, they were very distressed. The grandmother was under no illusions about what the arrangement meant in terms of ever seeing her granddaughter again; she had earlier placed her own young daughter to be adopted. But she and her son were determined to give the child a better life, and probably a longer life expectancy. The point is that the opponents of international adoption, who rightly discuss the loss suffered by birth families, rarely acknowledge the *right* of these families to make the choice of sending a child to a foreign family. It is an option many birth families are willing to choose. Even when birth families see intercountry adoption as the best choice for a child, however, many bureaucrats do not.

This chapter has focused on the benefits of international adoption, benefits that are often ignored in the debate about the viability of IA for improving children's lives. We next begin to look at the objections to IA, starting with the claim that it harms children by denying them their "birth culture."

To Save a Daughter

The previous chapter discussed the benefits to vulnerable children of being adopted internationally. As painful as the decision can be for them, birth parents who place their children for adoption by westerners are generally quite aware of these benefits. In this part of Isata's story, we recount the conditions that caused her birth family, the M.'s, to put her in the custody of TCH, from which she was adopted by the Sibleys in Oregon.

January 2013

We are driving through Freetown, Sierra Leone, in a rattling old Mercedes sedan driven by Shaun M., Isata's older brother by birth. Shaun is driving us back to our hotel after one of our visits. Suddenly, near an intersection that locals call PWD, Shaun pulls the car over. "This is where it happened," he says. He suddenly jumps out of the car, obviously expecting us to follow him, which we scramble to do.

Shaun was referring to events on the night of January 6, 1999, when the Revolutionary United Front (RUF) entered Freetown. The RUF was a ragtag army led by Foday Sankoh, whom the *Washington Post* described as "a psychopathic killer leading a band of brutalized and confused teenagers." The author continues, "[He] recruited many

TABLE 5. Adopted children of Jason and Becky Sibley, Redmond, Oregon

	Born	Birthplace	Addopted
Carlin Sibley	1996	Oregon	1997
Isata Sibley	1994	Sierra Leone	2002
Sia Sibley *Half-sister of GB Montgomery*	1998	Sierra Leone	2002
Shauna Sibley	1994	Sierra Leone	2004
Steven Sibley	1997	Sierra Leone	2004

of his young henchmen by making them murder their parents, then drugging them with cocaine."[1] After kidnapping children and forcing them into their army, the rebels would carve "RUF" into each soldier's chest or forehead with a razor. "The carving ensured [they] could not run away without the likelihood of being killed by government troops."[2] The RUF was notoriously brutal even by the standards of African wars. "Although mass killings have occurred elsewhere in Africa, the rebels have distinguished themselves by not killing their victims, but by mutilating them and leaving them as living symbols of terror."[3] In the year the RUF rebellion began, Ahmed Kabbah was elected president using a motto, "Give a Hand for Peace." Sankoh and the RUF hijacked the motto: "Give a Hand for Kabbah." They lined villagers up and chopped off their hands. The RUF was less a genuine rebel army than a criminal organization that wanted to control Sierra Leone's diamonds. It was supported by Liberian president Charles Taylor—who was later convicted of war crimes at the International Criminal Court for sponsoring this war.[4]

At the intersection in Freetown, we follow Isata's birth brother Shaun across the road and down to a jumble of small houses made of adobe that lies a few yards beyond, and a few feet below, the road. Shaun looks around and says, "things are different." An elderly man in an aluminum chair sits with a younger woman and a young child by a fire outside one of the houses. A couple of chickens peck around in the dirt. It's dusk, so the house behind them is dark and we realize with some embarrassment that we're in what must be their after-sundown living area. The elderly man seems only moderately surprised to see a handsome young Leonean man appear at his house trailing two older white people. Shaun begins speaking to him in rapid Krio, which is near enough to English that we can understand some words without actually following the conversation. Shaun is clearly moved to be in this place again. And dazed. But there isn't a lot to see—the houses are different and the old man wasn't here that night. We look around for a few minutes. We say to Shaun, "Is it OK to give him a bit?" He says yes. We pass the man some Leonean dollars and climb back to Shaun's car.

Earlier in the day, upon first meeting Shaun, his father [we'll call him Pa M.], and Abdul, another brother, had immediately launched into the story of January 6, 1999, and "how they lost Isata." Much later

Shaun, at our request, e-mailed us a more detailed telling of these events. What follows is a melding of Shaun's e-mail account and the story as told to us by (primarily) Pa M. on that first day of meeting. There are some generally unimportant points of inconsistency between the two versions and we have chosen to use Pa's version when there are disagreements.

January 6, 1999

[Shaun] The rebels attack our neighborhood around midnight. I am fifteen years old. Isata is five.[5] Everyone is asleep, hoping to wake up by five a.m. for the usual Muslim ceremonies, eating in the morning to prepare for the fasting during the day. [Many] of us are staying at the house that night. [Parents, four boys, Isata, a baby daughter and three aunts]. Those of us sleeping don't hear the gunshots around the neighborhood until our dad wakes us up and orders us all to get ready, whispering that the rebels are now in the city. We pack a few clothes and gather some food for the journey. The street in front of the house is filled with men, women, and children fleeing for their lives as the rebels are burning houses and killing innocent people. We hear gunshots at close range.

[Pa M.] My wife hides our money in her hair. We start out. The oldest son takes Abdul's hand. Shaun, the second oldest, I tell to take [five-year-old] Isata's hand. Ma takes the baby girl [a younger daughter] on her back. I take the other boy. The rebels have come into the city from the east side and are killing and burning as they come.

[Shaun] But the people in the street are unaware that the rebels are walking among them, even using them for protection. We walk on foot over two miles away from home, and reach a junction called PWD, where government troops are stationed, and we all stop because the government forces are checking the people going across the junction.

[Pa M.] So the government soldiers are in front of us and we're stopped and in a crowd and the rebel soldiers are coming up behind. We are caught in the middle. It is dark with lights from fires burning and some from the soldiers.

[Shaun] It is terrible as [the government soldiers] notice that the rebels are in our midst, there are so many gunshots as they are trying to retreat from the checkpoint at PWD. They instruct us to wait by a house close by the checkpoint to rest for a while. We get to the house and my dad orders me to look after Isata and on no account should I let go of her hand. I am looking for a place to rest.

[**Pa M.**] Suddenly there is a large explosion as an RPG [rocket-propelled grenade] is fired right over our heads. Everyone falls to the ground. Isata is scared and pulls her hand from Shaun and disappears.

[**Shaun**] The sound of the explosion is so terrible that the crowd is in disarray, which causes my attention to slip from my sister. She panics and runs. Then when my dad asks for her I don't know where she is! With so much confusion in our minds we start searching. At this moment I am no longer worried about the war. My sister is my concern. We search for fifteen minutes but don't see her. I have guilt in my head that it is my fault, that I should have taken care of her, that I should have never let her out of my sight. Finally, we hear a faint mewing sound and we find her behind a door. She is sitting down quiet, shaking with so much fright in her. My longest fifteen minutes of ever living on this planet was that night.

[**Pa M.**] It was the longest fifteen minutes.

[**Shaun**] After finding her my dad requests we should follow the crowd as the gunshots are getting worse. As we continue our journey, I carry Isata on my back and my dad is holding our remaining things with him. We walk another mile and finally get to the house of my dad's youngest brother. On reaching this place, the gunshots are increasingly terrible. My uncle advises us to go to the house of his friend where we spend the night. When we awake the next morning, I hear RUF fighters instructing residents to turn over government soldiers and "bring out your young girls."

[**Pa M.**] We hide and somehow the rebels do not find us.

1999–2002

By mid-February 1999, ECOMOG, a West African multilateral armed force, managed to drive the rebels out of Freetown, "leaving behind 5000 dead and a devastated city."[6] The disruption left much of the population hungry and homeless. (Including, incidentally, GB and Sia's family.) Most schools were closed, and infrastructure was in a state of collapse. TCH was offering help to destitute families.

[**Shaun**] We hear about The Children's Home from our mom, when she came home one day after the war saying that there is a program called TCH. She tells us that they are taking care of young children who are disadvantaged. They will feed them, clothe them and even help pay their school fees. My mother then registers my two younger sisters. This was unknown to my father. We don't know this is an orphanage until one day my mom comes home and says that there are other children living at the house.

[**Pa M.**] The whole thing with The Children's Home happens when I am out of Freetown back at my village. Isata's mother agrees that Isata will live there and she will be safe. My wife cannot read or write. So she signs the papers they give her with her thumbprint. She doesn't totally understand what adoption is or what she's signing. We visit Isata with the whole family once a week. We bring her favorite candy. Sometimes she cries when we leave.

[**Shaun**] Eventually TCH tells us they will be "flying [the girls] out to foster parents who would take care of them."

According to Shaun's e-mail, before she could go to the United States, Isata had to live for a time at TCH's orphanage. The family agrees. TCH also wants to take the baby, but Pa M. objects, saying she is too young. Both parents agree to have Isata go to America. But first—according to Shaun; TCH later disputes this—Pa M. insists on some conditions:

Every five years she will visit the M. family;
In ten years (when she is eighteen) she will return to Sierra Leone and stay if she wants to; and
There will be open communication between the two families and regular progress reports.

So, as Shaun reports, the M. family was quite eager to have Isata placed in a secure home with a family in America. "We let her go to America so that she will be safe and get a good education."

Isata leaves for America in 2002.

CHAPTER 2

Whose Culture Is Being Defended?

I am very proud that there is an adoption law and that our image as being the number one exporter of children has changed. Now our children have dignity, Guatemala has dignity.

Jaime Tecu', Former Official, Guatemalan National Adoption Council[1]

About a year after GB joined our family, we read a story in the *New York Times* about a surgeon who adopted one of the children he had treated pro bono in Sierra Leone.[2] The boy was about ten. Soldiers had killed his entire family, and a snake bite left him with a severely damaged leg that was being repaired at a hospital in Manhattan, where he lived with his new dad. Describing the boy's life in America, the article said, "[He] had built an impenetrable firewall against his past. He ignores questions about Africa and offers only obscure recollections: his family fleeing to the bush when soldiers invaded his village; his fear of ordinary soldiers and kitchen knives." That, we thought, is exactly like GB. Ever since reading that article we have used that term, firewall, to describe GB's disconnection with his African past. Except that GB's firewall is more impenetrable than that of the boy in Manhattan; while at first he offered a couple of memories, of soldiers in the night shining lights in their eyes, of a mean monkey at the orphanage, he quickly stopped offering *any* recollections of Sierra Leone and started answering all questions about his past with the same reflexive response: "I don't remember." All attempts to reconnect him with his birth culture were firmly resisted. No, thank you, he did *not* want to go hear the Sierra Leone All Stars sing in Iowa City. No, thank you, he did not want to go to the African Heritage Festival in Des Moines where he could sample authentic African cuisine. (We "convinced" him to go and he threw up on the way.) In researching this book, Mark traveled to Sierra Leone twice and Tinker once, but Gibrila flatly declined to tag along. "Maybe someday," he said.

This chapter asks whether objections to international adoption based on loss of birth culture are always about the child's well-being. Do they defend the rights of the child, or the rights of the group—ethnic, racial, or national—from which the child comes? As adoptive parents, we obviously want to believe we have done no great harm to our sons by separating them from the circumstances of their birth families, something we'll never know for sure. And we can hardly claim to have had a typical experience with international adoption. Our child, like the boy in the *Times* story, has deliberately hacked away at the emotional roots tying him to his home country.[3] This may be unusual for international adoptees.[4] So, any pronouncements we make on the importance of birth culture have to be taken with a grain of salt.

What Exactly Is Birth Culture?

On May 4, 1996, two plainclothes policemen escorted a ten-year-old named Sifiso Mahlangu onto a plane that would take him from London to South Africa. As *The Independent* reported, "Attempts to put the boy on an airplane [the previous day] were abandoned because of his distress."[5] The child was a Zulu. He'd been brought to London by his Afrikaans foster parent, a Mrs. Stopford, who had employed his birth mother as a housemaid in Johannesburg. Sifiso had effectively been in Mrs. Stopford's care even before she moved to London, four years earlier, when her husband died. At that time, the birth parents had agreed that the boy should go with Mrs. Stopford, so that he would get a better education. But when they discovered that Mrs. Stopford had started adoption proceedings, they understandably sued to regain custody of their boy.

Sifiso very clearly did not want to go back to the Transvaal. And expert testimony by a psychiatrist suggested that there would be long-term emotional consequences of compelling him to do so. But though the British court was under "no illusions whatever about the harm that return to South Africa will cause," they ruled in favor of the birth family.[6] The deciding factor was the child's original culture. "The child's development must be in the last resort and profoundly, Zulu development and not Afrikaans or English development."[7] Lord Justice Neil stated that the child had "a right" to be returned to his Zulu parents. Sifiso would have been only too happy to *waive* that right, but the court ordered that he return to South Africa.[8]

Sifiso's birth parents saw how unhappy their son was to be returned to South Africa, and of course it mattered a great deal to them. They promised that if after six months he was still determined to return to England, they would permit it. He was, and they did.

The so-called Zulu Boy case demonstrates just how powerful is the view that a child has an innate "birth culture" and that this culture plays a crucial role in his emotional development, irrespective of how and where he is raised. This view motivated the African Child Policy Forum announcement that every child has an inalienable right to be nurtured and reared in the "culture in which they are born," and it motivates the Subsidiarity Principle.[9]

Why is removing a child from her birth culture a violation of her human rights? There are many books and articles discussing this, but it should suffice to mention a few of the main arguments in reference to Africa, as the contentions tend to be the same for other countries. Academics, like J. L. Roby and Stacey Shaw for example, say that the problem is a question of "to what degree African children adopted in the United States would be fostered in their cultural identity, receive acceptance, and enjoy a sense of belonging in their families."[10] Similarly, Veronica Root argues that when children are "adopted by an individual living outside of Africa," it leaves "them without connections to their countries of origin."[11] Upon returning to Africa as an adult, therefore, the adoptee may have trouble communicating in a language she has lost; she will probably no longer be a citizen in her home country. "Many African children who are brought to the US and other Western societies will likely be perceived as 'black.' This means they could be subject to racial discrimination in their new country.... If their adoptive parents are not of a racial or ethnic minority themselves, the parents may have difficulty relating to the circumstance of their adopted child."[12]

Before we assess these arguments in more detail, we examine the extent to which these concerns are relevant in practice.

Is It a Right to Birth Culture, or National Pride?

Most scholars of organized international adoption consider the system to have originated with Harry and Bertha Holt, a couple from rural Oregon who, in 1955, adopted eight Korean War orphans.[13] The eight adoptees whom Harry and Bertha brought back from Korea entered what was already a large family. The Holts were so moved by this experience that they began arranging hundreds of adoptions of Korean children by American couples. At the time, it's fair to say, Harry and Bertha got mixed reviews. The Adoption History Project says, "In the press, the Holts were portrayed as heroic, selfless figures.... But many professionals and policy-makers in the U.S. Children's Bureau, the Child Welfare League of America, and the International Social Service devoted themselves (unsuccessfully) to putting the Holts out of business."[14] The professionals saw the Holts as dangerously amateurish religious zealots. Almost sixty years later, however, their organization, Holt International, continues to facilitate thousands of adoptions from around the world (including that of our son Kurt). But what's important about the Holts for our story is that for three decades the South Korean government seemed quite content to let them arrange the adoptions of thousands of the country's children. Until the Summer Olympics came to Seoul.

Some argue that it was the 1988 Olympic Games in Seoul that finally brought democracy to South Korea. Scholars still debate that, but there is no question that hosting the Olympics was a matter of great national pride.[15] In the site selection process, Seoul had unexpectedly beaten out the Japanese city of Nagoya, which had been the odds-on favorite to win the Summer Games. The Seoul Olympics were supposed to showcase the country's economic miracle. Moreover, hosting the event would redress the humiliation of having to withdraw from hosting the Asia Games in 1976 because the country couldn't afford to build the facilities. South Korea's self-image was riding on these Olympics.

It was no small national embarrassment, therefore, when the Western press wrote scathing reports about how South Korea gave away many of its children. A few months before the games were to begin, Matthew Rothschild published an article entitled, "Babies for Sale: South Koreans Makes Them, Americans Buy Them," in the American magazine, *The Progressive*. Rothschild's portrait of Korean adoption was extraordinarily unflattering. Most of the women, Rothschild wrote, were poor unwed mothers with low-paid factory or office jobs. He described how the babies were taken from their mothers immediately after delivery and placed in foster care until they could be sent to America or Europe: "For some of the Korean mothers, the experience hurts. 'Just after delivery, they are very upset,' says [social worker] Kim Yong Sook.... 'They have guilt feelings and avoidance feelings. I'd like to see my baby again, they say. Sometimes they have bad dreams.'"[16]

The article placed the blame on South Korea's apparent indifference about the fate of its misbegotten children. The director general of the Bureau of Family Affairs told Rothschild, "We have many children from unwed mothers, but few families who want to adopt. That's why we send our children to foreign families."[17] Korean society, Rothschild wrote, was highly patrilineal, which made families reluctant to adopt, and the culture actively discriminated against unwed mothers and their offspring. The article emphasized how commercial—virtually industrialized—the adoption process in South Korea had become: "One social worker... was employed by one of the four adoption agencies for several years, and she was appalled by the increasing callousness and the competition. 'It's really like dealing with a product instead of taking care of the mother and the child.... Our weekly staff meetings were all about numbers: How many babies did we get that week?'"[18] Indeed, the American embassy official charged with vetting the adoptions was quoted as saying, "Five hundred kids a month is an incredibly high number for just a humanitarian issue. One has to question where humanitarianism stops and business begins."[19]

A harsh exposé, surely, but so what? *The Progressive* was a magazine of modest circulation and was published, after all, in a foreign language. It seems unlikely that the South Korean public would even be *aware* of Rothschild's article, let alone be aroused by it. There was, however, an organization that was only too happy to translate the article and see that everyone was fully informed of its accusations. That organization was North Korea. They immediately serialized Rothschild's piece in *The People's Korea.* The North had long mocked its southern neighbor for "flunkeyism" toward the United States, and the adoption scandal was offered as further proof.[20] As a result of Rothschild's article, in May 1988 the *New York Times* published an article about Korean adoptions, and during NBC's coverage of the games, sports analyst Bryant Gumbel referred to South Korea's "primary export" of children.[21]

South Korea's reaction was swift and forceful. All adoptions were suspended for the duration of the Olympic Games. In 1989, the government published new guidelines that would annually reduce the number of adoptions with the goal that by 1996 only mixed-race and children with disabilities would be available to Americans. In the meantime, tax credits were implemented to encourage domestic adoption, and overseas placements were restricted to unwed mothers who gave birth at facilities managed by the adoption agencies.[22]

The reforms did not work quite as planned. There were too few domestic adoptions to meet the 1996 deadline, and, indeed, the 1997 Asian financial crisis resulted in so many abandoned children—dubbed "IMF orphans"—that foreign adoption quotas had to be increased. To stem the "export" of children, the government, in addition to increasing domestic adoptions, had tried to implement a Western-style long-term foster care system, a system that is much criticized in the United States. The government also promoted placements overseas in ethnic Korean households. These efforts were somewhat successful, but by the end of the 1990s still only about one-third of adoptions had become domestic.[23] Thus, such reforms as occurred in the Korean adoption system, though beneficial to some children, were not motivated by what was in the "best interest of the child." They resulted from a blow to national pride.

And such regulations as Korea made, even had the children's best interest truly been the key motivation, nevertheless had some unhappy consequences. The government tightened regulations so that the children of unwed mothers had to be registered before they could be adopted. Stephen Evans of BBC News (January 6, 2015) says, "The changes were made with good intentions. Adopted children might want to trace their birth parents so registering full details seemed like a helpful measure.... But the good intentions have led to unintended results: South Korean orphanages are now brimming with children who might previously have found a new life in a foreign family." Molly, the daughter of Bertha and Harry Holt, described the effect of the registration law on unwed mothers. "If they do [register], they can't ever marry because no husband wants to marry a woman who has had a baby. So now, so many babies are being abandoned. They used to have two babies abandoned per month and now they have 25 per month."[24] The abandoned babies are not eligible for overseas adoption. According to the US State Department's adoption website, the number of Korean kids adopted by Americans fell from 1,793 in 2003 to 128 ten years later.

In general, we think that the role of national embarrassment is underacknowledged in the debate over transnational adoption. As Bartholet puts it, "Political forces in the 'sending countries' have been condemning in increasingly loud voices the practice of giving their countries' children to the imperialist North Americans and other foreigners."[25] There is a sense of shame in sending vulnerable children abroad rather than taking care of them at home.

Examples abound. In 2011, the Reason Foundation, a libertarian group, produced a documentary, *Abandoned in Guatemala: The Failure of International Adoption Policies*, about how in 2008 the Guatemalan government shut down a private adoption system that had found homes for five thousand children in the previous year. Under pressure from UNICEF, a new law established a National Adoption Council (NAC) to centralize government control over adoption as required by the Hague Convention. "The plan was to promote in-country adoptions, but that plan hasn't worked. Last year, only 35 children were adopted by Guatemalan families."[26] Nevertheless, in the documentary, Jaime Tecu', a former NAC official, announces, "I am very proud that there is an adoption law and that our image as being the number one exporter of children has changed. Now our children have dignity, Guatemala has dignity."[27]

As of this writing, the number of children coming to America from Guatemala remains a trickle.

What Made Russia Ban Adoptions to America?

In April of 2010, Torry Ann Hansen, a thirty-four-year-old nurse and single mother from Shelbyville, Tennessee, put seven-year-old Artem Saveliev, whom she had adopted the previous September from an orphanage near Vladivostok, on a plane bound for Moscow. In his backpack he had candy, cookies, and colored markers. Hansen had told Artem he was going on an "excursion to Moscow." Hansen had paid two hundred dollars to a Russian tour guide, whom she had found online, to meet Artem at the airport. The blond-haired boy was delivered unannounced to Russia's child protection ministry with a letter from Hansen addressed "To Whom It May Concern." "This child is mentally unstable," the letter said. "He is violent, and has severe psychopathic issues/ behaviors." Hansen's note claimed that the employees of the orphanage and its director were definitely aware of the problems the child had, but "chose to grossly misrepresent those problems in order to get him out of their orphanage." She had given her best to the child, she said, but "I am sorry to say that for the safety of my family, friends and myself, I no longer wish to parent this child."[28]

Russian officials responded with outrage. Foreign Minister Sergey Lavrov said he was indignant at the way the child had been treated "as a parcel" and called for an immediate suspension of adoptions to America. Pavel Astakhov, the Kremlin's child rights commissioner expressed fury at the boy's return. "The adoptive mother broke all the rules and procedures by sending an adopted child back," he said.[29] "We must, as much as possible, keep our children in our country, and keep them safe here."[30] The day after the boy arrived, Astakhov interviewed him on state TV, asking the child about his life in America and especially about his adoptive mother. "'Did she hit you?' Astakhov asked. [Artem] said no, but motioned that she had pulled his hair."[31]

Commissioner Astakhov, forty-three at the time, was described by the *New York Times* as "an unlikely welfare crusader."[32] His educational background was a case in point: he graduated from the Higher School of the KGB.[33] He was one of Russia's leading private lawyers and also hosted a popular television show, "Hour of Judgement," in which he would adjudicate "the kind of cases often heard on 'Judge Judy' in the United States."[34] The versatile Astakhov also authored a series of novels featuring "a fearless renegade lawyer" who fights fiercely against corruption.[35]

Astakhov had proven quite adept at using the media and was especially skilled in exploiting television. In *Harper's*, Irina Aleksander described his June 2012 visit to the Ranch for Kids, a facility for troubled adoptees in Eureka, Montana, just south of the Canadian border. Almost all of the ranch's kids are Eastern Europeans. Generally suffering from in-utero exposure to alcohol and/or some combination of abuse and neglect in their home countries, these children had been sent to this facility by families who had difficulty coping with them. At the ranch, they received care and generally lived the orderly, consistent, and disciplined life that they required. The ranch owners had refused Astakhov permission to visit, but he came anyway, accompanied by a crew from Russia's state-owned news channel. Noting the empty grounds, he proposed that the ranch owners may have taken the children and fled to Canada—actually it was midafternoon, they were all in school. On his Twitter account Astakhov asked, "What is [this place], a pretrial detention facility? A penal colony? A trashcan for unwanted children?"[36]

What is most important about this story is that a few months later, in October of 2012, Astakhov began advocating for a ban on US adoptions of Russian children. And he would appear to have succeeded because, in December of 2012, Russia suspended all adoptions by American families—not foreign families, only *American* families. Having been proposed by the country's child rights commissioner, this ban would seem to have been clearly motivated by a sincere desire to protect Russia's children. But if so, the timing of the event was quite peculiar. On October 18, two months before the ban, the US State Department announced the "Agreement between the United States of America and the Russian Federation Regarding Cooperation in Adoption of Children." It had been more than two years in negotiation. The announcement averred that "each year... the lives of thousands of American families have been enriched by welcoming Russian orphans into their homes."[37] So whatever problems existed with placements in American families seemed to have finally been ironed out or not relevant for the vast majority of adoptions. Why suspend adoptions six weeks later? A closer inspection suggests a not-particularly-ulterior motive.

In 2007, Moscow police, acting on the orders of senior officials of the Interior Ministry, raided the offices of a London-based hedge fund called Hermitage Capital Management. They seized large numbers of documents and corporate seals. The following year, a thirty-six-year-old lawyer named Sergei Magnitsky testified in a Russian court that his investigation revealed that the Interior Ministry officials had engineered a fraudulent $230 million tax rebate for companies they had taken over using the confiscated documents and seals.[38] A month later, on the orders of the same officials he had testified against, Magnitsky was arrested on charges of tax fraud, charges that were widely understood to have been trumped up. He was never tried for these alleged offences, however. Under Russian law a prisoner can be held up to a full year without trial, and a few days before his year was to expire Magnitsky died in Moscow's infamous Butyrka Prison. An inquiry by the Kremlin's Human Rights Commission concluded that in the final hours of his life Magnitsky had been denied crucial medical care and that he might have been beaten.[39]

As you might expect, the Magnitsky scandal prompted a legislative response. But the response wasn't in Moscow, it was in Washington. In December of 2012, Congress passed the Sergei Magnitsky Rule of Law Accountability Act, which imposed visa bans and asset freezes on eighteen Russian officials—the "Magnitsky List"—deemed responsible for his arrest and subsequent death. The House Committee on Foreign Affairs said, "This bill... does what the Russian government should have done years ago, namely hold accountable those government officials and others who participated in the arrest, murder, or cover up of Magnitsky or who benefited from his death."[40] President Obama signed the bill into law on December 14, 2012.

Only one week later, the Russian Dumas passed a surprisingly similar law, one imposing sanctions on individuals who violated the fundamental human rights of citizens of the Russian Federation. Like the Magnitsky act, it was named for a hapless Russian who suffered an agonizing, wrongful death. This was a twenty-one-month-old boy named Dima Yakolev whose adopted American father tragically and inadvertently left him locked in a hot car for nine hours, as a result of which he died of heatstroke. The Yakovlev law did not just sanction "human rights violators"; it banned all adoptions of Russian children by *American* families. The bill was transparently *not* about protecting Russian children. Deputy foreign minister Sergei Ryabkov said, "Owing to certain sentiments that prevail in the U.S., including on Capitol Hill, our relations with the U.S. seriously lack what we call three basic principles—mutual respect, equal rights and noninterference in internal affairs."[41] Also, not surprisingly, there was the predictable element of national embarrassment. Duma member Yekaterina Lakova, who sponsored the Yakovlev bill said, "Normally, economically developed countries don't give away their children."[42] (Although we should note at least one developed country—the US—does "give away" some of its children for adoption, placing roughly two hundred primarily black and biracial infants a year in western European countries between 2003 and 2009.[43]) This legislation did not, apparently, require much soul searching on the part of the Russian government; President Putin signed the Yakovlev bill on December 28, two weeks after Obama approved the Magnitsky act.

The Russian adoption ban is another example of a politically motivated shutdown of adoption that was not—or, in this case, did not even claim to be—in the best interest of the children. In our next example, a country shut down adoption for, again, political reasons, but the political reasons were not their own; it was someone else's agenda driving the decision.

Romania: A Sad Cirque d'Adoption

Though Romania has sent fewer children to America and Europe in the past twenty years than such sending countries as Russia, China, or South Korea, we take special care describing the adoption situation there and devote more time to it than to those other countries. There are several reasons for this. In the wake of the collapse of communism, Romania had an enormous need for reforming child welfare, especially in its state-run orphanages. Also, because adoption began in earnest in Romania just after the totalitarian regime fell, it occurred in a comparative legal vacuum. For a short time, therefore, Romania represented the closest thing to an entirely unregulated adoption regime that had been seen before or is likely to be seen again. As such, it provides a highly instructive special case. Finally, more than in any other country, bureaucratic pressure on the Romanian system, both *for* and *against* the continuation of adoption, came from outside the system as well as within the country itself. It is in Romania more than anywhere else that we see the power of a single bureaucrat to have an enormous influence in disrupting adoption. So, Romania is worth examining in some detail.

Romania: The Ceaușescu Legacy

On Christmas Day 1989, Nikolai Ceaușescu and his wife Elena, who for twenty-four years had ruled Romania with an iron fist in an iron glove were given a forty-five-minute show trial in a military barracks, then promptly executed in the building's courtyard.[44] The trial and execution were aired on Romanian television to assure any loyalists that it was pointless to try to rescue the Ceaușescus—their dictatorship had ended. Images of their slumped and bleeding bodies appeared on the front pages of newspapers all around the world. Shortly afterward, international audiences literally gasped at television images of the appalling legacy that the Ceaușescus' rule had imposed on Romania's children.

Back in 1966, shortly after Ceaușescu was named general secretary of the Romanian Communist Party, it had become apparent that the country's population growth had almost ceased.[45] The regime launched aggressively pro-natal policies to increase the birth rate. Contraception was outlawed and marriages became virtually indissoluble, the number of divorces falling from twenty-six thousand in 1966, to just twenty-eight one year later. A woman who reached age twenty-five without having children, married or unmarried, was taxed as much as 10 percent of her income. Except in cases of rape, incest, or child deformity, abortion was forbidden to any woman until she was age forty-five, and then only if she had at least four children in her care. Police were stationed in hospitals to prevent abortions, with apparently great effect, as the number of legal abortions fell from one million in 1965 to fifty-two thousand in 1967.[46] As a result of these policies, from 1966 to 1967, the number of live births nearly doubled.

However, after a period of lax enforcement, the birth rate declined again by 40 percent. So, in 1984, the regime launched new pro-natalist policies so draconian they might have appeared in George Orwell's novel set in that year, *1984*. "Women under the age of 45 were rounded up at their workplaces every one to three months and taken to clinics, where they were examined for signs of pregnancy, often in the presence of government agents—dubbed the 'menstrual police' by some Romanians."[47] The minimum age of marriage for girls was lowered to fifteen and the taxes for childless women were increased. Women over forty-five seeking a legal abortion had to have five children now instead of four, and a party official had to be present during the procedure. If a child died, for any reason, local doctors could lose 10 to 20 percent of their salaries.[48]

But Romania, of course, was an already poor country and it was rapidly getting poorer.

> The debt crisis of the 1980s reduced the standard of living to that of a Third World country, as Romanians endured rationing of basic food items and shortages of other essential household goods, including diapers. Apartments were not only overcrowded and cramped, but often unheated. In the face of such bleak conditions, increased material incentives [to have children] that in 1985 amounted to [only] enough to buy 43 grams of preserved milk were not enough to overcome the reluctance of Romanian women to bear children.[49]

Tens of thousands of mothers, unable to care for children they had been virtually forced to bear, turned those children over to the state. By 1989, more than

150,000 children were in government care, under conditions so unsanitary that as many as 16,000 died of "easily treatable diseases."[50] They were housed in a network of hundreds of state-run institutions, "many of which were located in rural areas, away from public scrutiny."[51] Within months of the fall of the Ceauşescus in December 1989, however, these institutions would feel the glare of public scrutiny on an international scale.

In the fall of 1990, the ABC News show *20/20* ran a documentary about Romanian orphanages. It showed "young children in straightjackets, groups of mentally disturbed adolescents spending their days in bleak rooms sitting in eerie silence, babies nearly starving to death." In some places "babies were stacked on the shelves of a cart like loaves of bread."[52] Reporting on the show, the *Washington Post* said "[the camera] shows naked, underfed children sitting ankle deep in their own urine, scabrous children herded like pigs to 'bathe' in filthy troughs of black water, infants starving to death because of treatable conditions such as cerebral palsy and even anemia."[53]

The exposure of conditions in Romanian orphanages spawned an immediate and powerful reaction from horrified westerners. As Diane Kunz and Ann Reese wrote in the *Wall Street Journal* (February 4, 2005), "Financial aid and personal volunteers flowed into the country. Thousands of children were given permanent families by people who saw them as citizens of the world in need of nurturing homes not as the property of a sovereign state." Within a few short months, Romania overtook South Korea as the leading supplier of adoptive children to families in America. According to the then Immigration and Naturalization Service, between October 1, 1990, and September 4, 1991, 2,287 Romanian children were adopted by Americans.[54] UNICEF reported that within eighteen months of the horrid TV images, as many as ten thousand children were adopted into Western families.[55] By the end of the decade, the number had tripled.[56] It was not perhaps the perfect scenario; the American consul general in Bucharest said that only about half of the children, roughly five thousand, were actually adopted from institutions, and virtually none were severely handicapped like so many of those pictured on television.[57] The other children tended to be adopted directly from families. Nevertheless, international adoption quickly spared about five thousand Romanian children incarcerated in some of the world's most nightmarish "orphanages." Yet IA quickly aroused the hostility of some powerful bureaucrats both inside and outside the Romanian government.

In March of 1991, freelance journalist Kathleen Hunt reported on "The Romanian Baby Bazaar" in an article for the Sunday *New York Times*. Hunt described the "hundreds of adoptive parents who have poured into the country since the liberalization of Romanian adoption law last August [1990]," many no doubt attracted by the short wait time for white toddlers and babies. Some of these parents were working with registered adoption agencies; others worked through lawyers who, "for a substantial fee" that could be as high as $15,000, could deliver a baby to the visitors' hotel.

"And then there are Americans and Canadians of modest means," Hunt reported, "who come on group 'tours,' hoping to find and adopt a child for under $5,000." Many such hopefuls congregated in the lobby of the President Hotel in Bucharest, formerly a guesthouse for Communist elites, to meet people like M., "a suave Romanian in a double-breasted Italian suit" who would promise a prospective adopter he could find her a baby "the following day." M. typified a burgeoning class of extralegal adoption entrepreneurs. After thirty-seven years in Australia, M. had returned to Romania the previous summer and become "one of the leading black-market money-changers at the hotel and recently began applying his broker's skills to babies." No doubt the authors of the Hague Convention had people just like M. in mind when they wrote Article 11 of the convention a couple of years later, stating that agents pursue "non-profit objectives" only.

The glare of this negative publicity forced the Romanian government to try to end what one reformer identified as "the black period of Romanian adoptions, from August 1, 1990, to July 16, 1991."[58] Said reformer was Dr. Alexandra Zugravescu, a sixty-six-year-old Bucharest pediatrician who headed the new Romanian Adoption Committee (RAC), which began overseeing adoption under Law 11/1990.[59] That law had revised the old Family Code of 1954. Dr. Alexandra Zugravescu's job was, as she put it, to wipe out the "dirty business of baby trafficking."[60] She expressed deep embarrassment that her country had become known internationally as a place to buy a baby. "It pains me that this could happen," she said. Dr. Zugravescu was quite explicit about wanting to eliminate all private adoptions. Indeed, although the stated goal, as with all adoption law, was to protect the best interests of the child, the big fear seemed to be that someone, somewhere, might be making some money. Or at least, more money than they should be making. "Improper financial gain" seemed to become the new mantra of the adoption regulators. In a 1995 article Zugravescu explained,

> The purpose of the new regulations... is to prevent trafficking in children
> or improper financial gain through adoption. A parent, guardian, or
> foster parent who claims or accepts money or other material goods... in
> exchange for a child's adoption, can expect a sentence of imprisonment

from one to five years. The same penalty applies to a person who obtains improper financial gain through acting as an intermediary or facilitator in a child adoption.[61]

The new system, Zugravescu said, seemed to be "the only one capable of stopping trafficking and improper financial gain either by biological parents or other persons involved in the adoption proceedings." So, under the new regulations it was not illegal in Romania to run an orphanage in which children wallowed in their own filth, nor to abandon a child to live in such a place, but to gain financially for helping a child escape that institution or to escape family conditions that might put her there, was a crime. A serious crime: Law 11/1990, mandated "prison for those who make money by mediating or facilitating adoption."[62] As there was a great deal of money to be made through such facilitation, and as it could only be made by someone willing to risk prison, it should not surprise us to meet shady characters like M. stalking the lobby of the President Hotel.[63]

On July 17, 1991, after ten thousand children had found new homes in America and Europe, all adoptions by foreigners were suspended; the RAC wanted to control the system. When adoption resumed in April of 1992, the system had indeed been radically "reformed." A 2011 report by USAID describes the RAC's approach to removing money from the allocation of adoptable children.

> This methodology employs a "point system" to value the contributions
> made by Romanian and foreign adoption agencies to the local govern-
> ments for specified social service purposes. The contributions—which
> may be in the form of money, goods, or services—are then assigned
> points at the local level, and reported periodically to the central adoption
> authority, the Romanian Committee on Adoption (popularly, the RAC)....
> The RAC then assigns to adoption agencies the right to place specific
> adoptable children, ostensibly on the basis of the points they have
> earned.[64]

The report noted that "it is this periodic assignment of points that some critics have described as an 'auction,' at which agencies gain access to children according to the contributions they have made."[65] In other words, the reform had by no means eliminated the allocation of children to the highest bidders. What it had done was launder payment into points and shifted those payments from the facilitators and the birth families into the coffers of the government.

Specifically, to the agencies responsible for child welfare, among which the RAC, of course, was primary.

Theoretically, this should have been a good thing; Western money could be used to buy food and supplies for orphanages instead of, for example, double-breasted Italian suits. But if reorganization of the adoption procedures actually channeled more money to the child welfare system, the resulting improvements were superficial. In 1996, the *New York Times* reported that "Romania's orphanages are as full now as they were [in 1989] even though contraception and abortion have since become legal." The Western aid agencies that "poured in [in 1990] to improve the miserable lives of abandoned children.... Today they say they have failed, except in some of the basics like new paint and better heating."[66]

So, in revising the adoption laws, the Romanian government had clamped down on the removal of children from the country, but it failed to address the conditions that precipitated their departure. For example, Doctors Without Borders (DWB), the respected Belgian humanitarian group, stated, "There are so many abandoned children because there is no social policy by the Government for parents to keep their children.... The Government hasn't trained any social workers to encourage families to take their children home or take them back after they have been in an institution for a while." DWB withdrew in 1995, "rather than abet what it considered the intolerable Government policy of perpetuating institutional custody for children." In these institutions, the organization reported, "the children are left as they were during the Ceausescu era, prisoners in their cribs. Romanian orphans, it is estimated, receive five to six minutes of attention a day. Attendants still loll in the corridors, smoking and drinking coffee, leaving the children to rock in their cots."[67] DWB was unable to persuade many staff members to lift the children out of their cribs and hold them more often. In its farewell report, DWB warned that the long-term psychological consequences of this treatment would haunt the country for decades to come.

The important point here is that for a government besieged by an avalanche of bad press, the self-entitled, rich Western couples and their greedy, unscrupulous local agents made a convenient target of attack. It's much cheaper to pass a regulation than to expend resources addressing a huge social problem, especially for a country so short on resources. Although adoption had helped thousands of Romanian children and could help more, the squalid institutions still held *scores* of thousands of children, and general poverty continued to grip *hundreds* of thousands more.[68] Realistically, adoption could, at best, extract only a tiny fraction of these vulnerable and needy children. Considering the enormous deprivation facing Romanian children, both in and out of institutions, the "improper financial gain" of adoption facilitators might not have been the most urgent problem for the government to address—but it was surely easier than fixing the social welfare problem. Or, at least, it was easy to *appear* to have addressed it.

Also, the images of warehoused institutionalized children and the reports of an international adoption melee were more than just an embarrassment to Romania's national pride. They were impediments to an almost desperate national ambition: joining the European Union (EU). In a 1993 meeting in Copenhagen, the EU had agreed to accept Romania's application for membership contingent upon the country satisfying certain requirements, not the least of which was improving child welfare. "Considering the living conditions of children in public care as a human rights issue, the European Commission paid special attention to this topic in all the reports provided about Romania's application for membership."[69] By 1998, the EU *Commission's Report on Romania's Progress towards Accession* reported, "There is encouraging evidence the number of children re-integrated into their families or adopted by foster families has increased." But there was scope for further improvement, "in particular by promoting the reintegration of children into their families."[70] Ideally, the EU asserted, institutionalized children should go back to their families; as a second-best they might be adopted by local foster families. Was there any role for adoption *outside* the country? No. After the 1999 appointment of Emma Nicholson to shepherd Romania into the European Union, there was definitely no role for international adoption.

Romania: "Curse You, (Red) Baroness"[71]

Like many people active in international adoption, the Baroness of Winterbourne is the kind of person you can genuinely admire on one level and profoundly disagree with one another. Given her extraordinary role in the saga of Romanian adoption, it is worth taking some time to consider exactly who she is. Born in 1941, Emma Nicholson is the daughter of a wealthy English family with an impeccable social pedigree. "Her ancestors—including three uncles, 10 cousins, a grandfather and three great-grandfathers—had sat in Parliament since the 17th century."[72] Her early life was pioneering in a number of ways. She won a scholarship to the Royal Academy of Music despite being nearly deaf. In the 1960s, she was a successful systems analyst in the then solidly male world of computer programming. It was her IT skills that eventually led her to the Save the Children Fund, to try to "sort out their computer system," ultimately raising millions of pounds in donations for their international operations. Eventually she "joined parliamentary groups on Romanian orphans and Iraqi Shias; she became chairman of the charity Blind in Business; she became a director of Shelter."[73] Later, this work led her into international adoption.

According to a 1995 profile of Nicholson in *The Independent*, "She visited the marshy border between Iran and Iraq after the Gulf War... [and] decided to give a temporary home to a young refugee called Amar.... She took him to hospital to have his burnt face rebuilt... but planned to find him Arab foster parents. Gradually she changed her mind. Today, Amar is 14 and her adopted son, 'a constant joy.'"[74] When she first entered politics in the mid-1970s, there was no question about which party Nicholson would choose. "As a family, on both sides, we had been members of the parliamentary Conservative party since its inception in the eighteenth century."[75] Here again, she had to confront a wall of maleness—the application form to become a Conservative candidate for Parliament asked her about *her wife*. Initially the party elite rebuffed Nicholson. It was only the patronage of Margaret Thatcher, who made her a party vice chairman that paved the way for Nicholson to run for Parliament and win a seat.

But by the mid-1990s Nicholson had decided that the Conservative Party was just too *conservative*. As she would tell the BBC, the Conservative Party was no longer the "One Nation" party she had joined. It was a party of anger: "angry with specific parts of the nation, single mothers, asylum seekers, people from ethnic minorities, people of different religions."[76] She told *The Independent* that "the last straw for her was the sight of pregnant women in chains at Holloway Prison."[77]

A few days after Christmas 1995, Nicholson, in a courageous move, crossed the floor to the Liberal Democrat Party. Fortunately, her career in the Commons ended shortly thereafter when, in 1997, she was made a lifetime peer, serving the Liberal Democrats in the House of Lords. In 1999, she joined the European Parliament, becoming vice chairman of the Committee of Foreign Affairs. And the baroness became the EU's rapporteur for Romanian accession to EU membership, in which role she attracted significant praise, but a bit more public vilification as well.

Thus, Emma Nicholson is an extraordinarily formidable individual who has established, in both her personal and her professional life, an obvious commitment to the welfare of orphaned and abandoned children. Naturally, that commitment carried over to her role in guiding Romania's application to the European Union, an application more dependent upon her good opinion than that of any other person on Earth. None of this was lost on Romanian officialdom. In her (self-published) book *Romania for Export Only*, which she dedicated to the baroness, former EU staff member Roelie Post describes a meeting of aid agencies held near Bucharest. "On entering the first thing one saw was a huge banner: *Our Children—Our Top Priority.* The Romanian Government," Post says, "really did not spare efforts to impress the Baroness."[78] To the Romanians, it must surely have seemed like good policy to *do* things that the baroness approved of, and to *not* do things the baroness *dis*approved of. And one thing the baroness definitely disapproved of was international adoption.

It's no great exaggeration to say that the baroness's embrace of the Subsidiarity Principle—that international adoption should only be a last resort—was bear-like in its ferocity. Even children in the poorest families, whose parents *wanted* them to go to what they considered a better life abroad, were not suitable for IA, she thought. In a CNN interview on June 11, 2002, she said that "it was a mistake from the beginning to assume that for a child, a foreign adoptive family is better than the family which cannot care for him. This is totally false." The birth culture and the birth family were too important to be discarded.[79]

Worst of all, to Nicholson, was the idea that people accepted money for placing their kids for adoption. "What I uncovered [in Romania] was massive trafficking of children. Some of that trafficking was going under the false name of inter-country adoption," which was "just a cover up phrase that was being used to sell children globally." She was not persuaded that these children had been comfortably settled in families abroad. "Many times the children have just disappeared. There are about 30/40/50 thousand children completely untraceable."[80] Tens of thousands of "untraceable" children?

To some, her anxiety about child selling could appear paranoiac. Charles Nelson is a Harvard neuroscientist who, in 1999, with a team of American scientists, launched the well-respected Bucharest Early Intervention Project, a clinical assessment of how institutionalization affects child development. The project was funded by the MacArthur Foundation. One day in June of 2002, Baroness Nicholson appeared at the study's Bucharest lab "uninvited and unannounced."[81] Nelson later told a reporter that "She [the baroness] goes to the press and says that we're doing a study, using high-tech American measures, to identify the smartest orphans so we can sell them on the black market." As Nelson reported this, he was "practically sputtering." While the baroness later denied accusing the scientists of trafficking, she was steadfast in believing that the MacArthur study was illegal and unethical.[82]

Of course, the baroness was not alone in criticizing Romanian adoption; UNICEF was also a strong supporter of the Subsidiarity Principle. But even on the spectrum of opposition to intercountry adoption, it's hard not to see her views as extreme. "Child Trafficking is the fastest growing organized crime in the globe," she said, "and so the use of the word of intercountry adoption was just a false piece of sticky plaster over a very evil thing indeed."[83] She would tell *Deutsche Welt*, "We really uncovered horrors of a scale and dimension you would wish never to know about."[84]

Nicholson was determined to stop this "evil thing" by whatever means were available—and, to her, considerable means *were* available. In an April 2001 report, the Commission for the External Affairs of the European Parliament asked for the suspension of negotiations for accession. Among the problems cited was the issue of abandoned children. "According to Emma Nicholson, the Romanian State encourages abandonment of children, government officials being connected with the international agencies practicing adoption."[85] As if the negative recommendation weren't enough, Roelie Post, the EU staff person cited earlier, stated that in 2001 Nicholson even considered suing Romania.[86] By letting children be adopted outside the country, the baroness claimed, Romania had violated the UN Convention on the Rights of the Child (UNCRC), which it had recently signed. Could the Romanian government be brought before the Strasbourg Court on Human Rights? At a dinner, also attended by Post, the baroness pitched this idea to an experienced Romanian human rights lawyer. "To our surprise," Post reported, "[the lawyer] was not enthusiastic." Post found it "hard to believe" that one of the most prominent human rights lawyers was "not at all interested in intercountry adoption [as a human rights violation]." In fact, she said, "It was... surprising that none of the human rights NGOs, so actively monitoring Romania on other issues, had shown interest either."[87]

Still, for all practical purposes Romanians had become sinners in the hands of an angry Baroness, and they knew it. In July of 2001, the government announced a "temporary" moratorium; international adoption was entirely shut down.

Some Europeans did not celebrate Nicholson's victory for human rights. Within a month of announcing the moratorium, Romania hosted French minister Lionel Jospin, who asked what would happen to the five thousand children whose adoptions were already in progress when the moratorium began.[88] In Bucharest, he met with a number of NGOs that pleaded with him to get adoption reopened. And while the moratorium had been implemented to appease the European Commission, it got decidedly mixed reviews in the European Parliament. Some members of Parliament (MEPs) fought hard for individual constituents who had children stuck in the adoption pipeline. And these weren't all just ordinary, run-of-the-mill MEPs, either. For example, a former EP president, Jose Maria Gil-Robles, came to see the director general of the European

Commission complaining that a thousand Spanish families had paid a lot of money to start adoption procedures, only to have them blocked by the moratorium.[89] Silvio Berlusconi made a similar appeal on behalf of Italian families while he was actually *president* of the EU.[90]

And when not calling for a renewal of adoption in general, many prominent politicians were petitioning the Romanian government for individual exceptions to the moratorium—that is, for the approval of the adoptions of specific children. The list of names leaked to the press by the Romanian opposition included a number of MEPs, plus US senators John Kerry and Edward Kennedy, among other US congresspersons. More embarrassingly, the list included the current president, and a past president, of the European Commission *itself*. In other words, a request to approve specific adoptions came from heads of the very organization that pushed for adoption to be suspended in the first place.[91]

So cacophonous were the signals and countersignals from within the EU that the European Commission's director for enlargement, Eneko Landaburu, had to make absolutely clear his position on the subject: "I am neither for nor against international adoption!" he said.[92] Ah.

And, of course, pressure also came from the main recipient of adopted Romanians: the United States. As early as 1996, in hearings before the Senate Finance Subcommittee on International Trade, congressman and former ambassador to Romania David Funderbunk opposed extension of the country's Most Favored Nation Status. Among other problems, he said that "over 100,000 orphans continue to live in horrific conditions when many could be more easily adopted by Americans."[93] By 2001, with the moratorium in place, the Americans got tougher. Not being in Europe, of course, the United States can't determine EU membership, but it *is* on the North Atlantic and has a lot to say about who gets into NATO. Which Romania very much wanted to join as well. In October, Prime Minister Adrian Nastase met with Secretary of State Colin Powell in Washington presumably to discuss Romania's NATO application. But "after a short introduction Powell switched to the subject of intercountry adoptions. These had to be resolved before accession to NATO could be further discussed."[94]

Under this barrage of complaint, the moratorium may have leaked a bit, but it didn't crack—the baroness' finger still firmly plugged the dike. In 2004, when 105 children slipped through to families in Italy, for example, Nicholson accused Romania of violating the moratorium and again asked that accession talks be suspended. That did it. In June, Romania passed Law 273/2004, which virtually shut down international adoption.[95]

Pressure on the moratorium rose in inverse proportion to the time remaining until the EU vote on Romanian accession, scheduled for October of 2006. In April of that year, the US Houses of Representatives voted on Resolution 578 which called upon Romania to "amend its child welfare and adoption laws to decrease barriers to adoption, both domestically and Intercountry."[96] Sponsor Christopher Smith (R-NJ) said that as of December 2005, 76,509 children were currently in Romania's child protection system, and only 333 children had been adopted domestically in 2005. The bill passed the House unanimously.

As the October deadline approached, pressure increased. On June 12 of 2006, the *Financial Times* ran a full-page ad signed by thirty-four NGOs that accused Romanian officials of running a "Guantanamo for Babies.... EU officials and celebrities are given carefully guided tours of 'new and improved' children's facilities wholly unrepresentative of the real Romania. Thousands of abandoned children still endure appalling conditions."[97] Local adoption was often infeasible, the ad claimed, because "many [abandoned children] enter a legal 'no man's land' where, because they do not have birth certificates or consent from the abandoning parent, they cannot be fostered or adopted [domestically], and often are not eligible for medical treatment or education." Much of the blame was laid directly at the feet of Emma Nicholson. "Her recent description of Romania as a 'model' for childcare is incomprehensible to those living with the reality."

Attentive readers would be surprised if the baroness took this affront lying down. The very next day, the *Financial Times* published Nicholson's response. "Romania banned international adoptions in 2001 because it was an evil trade in children," the baroness said. Many signatories of the ad, she said, "have a strong financial interest in the resumption of the highly profitable international adoptions business."[98]

One is tempted to conclude that the status of international adoption from Romania seemed to come down to a simple question. Of whom was the Romanian government most afraid: i) the leading politicians on the European Continent, ii) the world's only remaining superpower, or iii) a single British baroness? In the end, Romania was welcomed into the European Union without ending the moratorium on international adoption. It is still in place as of this writing.

It is hardly surprising that domestic Romanian adoption has not managed to take up the slack. The number of children in state care is approximately the same as in 1979, about seventy thousand. Tens of thousands more are thought to be living on the streets.[99] In a 2014 article about the Bucharest Early

Intervention Study, Virginia Hughes wrote, "A taxi driver in Bucharest told me a story about friends of his, native Romanians, who have been trying to adopt a Romanian orphan for years. The regulations seem ridiculous; for example, children can't be adopted until the state has attempted to make contact with all of their fourth-degree relatives."[100] In practice this means "all relatives as distant as the siblings of grandparents must also sign away rights to the child."[101] Bogdan Simion, executive director of SERA Romania, a nonprofit foundation that helps support child welfare, says, "It is not a system for children's rights. It is a system for parents' rights."[102]

What lessons can we draw from the *cirque d' adoption* that was the politics of child welfare in post-Ceauşescu Romania? As in our other examples, while the "best interest of the children" was always touted, it would be hard to argue that it motivated most of the actors most of the time. We saw that when Dr. Zugravescu of the Romanian Adoption Commission said, "It pains me that this could happen," she was referring not to the horrific conditions in the country's orphanages, but to the "dirty business" of baby buying. Also, the on-again-off-again Romanian adoption policy was clearly driven by a desire to meet the conditions for joining the European Union. Requests by MEPs and American congressmen for exceptions to the moratorium came from constituent pressure, as did calls for the restoration of adoption. And the baroness? Emma Nicholson's credentials as an ardent defender of child welfare are well established, but was this really her primary concern in Romania? In their 2005 op-ed in the *Wall Street Journal*, Kunz and Reese say that "Lady Nicholson has been conducting a one-woman war against intercountry adoption (ICA).... Her view is that ICA is a cover for child trafficking and is also beneath the dignity of the member states of the EU." Our own interpretation is that the baroness was determined to stamp out baby buying and was willing to shut down one hundred viable adoptions to eliminate one she saw as illegitimate. She may honestly have seen this as in the best interest of the Romanian children, but we, and many others, are highly doubtful.

What Is Being Nurtured: Children or Old Grudges?

Interethnic or interracial adoption has occasionally been referred to as a form of "cultural genocide."[103] On the face of it, international adoption seems to be the very *antithesis* of genocide in that its purpose is not to exterminate people of a different race but to love and nurture them as members of one's own family. But contemporary adoption often suffers from guilt by association, that is, by association with awful past practices that seem to have something in common with current adoption. As an example, consider the "adoption program" under-taken by the very people who, through their inhumanity, introduced the con-cept of genocide into human vocabulary.

While Harry and Bertha Holt are relatively well known as founders of the first large-scale international adoption program of the postwar period, an even bigger program was launched by someone considerably more famous than the Holts, but whose name is not usually associated with adoption: Reichsführer-SS Heinrich Himmler, chief architect of the Nazi Holocaust. He was motivated by a perceived threat to the German population. Because Germany lost so many young men in World War I, a large fraction of interwar pregnancies occurred out of wedlock. As many as eight hundred thousand were aborted every year.[104] To stem the loss, in 1935 Himmler created the Lebensborn ("Spring of Life") Society. The society ran a number of homes where "racially acceptable" young women could secretly bear illegitimate children, often fathered by married offi-cers in the SS or Wehrmacht.

But encouraging illegitimate birth was not popular with the German public. In 1939, Nazi conquests in Eastern Europe gave Lebensborn an alter-native opportunity to expand the German population. Himmler's *Ostplan* (General Plan for the East) ordered that ethnic Poles were to be either expelled from the conquered territories or enslaved.[105] As historian Lynn Nicholas reports, "Getting rid of the Poles was important to the [Nazis] but they were determined to make quite sure that not a drop of possible German Blood be wasted in the process of ethnic cleansing."[106] In May of 1940, a top-secret memo entitled *The Treatment of Racial Aliens in the East* ordered that "racially selected children were to be abducted and Germanized."

SS doctors began combing Polish orphanages for children who appeared to have Nordic ancestry. Those aged two to six would be fostered or adopted by German families; those between six and twelve would be sent to German boarding schools. Two examples are Alodia and Dalia Witaszek, who went to Germany after their mother was sent to Auschwitz and their father, a member of the Polish underground, was hanged by the Nazis.[107] "They beat German into our minds until we didn't know what was what anymore," Alodia recalled in an interview sixty years later. "If we spoke Polish, they would beat us or lock us in dark rooms for hours." Polish children who refused or were unable to become suf-ficiently Germanized were usually sent to the Kalish extermination camp.

When orphanages failed to provide enough racially valuable adoptees, the SS began kidnapping children, literally taking some from their parent's arms.[108] Great care was taken that the adoptive parents back in Germany not know the children were originally Polish. They were designated as "German orphans from the regained Eastern Territories."[109] The number of kidnapped children is uncertain; it may be as high as two hundred thousand for Poland and another thirty thousand from Russia and other countries.[110] It's estimated that despite the postwar efforts of the United Nations Relief and Rehabilitation Administration, only 15 to 20 percent of the Polish children were ever returned to their original families.[111]

Or consider another example, a more recent genocide. We have visited the room in the former presidential palace in Kigali, Rwanda, where in 1994 the Hutu government planned the massacre of the country's minority Tutsis. The plans were launched when parties unknown fired a surface-to-air missile that crashed the president's plane literally into his own backyard—the wreckage is still visible a hundred yards or so behind the house. Over the next three months, some eight hundred thousand Tutsis were systematically slaughtered while the West stood by and did nothing. In a country so ravaged by ethnic hatred, it's not surprising that Mr. Nzaramba, Rwanda's assistant to the minister of Gender and Family Promotion would ask Mark, with genuine curiosity, "Why do Americans want to adopt these children?"

While the Tutsi had generally formed a political elite within Rwandan society, before colonization the lines between them and Hutus had been relatively porous. The language, religion, and cultural traditions did not systematically differ between the two ethnic groups, the biggest distinction, perhaps the only distinction, between them being in whether they made a living through raising cattle or farming. But colonial governments, Germany before World War I and Belgium after, used the Tutsi to administer colonial rule on the local level. They were provided with more education, land, income, and power. In 1933, Belgium decided to issue an identity card to each Rwandan, on which was stamped his or her ethnic "identity." To establish this identity, they measured the length and width of noses and the shapes of their eyes as well as counting the number of cattle they owned.[112] Under Belgium, French became the language of the elite, which eventually became the Hutu majority. The Belgians left Rwanda in 1962, but they did not take the resentment with them. It exploded into deadly violence on several occasions, even before independence, with the 1994 genocide being the most recent and most horrific.

In a subsequent visit to Kigali, we were told by Mr. Nzramba that some people had demanded to know why his ministry had placed Rwandan children with French families when the French, wanting to maintain Rwanda as French influenced, had sided with the Hutus in the war. He explained to them that a country's foreign policy was not a criterion for deciding whether a child could get a good home there. Thus, in Rwanda, part of the opposition to intercountry adoption was the result of ill-feeling toward France for supporting the génocid-aires and toward other Western countries for doing nothing to stop the geno-cide. But the Rwandan example also shows that one needs to acknowledge the relevance of the colonial legacy in motivating anti-foreign-adoption sentiment.

Intercountry Adoption as the New Imperialism

Colonialism was generally disastrous for indigenous peoples, and in many places the effects have yet to wear off. International adoption stirs up memories of previous exploitive relationships with colonial powers. As Bartholet explains, "[Adoption] can be seen as the ultimate kind of exploitation... namely the taking by the rich and powerful of the children born to the poor and power-less."[113] Of Latin American adoption, for example, Fieweger says, "Traditionally, these third-world republics have been providers of natural resources, purchased at bargain prices by the developed world, first Spain, then England, and today, the United States. Many Latin Americans object to international adoptions because, as they see it, Latin American children have become another natural resource in demand in the developed world."[114] So by this argument, adop-tion is a form of neocolonial resource extraction; only now what's being taken is the most precious resource a country has: its children. Fonseca describes an article published in 1987 by a famous Brazilian journalist: "She insists that intercountry adoption, with its salvationist overtones permits foreigners to feel like 'the pure, the saviors,' in relation to Brazilians seen as 'indigents, delin-quents, murderers, hunger-stricken, underdeveloped.' Rather than tolerate such an affront to national honor, the journalist declares, referring to the children adopted by foreigners: 'I prefer to cry over their deaths rather than to suffer the shame of them alive.'"[115] So here we have someone explicitly weighing national honor against the best interests of the child and declaring national honor to be the winner.

Of course, Western imperialists did more than extract natural and human resources from their colonies. An important part of colonization, especially when colonials needed to self-justify brutal repression, was the saving of pre-sumably benighted native souls through the spreading of Christianity. In describing Guatemala, for example, Adriaan Van Oss says that the one irre-ducible idea underlying Spanish colonization of America was Catholicism.[116] And while overt colonization has ended, the propagation of Christianity in the so-called Third World has certainly not—adoption continues to play a sig-nificant role in this sphere. Indeed, Bertha and Harry Holt were fundamen-talist Christians. Until professionalized in the 1960s, Holt adoptions were "by proxy," meaning children entered American families sight unseen, and the Holts asked only that applicants be "saved persons" who could pay the cost of children's airfare from Korea.[117] This model infuriated adoption professionals. And even some Holt admirers, such as author Pearl Buck, were disturbed by the couple's religious conservatism. When we were adopting through Holt in 1991, we were asked to supply a description of our personal relationship to God through Jesus Christ. When we explained that the relationship was at best "distant," we were allowed to substitute a statement of our moral values. We have been surprised by how much Christianity suffuses the adoption and orphan-care community in Africa.

In *The Child Catchers*, Joyce analyzes the adoption movement among evangelical Christians. This movement, according to Joyce and to many of its advocates as well, is motivated in large part by principles that are based, not surprisingly, on scripture. Accordingly, adoption responds to the biblical injunction to care for "widows and children" and "the poor." Also, many influential evangelicals think the adoption of needy children mirrors the adoption by God of born-again Christians. Promoters of this scriptural model of adoption include Rick Warren of Saddleback Church; Jedd Medefind of the Christian Alliance for Orphans; Russell Moore, author of *Adopted for Life: The Priority of Adoption for Christian Families and Churches*; and Tony Merida and Rick Morton, coauthors of *Orphanology: Awakening to Gospel-Centered Adoption and Orphan Care*. In her critique, Joyce says that the Christian adoption movement has at least two political motivations in addition to, or perhaps complementing, the biblical motivations. She argues that the movement seeks to reclaim from political liberals the issues of social justice and also that it uses adoption to offer an alternative to abortion, which, of course, evangelicals vigorously oppose. As Joyce sees it, the evangelical adoption movement extends the age-old colonial mission to convert natives to Christianity, part of the "Great Commission" to spread the Gospel. In this sense, she likens it to a continuation of "imperialism by other means." Adoption is a tool to replace the culture of developing countries with Western religion.

We're surprised to find ourselves in much less sympathy with Joyce's view than we might have been a few years ago. As we stated above, the Christian right generally opposes some of the social justice measures that we hold dear: gay rights and a woman's access to an abortion, for example. And we have the severe anxieties about the growing political influence of the religious right that we assume people like Joyce do. Our discovery of the deep connection between international adoption and evangelical Christianity, however, has made us less, rather than more, antagonistic toward the evangelical community. In our exploration of international adoption, we have made connections with very religious people whose determination to improve the lives of others in very practical ways is real. Adoption and orphan care are areas in which the Christian right not only supports social justice but actually *does* social justice. In other words, rather than talking about the plight of the world's poor, as we academics like to do, lots of these folks go abroad and do something about it, doing hard work in hard countries by building schools and orphanages, for example. We respect that. We may not entirely appreciate their spiritual motives, but economists are more concerned with outcomes. So, given our antipathy to so much of the evangelical political agenda, it's refreshing to be able to put international adoption on the other side of the ledger. Unlike perhaps Joyce, we would prefer to see not less adoption by fundamentalist Christians, but more adoption by secular humanists.

Rumors

On March 29, 1994, June Weinstock, a fifty-one-year-old American environmental consultant from Alaska, huddled for five hours in the police station of the village of San Cristobal Verapaz, Guatemala, with the local police chief, while outside a crowd of a thousand villagers tried to hack their way in. The villagers believed that Weinstock was responsible for the disappearance of an eight-year-old girl who got separated from her mother in the Easter crowd that morning. Even after the child safely reappeared, the crowd still tried to attack Weinstock. Tear gas failed to disperse them. Eventually she was dragged from the station and beaten with sticks and pipes until the police chief untruthfully persuaded the crowd that she was dead. In a coma, she was flown back to Guatemala City, and eventually to Fairbanks, still unconscious, ultimately suffering permanent brain injury as a result of the attack.[118]

Even less fortunate was Tetsuo Yamahiro, who was killed, along with a Guatemalan bus driver, when a mob attacked him and twenty-two other Japanese tourists as they visited a Mayan market in the village of Todos Santos Cuchumatan in May 2000. According to a police spokesman, "The tourists were taking pictures of women and children in the market when someone started to scream that they were stealing children and a crowd of 500 villagers quickly closed around them."[119] They attacked the tourists with sticks and stones. Police used tear gas to break up the crowd.

Why did these Guatemalan crowds believe that foreigners were stealing their children? In April of 1994, the *New York Times* reported, "Fed by rumors that Americans were coming to kidnap children, cut out their vital organs and ship them to the United States for transplantation, an extraordinary wave of panic has swept Guatemala over the last month."[120] In fact, rumors that international adoption was a front for the harvesting of children's organs had been circulating in Latin America for some time. Moreover, belief in these horror stories was not confined to poor and poorly educated indigenous people in remote villages: "In 1988 rumors about the traffic of organs were dignified by a federal prosecutor [in Brazil] who claimed to have sound evidence that Brazilian children adopted abroad were being used as guinea pigs in scientific experiments as well as for organ transplants."[121] Nor were these rumors given credence only in Latin America. In October 1993, a French deputy in the European Parliament reported that by his estimate only one thousand of four thousand Brazilian children who were "adopted" by Italians survived; the rest "had supposedly died from abuse or had been killed, their organs harvested for future transplants."[122] Otherwise reputable sources fanned the flames. According to a 1994 report to the United Nations, Todd Leventhal of the United States Information Agency stated that the organ transplant rumors were promoted in "British/Canadian and French television documentaries, a book published in Spain, a paper by the director of the World Organization Against Torture, a resolution by the European Parliament, numerous press articles, and the January 14, 1994 report of the U.N. Special Rapporteur on the Sale of Children, Child Prostitution, and Child Pornography."[123] None of these sources contains any credible evidence of child organ trafficking, however, Levanthal said.[124]

Not only was the organ theft unverified, it was largely infeasible. Medical experts had testified that successful organ transplantation requires a large number of people using sophisticated medical technology, and that given "the extremely short amount of time that organs remain viable for transplant... such operations could neither be organized clandestinely nor be kept secret."[125] These facts made little dent in what seemed to be a "worldwide wave of hysteria" over trafficking in children's organs.[126]

Though we have argued that much opposition to international adoption is not really about the best interests of the child, the hysteria over organ trafficking is surely an exception. The mobs in the Guatemalan villages were horrified not about what was happening to their ethnic group, or to their nation, or even to themselves; it was about an outrage to innocent children. Even here, however, the glass darkens slightly when looking at the evidence. The April 1994 *New York Times* article stated that after a civil war that caused one hundred thousand known deaths and forty thousand disappearances, "the hold on power by civilian leaders is precarious." The propagation of these horror stories may have been politically motivated. "Diplomats and human rights advocates fear that the rumors are part of a campaign [by the military] to destabilize the administration of President Ramiro de Leon Carpio by weakening the influence of the United States Government, which has been an important source of support for the embattled Guatemalan leader."[127] So while it is clearly in the best interest of a child to prevent her murder at the hands of organ thieves, even here the arousal of panic may have partly served some other political purpose.

Today, fortunately, comparatively few take seriously the stories of adoption as a mask for trafficking in human organs. While hysteria may be resistant to logical argument, it eventually subsides in the absence of direct evidence. But that sorry tale of murderous paranoia suggests once again that antipathy to international adoption on the basis of the best interest of the child should always be examined for ulterior motivation.

In this chapter, we argued that much of the criticism of international adoption, rather than being motivated by what is in the best interest of the child, is actually motivated by national pride, national interest, or national resentment over past injustices. These motivations are understandable, to be sure, but are not good justifications for abandoning international adoption as a viable option for children needing permanent families. Instead, policy decisions such as those affecting international adoption should be judged by comparing, to the extent possible, the costs and benefits to the children and their families. That is not what has happened with the adoption policies we described here. The best interest of the child was always given lip service, but rarely played a decisive role.

Is It Culture? Or Is It Really Race?

But the fact that much opposition to removal of a child from her birth culture is motivated by national interest or national pride does not allow us to dismiss the notion that international adoption is ultimately not the best option for her. This brings us back to the original question in the Zulu Boy case: is it harmful to the child if she is raised outside of the culture to which her genetic ancestry links her? Some people consider the answer to be obvious. David Smolin—one of those people we admire but disagree with—asks what happens when we try to Americanize, for example, one of the many thousands of Korean girls who are adopted by white families in the United States. "It would take a willful blindness to deny the Korean adoptee's family ties to Korean parents and the nation of Korea. Indeed, the Korean adoptee cannot escape the obvious—that her physical body did not descend in any way from her adoptive parents. Every part of her physical appearance points back to Korea."[128] That seems reasonable enough, but this begs a question: seeing this child in a mall, would most Americans know that she was from Korea? Or might they think she was from China or Vietnam or Cambodia? These are very different places with very different cultures. Every part of her physical appearance points back to Asia, yes, but to Korea? In the last thirty years, we have taught literally thousands of students from Asia and Africa, and we can certainly distinguish at first sight a South Asian from an East Asian or an African. But will we know a Bengali from a Nepali, or a Tibetan from a Han Chinese? We will not. This is perhaps to our discredit, but we are hardly unique in this failure. Sierra Leone in West Africa has culturally little in common with Rwanda in Central Africa, but, in Kigali, a local man tried to speak to GB in Kinyarwandan because our son was obviously African. In America, he is not obviously an African; he is perceived as African American.

The point is that when critics of international adoption talk about *culture* what they are almost always referring to is *race*. Currently most transnational adoption is also transracial, and, when it is not, it seems to arouse much less anxiety about cultural loss. Is there much fretting that children adopted from Russia will no longer be Slavic, or that Romanians will lose their Balkan heritage? Not very much.[129]

It can be argued, therefore, that the primary objections to *transcultural* international adoption are in fact objections to *transracial* adoption. Opposition to placing children of color in white families has been long and bitter, but it did not originate in the international sphere—it started with American families adopting American children. We next look at the history of how transracial adoption has had to struggle to gain acceptance. We see how the regulatory regime of adoption made it harder to pursue transracial placements and the costs that this imposed on children.

Birth Culture Shock

In the preceding chapter, we argued that fears of children losing their culture are often really fears about cultures (nationalities) losing their children. We have argued that sometimes policy makers use loss of birth culture as an excuse for opposing international adoption. However, as we see in this section of Isata's story, even some birth parents who are willing to release their child for adoption may have concerns about them keeping their cultural heritage. Failure to arrange in advance how birth culture will be handled in the adoption—and such failure is virtually guaranteed under the Hague system—can lead to significant conflict eventually.

October 2012
Ten years after arriving in Oregon with Jason and Beckie Sibley, Isata is eighteen years old, a cheerful and pretty young woman, happy in her family with her (adoptive) parents, four (adopted) siblings—as we see later, two more Leonean children had been added to the family—all between fourteen and eighteen years old, and two grown siblings (who are birth children). Her parents recently have allowed the oldest of the young adopted group, including Isata, to get on Facebook. Isata's mom had homeschooled her from when she arrived because she didn't want Isata to stand out or be made fun of because she was older and hadn't been in school continuously, especially as she was learning English. Beckie initially homeschooled the other kids as well, though they all eventually graduated from the local public high school. In October 2012, Isata was rarely thinking about her family in Sierra Leone anymore and had accepted, sort of, that they had not been her parents. One night on Facebook, she received a "friend" request from someone with a long African name. The last name looked like the last name she remembered. The picture that went with the name looked like the older brother she remembered from Sierra Leone. She went to Beckie. "A man is trying to friend me on Facebook," she said. "I went to his

profile and there's a picture of me there. I think he's my brother." Within a week, the Sibleys got a call from Pa M., Isata's birth father in Sierra Leone. The Sibleys were shocked to discover, after all these years, that the story of placement by an aunt and uncle and the death of Isata's birth parents was simply a lie. Someone—presumably The Children's Home?—had made that up.

They expected cultural differences when the M. family found Isata on Facebook. After ten years of no contact with their daughter, and without even knowing whether she was still alive, the M. family was overjoyed to communicate with her via Skype. Almost immediately a reunion was planned in Freetown for January of 2013. Beckie and Isata began raising money from family, friends, and church members for the two of them to fly to Freetown. But even before those plans could be consummated, cultural clashes emerged between Isata and her birth family.

According to Beckie and Isata, by Facebook message Isata was asked, primarily by Pa M., about why she had abandoned her native language, her native culture, and her religion (Islam). She was made to understand that she would eventually be expected to help them financially. She was reminded that one of the main reasons she was sent to America was so that she would be educated and one day return and help her family. She should earn money now to help support her family. It was what was expected of an African daughter. Isata's birth and adopted cultures were indeed very different, and she was suddenly caught between them.

Isata was frustrated to the point that she nearly canceled the trip. She told Beckie she wanted to end all contact. Beckie was worried that they would pressure Isata to stay in Sierra Leone once she got there. So, prior to the visit, with Isata's approval, Beckie wrote a long e-mail to Pa M.

"You have all indicated that you are disappointed in her for forgetting her culture, language, and sense of obligation to your family," Beckie said. "She does not want to feel sad or angry after communicating with you; yet she often does because you blame her for being American, for losing her language and culture. This is not fair to her; it is not fair to us. She does not deserve this criticism by the very people who sent her away."

When we, the authors, met with the M. family in Freetown in January 2013, just before the planned visit of the Sibleys, they were very upset, especially Pa. He showed us the e-mail from Beckie and some more e-mails back and forth between the two. Eventually, however, despite some hard feelings expressed in that exchange, and with a little feather-smoothing by the authors, explaining some differences between the two cultures, the reunion happened.

Isata describes her experience of the event:

> Before the reunion I was very nervous. I thought they might not like me. I'm so different than when they saw me last. When I saw them at the airport, I first noticed my little sister who was so much bigger. She had been a very little girl the last time I saw her. We were the first two to hug and we cried. We had been so close before I went to America. Everyone seemed happy to see each other.

Shaun M. describes the scene at the airport:

> I hugged her over five minutes, crying as it was a very long time since I last saw her, over ten years. I was very glad to also see Madam Beckie who had been taking care of Isata all this while.…
> As we were in the Ferry crossing (from the airport) we were very glad as Madam Beckie took photos of us together. We continued the happy mood when finally we reached at the Ferry Terminal where other family members were waiting to see them. During this period there were tears of joy flowing through each family member as Madam Beckie continued taking photos of these moments.

In interviews with the authors, Isata, Shaun, and Beckie agree that the reunion went really well, with only minor glitches. The M. family had wanted everyone to visit Pa's village up country (so Pa could proudly show off his daughter's return). But the Sibleys would have had to pay to rent vans to carry everyone and buy food, and that was beyond their means, so they begged out of the village trip, and the M. family accepted that with good grace. All parties were happy with the visit and cried at the end. Isata said she planned to return to Sierra

Leone in a couple of years and live there for a year to get closer to her family and to work.

We think there are a couple of points to make here. It could be argued that Isata had, as some adoption scholars would say, lost her birth culture. But this loss was less a problem for her than for the adults who remained behind. It was the M. family, not Isata, who objected to what she had become in her new life in America. Nevertheless, their problems and issues should not be ignored.

But also, the M. family had certain expectations regarding how the adoption would proceed, and these expectations were not met. We believe that this problem arises because the birth and adoptive families do not meet prior to the adoption. As we will explain, the Hague Convention, which currently governs most of international adoption, specifically discourages pre-adoption contact between birth and adoptive families. This makes it difficult, if not impossible, for both sets of parents to negotiate an adoption arrangement that is mutually satisfactory in terms of preserving birth culture, or indeed in terms of any other aspect of the adoption.

CHAPTER 3

Is It Culture or Race?

I am the better woman, the wiser human being, for having my two black children. And I hope and believe they are the better, too, and the more understanding of me and my people because of their white adoptive parents.

Pearl S. Buck[1]

In 1989, the Supreme Court of the United States was asked to decide whether twenty-nine-year-old Jenny Bell had been residing on the Choctaw Reservation in Mississippi in December of 1985. This seems like a question that requires, say, a phone book, not the judgment of the highest court in the land. There was certainly no question of where Jenny had been *living* at the time. She had been living with Orrey and Vivian Holyfield in Long Beach, Mississippi, two hundred miles from the reservation, waiting for her twins to be born. The twins were to be adopted by the Holyfields. But where did she officially *reside*? It turns out that this mattered a great deal for the future of her children.[2]

Intermittently here we use the story of Jenny Bell to illustrate the power of race in adoption, specifically how racial identity was directly codified into adoption law in response to the demands of a minority group.

The Never-Ending Interaction of Race and Adoption

Perhaps we should not have been surprised to find that in the last few decades so much opposition toward international adoption centers on the issue of race. But we are not alone in this. When she first considered adoption, Elizabeth Bartholet, an author on adoption and discrimination, was "stunned at the dominant role race played" in adoption,[3] sometimes in unexpected ways. In

Family Bonds, she describes a visit to one of Lima's most elite pediatricians, whom she had consulted after three other doctors had failed to relieve her infant son's nausea and diarrhea.[4] In the summer, she'd been told, unclean water made sickness common among Lima's infants and many died. Bartholet was desperately afraid that Michael would not live through another three weeks of illness. Without even looking at Michael, however, the expensive pediatrician calmly reassured her. Not to worry, he explained, he could get her *another* baby from among those left at the hospital by poor mothers *and* have Bartholet's name placed on the birth certificate. She would be the official mother of the baby he provided. The tedious and uncertain adoption process could be entirely bypassed with the stroke of a pen! Only when Bartholet firmly explained that she wanted him to save *this* child, her new son, did the doctor bother to examine Michael.

"Oh, I see, I understand," he said. "What an extraordinary child." Michael did not look at all like the mestizo or Indian children who were normally placed for international adoption. The doctor glanced knowingly at Bartholet. "Entirely white," he continued, "not even any Mongolian spots" (the dark patches that often appear on the backsides of non-white newborns). "It was overwhelmingly clear," Bartholet wrote, "that Michael's value had been transformed in the doctor's eyes by his whiteness. Whiteness made it comprehensible that someone would want to cure and keep this child rather than discard him."[5]

Jenny Bell Leaves the Reservation

The aforementioned Jenny Bell was living on the Choctaw Reservation with two children when she discovered she was pregnant with twins by a married man with two kids of his own. Like her, the father was a "full-blooded" Choctaw. She tried, unsuccessfully, to find someone on the reservation to take the twins. An aunt was willing to take one, but Jenny did not want the twins to be separated. Meanwhile, Orrey Holyfield was a middle-aged Methodist minister of fragile health, because of which, and because of their age, he and his wife Vivian had been rejected by multiple adoption agencies. A friend who taught on the reservation connected them with Jenny Bell. Unable to find someone on the reservation willing to take them, Bell decided to release the twins to the Holyfields. The genetic father agreed and everything was arranged through a private attorney. Bell moved in with the Holyfields a few months before the babies came. The twins, Seth and Beth, were born on December 29, 1985, and "twelve days later, Jenny executed a consent form before the chancery court of Harrison County, Mississippi, relinquishing her parental rights. The following day, Windell Jefferson, the twins' father, did the same."[6] Within a month the adoption was final, and Jenny Bell moved back to the reservation.

Because all parties had agreed to this adoption, the chancery court was not required to inform the tribe that this adoption had taken place. But, as a courtesy, they did.

The Midcentury Cult of Racial Matching

The adoption of Jenny Bell's babies by the Holyfields would have been unthinkable in 1950. From the 1930s to the late 1960s, the prevailing view among adoption professionals was that children should be placed with families that they "matched," meaning that it should appear to the outside world that the adoptive child had been born into the family. As historian Ellen Herman puts it, "According to the matching ethos, the best adoptive families never betrayed their adoptive status by declaring their difference.... Successful matching erased itself, making the social design of adoption invisible."[7] Matching occurred along just about every characteristic including religion, intellectual ability, and emotional temperament. Because not all characteristics are obvious at birth, delaying placement for six to nine months, sometimes longer, during which time more physical traits become evident and even intelligence could be tested, was considered an acceptable tradeoff for getting a better match.

Most obviously, matching required that children *look* like their new parents, racially and ethnically. In her book, *Kinship by Design*, Herman uses case records from the 1940s to 1960s to exemplify the struggle to achieve physical resemblance. The requests could be quite specific.

> "Your agent promised me a nice red-haired boy," noted one applicant early in the century, "I have a red-haired wife and five red-haired girls and we want a boy to match."... Another couple said "they were willing to consider a child of Hungarian heritage or with an Italian strain providing that their coloring was not too much of a contrast."... In New York, Mr. and Mrs. B explained that although they were Jewish themselves, they did not want a child who was "heavy Jewish looking" and therefore preferred one who was "half-Jewish."[8]

An infant's racial background is less apparent at birth than many might suppose. For example, some African American babies look relatively Latino at birth—as our son did; hair can change color and texture; eyes and skin can develop darker pigmentation. Adoptive parents rarely welcomed surprises. "In [some] cases, telling prospective parents about a child's ambiguous racial identity had proved an obstacle to any adoption at all, or a source of shame so profound that adoptions were disrupted."[9] Adoption agencies consulted prominent anthropologists who examined hair and facial features—would this child ultimately be able to "pass for white?"[10]

The cult of matching could even cause international scandals. In February of 1954, an attorney was arrested at the Montreal airport as he was attempting to leave Canada with his wife and parents. He was charged with aiding an illegal adoption ring by teaching them how to falsify birth documents. The *New York Times* reported that "authorities had been investigating the ring, which they think sold most of the children in the Eastern United States to childless Jewish couples who paid prices ranging between $3000 and $10,000."[11] Why mostly Jewish couples? The Jewish community produced fewer unwed mothers than society as a whole, but even couples willing to take non-Jewish (white) infants faced a serious bottleneck. In *The Traffic in Babies*, author Karen Balcom explains that, as late as the 1960s, most states and provinces had laws "restricting the placement of children across religious lines or strongly recommending that children be placed with families sharing the same religious heritage as the birth family."[12] Some Canadian adoption agencies, therefore, took advantage of loopholes in the cross-border adoption procedures to supply this "niche market" of Jewish couples.

In this prevailing climate of racial matching, therefore, it was extraordinary that in 1958 the government launched the first program to deliberately create interracial families: The Indian Adoption Project.

The Choctaws Respond to Jenny Bell's Adoption

When the Harrison County Chancery Court sent notice of the Holyfield adoption to the tribal court of the Mississippi Choctaws, the tribe immediately tried to stop it. In March 1986, the tribe filed a motion with the court to vacate the adoption of Seth and Beth on the grounds that it violated the Indian Child Welfare Act (ICWA) of 1978. Under the ICWA, tribal courts had jurisdiction over all custody matters involving *all* children of members of the tribe. And not just on the reservation. If a child eligible to be fostered or adopted lived on tribal land, jurisdiction belonged exclusively to the tribal court; if the child lived off tribal land, jurisdiction was shared between the tribal and state courts. This was precisely the reason that Jenny Bell had delivered her baby in Long Beach, two hundred miles away, to prevent the tribal courts from interfering with the placement. But, the tribe argued, Jenny's twins were "Indian children" under the provisions of the ICWA, and therefore could not be placed for adoption without tribal approval.

The ICWA was a backlash against what was widely considered, at the time it was launched, the most racially progressive adoption program ever undertaken by the US government.

The Indian Adoption Project (IAP)

In 1958, the Bureau of Indian Affairs (BIA) and the highly respected Child Welfare League of America (CWLA) collaborated in developing the Indian Adoption Project (IAP). It responded to complaints by state welfare authorities that the Native American children needing out-of-home placement far outnumbered the Indian families who might foster or adopt them. Some of these kids needed to go to families of other races, presumably mostly to white folks.

Officially, the IAP removed 395 children from reservations and placed them for adoption in non-Indian families, with a later extension placing approximately 250.[13] Who were these children and why were they taken away from their families? Not surprisingly, people associated with the project answer those questions quite differently than do its (mostly) Native American critics. Giving the official reasoning, David Fanshel, commissioned by the CWLA to evaluate the program, wrote, "[The children] came from family situations where the oppression of poverty and the meanness of daily life—so familiar to American Indians—had exacted its toll. The children were identified by social workers on the reservations as being at risk of growing up without any semblance of family life."[14] Project director Arnold Lyslo, said,

> It had been apparent for some time from the reports of Area and Agency Welfare Staff of the Bureau of Indian Affairs, that many children who might have been firmly established in secure homes at an earlier age through adoption had been passed from family to family on a reservation or that they had spent years at public expense at federal boarding schools or in foster care. They never had the security of family life to promote their development and assure their future.[15]

How did removal from their families and placement in white homes affect the lives of these children? Unusually, for that time period, the IAP included a one-year and a five-year follow-up evaluation of the children and adoptive parents (though not birth parents) because, as principal evaluator Fanshel put it,

"Adoption across racial lines is a comparatively rare experience in the United States, [and] there was interest in establishing whether such placements were viable from the perspective of both parents and children."[16] Overall, the results were reassuring. Eight out of ten children were doing "quite well" and only one in ten showed problems that "make his future adjustment seem uncertain."[17] Thus the IAP was a progressive, boldly interracial program to help children in serious need, which, according to a careful scientific evaluation study, showed overwhelmingly positive outcomes on the children and their adoptive parents. At the completion of the project, director Lyslo proudly said, "One can no longer say that the Indian child is the 'forgotten child.'"[18]

Yet, within a few decades, the Child Welfare League of America would publicly apologize for cosponsoring this project. What happened?

Jenny Bell Meets Blood Quantum Rules

The Indian Child Welfare Act, under which the Choctaws were suing the Holyfields, defines an "Indian child" as any "unmarried person who is under age eighteen and is either (a) a member of an Indian tribe or (b) is eligible for membership in an Indian tribe and is the *biological* offspring of a member of an Indian tribe" (emphasis added).[19] A child is an Indian child simply by being "eligible for tribal membership." And who defines eligibility for membership? The tribe itself. By what method? Blood quantum rules.

Traditionally, Native American tribes did not use racial heritage to determine inclusion.[20] In colonial times, even captives were sometimes incorporated into the community, like the fictional John Butler in Conrad Richter's *The Light in the Forest*, a kidnapped white child who is called True Son by his Lenni Lenape father.[21] The blood quantum concept, not surprisingly, was invented by whites. In 1705, the Virginia legislature voted to deny civil rights to all "Indians," "Negroes," and "mulattoes," defining a mulatto as anyone with one-half Indian blood or one-eighth Negro blood.[22] Thus was first quantified, perhaps, a racial contempt ratio: Indians were only half as good as whites, but still four times better than Africans. Tribes were first made subject to blood quantum rules, again not surprisingly, by the US government. In the late nineteenth century, the government needed to determine who was eligible to sell the properties it had created by carving up and privatizing what had originally been the tribes' communal land.[23] This, it was thought, would speed the "civilizing" process. The more white you were under the blood quantum rules, the more economic freedom the government gave you. For most tribes, the blood quantum concept stuck.

About two-thirds of the 304 federally registered Indian tribes have eligibility requirements based on blood quantum rules.[24] Among the tribes using them, blood quantum rules for tribal membership vary quite a bit. Only six tribes have requirements as strict as one-half (at least one parent), and fewer than another twenty require at least one grandparent (one-quarter).[25] The requirement for the Choctaw Nation was one thirty-second, one great-great grandparent.

The Choctaws claimed that Jenny was a resident of the reservation when the twins were born, even if she wasn't physically living there. It was her permanent home, as evidenced by her having returned there after the babies were turned over to the Holyfields. Typically, children born out of wedlock are legally domiciled with the mother. So, in spite of Jenny's sojourn to Long Beach, the tribe argued, Seth and Beth were legally residing on the reservation at birth, meaning that under the ICWA, the tribal court had *exclusive* jurisdiction over the children. The Holyfield adoption must therefore be vacated.

The chancery court did not agree. The twins were not domiciled on the reservation because they had never lived there, and, moreover, both biological parents voluntarily gave their parental rights to the Holyfields. An appeal to the Supreme Court of Mississippi failed to overturn the lower court's ruling. The state supreme court noted that not only had Jenny willingly surrendered her twins, but she had given birth off the reservation *specifically to avoid* interference by the tribal court. This was not a case of recovering a lost child, the court said. Both sets of parents wanted the adoption to take place. The tribal court, therefore, did not have the exclusive jurisdiction that it claimed.

But the Choctaws would not give up the fight. Why not? In refusing to concede jurisdiction in the Holyfield case, the Mississippi Choctaw Tribe might appear slightly stubborn. After all, as the lower courts noted, none of the parties to the adoption opposed it in any way. Who was being harmed? To compound the strangeness, Orrey Holyfield, the adoptive father, had a paternal grandfather who was a full-blooded Choctaw. Thus, Orrey was one-quarter Choctaw, which meant that under the tribe's own definition, the twins were actually being adopted by a Choctaw Indian. So what exactly was there to complain about?

As legal scholar Solangel Maldonado explains,

[The Tribe] feared that if the *Holyfield* decision were allowed to stand,
Mississippi state courts improperly exercising jurisdiction over tribal
children would routinely place them in non-Indian homes, thereby
providing incentives for non-Indian families from all over the country

to come to Mississippi for tribal children. In other words, the Tribe feared that Mississippi would become "a mecca for black marketeers in Indian children."[26]

The tribe appealed to the US Supreme Court.

Backlash Against the Indian Adoption Project

The Indian Child Welfare Act, the basis for *Mississippi Choctaw v. Holyfield*, was spawned by strong tribal reaction to the Indian Adoption Project. Tribal resistance to the IAP crystalized in 1968, when county welfare officials removed a six-year-old boy named Ivan Brown from the care of his grandmother on the Devil's Lake Sioux Reservation in North Dakota. She was his grandmother, not genetically, but by tribal tradition. At sixty-three years, the woman was considered by the county welfare service too old to care for Ivan, and they took him away. The tribe asked for the help of the American Association of Indian Affairs (AAIA) in New York, which sent a young, long-haired Native American lawyer named Bertram Hirsch, who would turn the tide of Indian adoption policy.

At Devil's Lake, Hirsch was shocked to discover, "a quarter of the tribe's children had been placed off the reservation—either in boarding schools, white foster homes, or adoptions."[27] Over the next two years, further investigation in sixteen states with large Indian populations showed similar statistics: 25–35 percent of native children were off the reservation whether in boarding schools or with mainly non-Indian adoptive or foster families.[28] Although the vast majority of these "removals" were not adoptions or foster care placements, but children attending government boarding schools off of the reservation, to opponents of the IAP, the key fact was that large numbers of Indian children were required to leave their homes, even if only temporarily. Hirsch's investigation galvanized Indian opposition to any removal policy, with the AAIA leading the fight.

In civil-rights-era America, the protests of Native American tribes against child removals could not long be ignored by the federal government. By 1974, a sympathetic young senator from North Dakota, James Abourezk—the Senate's first Arab American—had begun congressional hearings on Indian child welfare reform. Abourezk's opening remarks to the Subcommittee on Indian Affairs revealed his attitude about the importance of birth culture. "[State welfare] Officials would seemingly rather place their Indian Children in non-Indian settings where their Indian culture, their Indian traditions, and their entire Indian way of life are threatened."[29] Why, he asked, didn't the Bureau of Indian

Affairs and the Department of Health Education and Welfare provide more support for families with the goal of helping them remain intact? Over a two-year period, families testified about egregious instances of improper removal; tribal leaders described the treaty violations and loss of sovereignty; psychiatric experts described the harmful effects of child's placement in a non-Indian family. As Navajo legal expert Leonard B. Jimson saw the problem,

> A judge who thinks in terms of the comfort and stability of a middle-class Anglo home may unconsciously think about this when he looks at a Navajo hogan where people do not have these same comforts. He may not see the importance of raising children to speak Navajo or to know their own culture and religion, because he assumes that all Navajos want to speak and think like Anglos, and this is best for them. In short, the way that the caseworker and judge look at family life may be so different that Navajo people cannot ever satisfy them, even though they also want to do what is in "the best interests" of the children.[30]

The end result of the protests was the Indian Child Welfare Act (ICWA) of 1978. The purpose of the ICWA was to "protect the best interests of Indian children and to promote the stability and security of Indian tribes and families."[31] Thus, it was concerned with the costs of adoption to two parties: harm to the child and harm to the tribe. Under some circumstances, of course, those goals may have been in conflict. The ICWA made sweeping changes in the power of state agencies over Indian children. Under the act, tribal courts had jurisdiction over all child-custody matters involving members of the tribe, and thus would resolve all conflicts. If the child lived on tribal land, jurisdiction was exclusive; if the child lived off tribal land, jurisdiction was concurrent with state courts. Thus, the state had no authority to remove an Indian child from any home on the reservation without the tribal court's permission. And if a member of the tribe lived off the reservation, how did we know she was a member of the tribe? The tribe deemed her so, primarily on the basis of blood quantum rules. Hence, for the first time at the national level, the Indian Child Welfare Act formally, legally codified race as a key factor in determining who was allowed to adopt whom.

The Jenny Bell Case Goes to the Supreme Court

Basing its decision on the ICWA, the US Supreme Court sided with the Mississippi Choctaws. Jenny couldn't circumvent tribal authority just by fleeing the reservation to have her babies. Writing for the six–three majority, Justice Brennan said, "Tribal jurisdiction under [ICWA] was not meant to be defeated by the actions of individual members of the tribe, for Congress was concerned not solely about the interests of Indian children and families, but also about the impact on the tribes themselves of the large numbers of Indian children adopted by non-Indians."[32] So, the fact that the birth parents wanted to place the twins with the Holyfields was insufficient to allow the adoption—the rights of both sets of parents did not outweigh those of the tribe. What about the rights of Seth and Beth, who were three years old now and had spent their entire lives with the Holyfields? "It is not ours to say whether the trauma that might result from removing these children from their adoptive family should outweigh the interest of the Tribe—and perhaps the children themselves—in having them raised as part of the Choctaw community." In the court's view, the ICWA was passed to protect the sovereignty of Indian tribes in deciding custody matters for tribal children, generally as defined by race. That sovereignty outweighed the rights of the birth parents and the rights of the children. More accurately, perhaps, the decision said that it was up to the tribal court to weigh the interest of the tribe, the children, and both sets of parents.

An interesting postscript to the story is that when finally given jurisdiction, the tribal court supported the adoption. They ruled that the advantage to the Choctaw Nation of retaining the twins did not justify the painful separation of Beth and Seth from the only parents they really knew. But that decision was made by the Choctaw Nation and no one else.

Lessons of the IAP

When launched in 1958, the Indian Adoption Project might have seemed a logical extension of the civil rights movement then sweeping America, a chance to create not just multiracial communities, but multiethnic families as well. Instead, it triggered a backlash of congressional proportions in the form of the Indian Child Welfare Act. At a meeting of the National Indian Child Welfare Association in 2001, the executive director of the Child Welfare League, Shay Bilchik, formally apologized for the organization's sponsorship of the IAP. "No matter how well intentioned and how squarely in the mainstream this was at the time," he said, "it was wrong; it was hurtful; and it reflected a kind of bias that surfaces feelings of shame."[33] If white majority America believed that adopting minority children would help atone for centuries of oppression, some voices within the minority communities were loudly proclaiming that it wouldn't. In fact, just as reaction to the Indian Adoption Project gathered steam among Native Americans, elements in the African American community began protesting the placement of black children in white families.[34]

Opposition to White Families Adopting Black Kids

During the immediate postwar period, transracial adoption of blacks by whites had appeared to be gaining acceptability. According to the University of Oregon's Adoption History Project,

> The National Urban League Foster Care and Adoptions Project, founded in 1953, and Adopt-a-Child, founded in 1955, took big steps toward promoting "Negro" adoption nationally. Adopt-a-Child lasted for five years, received more than 4000 inquiries from around the United States and the Caribbean, and facilitated the placement of more than 800 children before running out of money.... [Even] some states with overwhelmingly white populations... initiated projects: The Children's Home Society of Minnesota launched PAMY (Parents to Adopt Minority Youngsters) and the Boys and Girls Aid Society of Oregon sponsored "Operation Brown Baby."[35]

But this apparently rising tide of white families adopting black children ebbed sharply, and quite abruptly, in 1972.

The year 1972 had begun auspiciously enough for transracial adoption. In January, Nobel Prize-winning author Pearl Buck, then eighty, published an essay about her experience of adopting two black girls (among many other children). The daughter of American missionaries, Buck had spent her youth as a racial outsider. "In China, I was the wrong color, for my skin was white instead of brown, my eyes were blue instead of black, and my hair light instead of dark."[36] Biographer Peter Conn says, "Pearl was one of the few white Americans who grew up experiencing some of the sense of isolation and presumed inferiority that American blacks have known in white America."[37] After World War II, Buck and her husband adopted two girls, one from Germany and one from Japan, each of whom was the offspring of a local woman and a black soldier of the American occupation. Both children, like American Korean children born during the Korean War, were despised within the communities of their birth. Buck's essay said,

> I would not have missed the interesting experience of adopting children of races different than my own. They have taught me much. They have

stretched my mind and heart. They have brought me, through love, into kinship with peoples different from my own conservative, proud, white ancestry. I am the better woman, the wiser human being, for having my two black children. And I hope and believe they are the better, too, and the more understanding of me and my people because of their white adoptive parents.

At least I know that there is no hate in them. No, there is no hate in them at all.[38]

Two months later, in March of 1972, a panel of federal judges in New Orleans found that a Louisiana law prohibiting "biracial" adoption violated the equal protection clause of the Fourteenth Amendment. The justices ruled, "To justify the classifications in the statute the [state] must convince the court that under all circumstances it is against the child's best interest to have racially different parents."[39] Thus, transracial adoption had achieved what appeared to be a significant legal milestone against racist adoption laws.

But ironically, in June 1972, the National Association of Black Social Workers (NABSW) attempted to do just what the judges in New Orleans had challenged the state to do: convince the nation that *under all circumstances* it is against the child's best interest to have racially different parents.

The NABSW's Denunciation of Interracial Adoption

The fourth annual meeting of the National Association of Black Social Workers was held in Nashville in June of 1972. Similar to that of the American Indian tribes, the stand taken by the NABSW at their meeting was that adoption of their children by the white majority was a threat to the very survival of their culture. In a statement that launched what the *New York Times* called "A Furor Over Whites Adopting Blacks," the NABSW took a position on transracial adoption that contained no hint of equivocation.[40] "The National Association of Black Social Workers has taken a vehement stand against the placement of black children in white homes *for any reason*" (emphasis added). In announcing the position statement to the press, the association's president and cofounder, Cenie Williams, went so far as to invoke the g-word: "We have committed ourselves to go back to our communities and work to end this particular form of genocide."[41] A later NABSW president, William Merritt stated even more strongly, "It [placing black children with white parents] is a blatant form of race and *cultural genocide*."[42]

Part of their argument was about motivation. Why, after all of these years, the black social workers asked, were white families suddenly interested in black children? Because, they argued, in the face of a low supply of adoptable white infants and children, mainstream society had performed a hypocritical about-face in how it defined blackness. "Those born of black-white alliances are no longer black as decreed by immutable law and social custom for centuries. They are now... bi-racial, emphasizing the[ir] whiteness." The system was set up to benefit the majority, not minorities: "Transracial adoption [is] an expedient for white folk, not... an altruistic humane concern for black children."[43] This point seems undeniable at least for some white adopters.

But the NABSW's main argument was framed, as arguments about adoption usually are, in terms of the best interest of the child: "Only a black family can transmit the emotional and sensitive subtleties of perception and reaction essential for a black child's survival in a racist society." The oft-expressed counterargument that determined white parents could instill racial pride in their black children was dismissed: "The attempts by white adoptive parents to learn techniques to care for black children (hair, etc.), to get to know more African Americans to provide more Black role models, to teach African American cultural traditions and history are worse than useless because they make the transracially adopted child feel different within the family.... Superficialities convey nothing of worth and are more damaging than helpful."[44]

But surely a permanent home in a white family was far better for a black child than foster care or institutionalization, wasn't it? Yes, said the NABSW, but this was a false dichotomy; there would be plenty of homes for these children if the system would stop discouraging black parents from adopting them in sufficient numbers. Social services agencies should quit requiring black adopters to meet the standards that screened many potential black adopters out and left only white, middle-class, intact families, standards such as high minimum-income rules and insistence on home ownership.[45] Also, with appropriate financial help, black children could be reabsorbed into their extended families. And the adoption process in general could be made more welcoming to black prospective adoptees and easier for them to negotiate. These reforms, said the NABSW, would make transracial adoption largely unnecessary.

More than forty years later, some of the language of the NABSW statement sounds harsh: "Our society is distinctly black or white and characterized by white racism at every level. We repudiate the fallacious and fantasied reasoning of some that whites adopting black children will alter that basic character."[46] The NABSW statement was made only four years after Martin Luther King Jr. was assassinated in Memphis, eight years after three civil rights workers were murdered in Mississippi's Freedom Summer, and nine years after four black girls were killed when their Birmingham Sunday school was bombed by the KKK. At this writing, the Black Lives Matter movement is protesting police shootings of unarmed black men. One need not agree with all of the NABSW statement to empathize with its rage.

The NABSW statement was severely criticized by some prominent members of the black community. James L. Curtis, a black psychiatrist at the Cornell University Medical College, called it "the most destructive position that could be taken," arguing that "the practice in this field is almost uniform in believing that a child has a right to grow up in an adoptive home if one can at all be obtained for him."[47] Nor did it represent the majority view among African Americans. For example, a survey of 150 black families in Dayton conducted by Howard, Royse, and Skerl found that the majority of respondents (56 percent) had an "open attitude" toward whites adopting black children, and only a small minority (7 percent) were "most unfavorable" toward it.[48]

But whether or not the NABSW position enjoyed popular support, even within the black community, its effect on adoption professionals is hard to discount. Some effects were obvious. For example, the Child Welfare League of America, which had revised its adoption standards in 1968 to make them friendlier to interracial adoption, *re*-revised them in1973 to state that same-race placements were *always* better.[49] The direct impact of the NABSW statement on the behavior of adoption professionals, the people approving placement decisions, is harder to observe, however. As Bartholet put it, "Those in a position to know what today's racial matching policies look like are often reluctant to disclose what is going on for fear of attack by people on different sides of the matching issue." But her interviews with "leaders in the adoption world and experts on racial matching policies" led Bartholet to the conclusion that "race is used as the basis for official decision-making in adoption in a way that is unparalleled in a society that has generally endorsed an antidiscrimination and pro-integration ideology."[50]

But even if attitudes toward interracial adoption had been chilled by the NABSW statement, were there fewer actual transracial placements? That question, too, is not so easily answered, though the prima facie case for a retrenchment may look pretty persuasive: "By 1973 the numbers had fallen to 1091, less than half that of the peak year, 1971; in 1975 there were only 831 transracial adoptions."[51] Again, however, that evidence is not entirely conclusive: at the time, adoptions of all kinds fell sharply, especially after 1973, when *Roe v. Wade* made abortion legal throughout the United States. Still, transracial adoptions fell much faster than adoptions in general.[52] Overall, the sum of the evidence, empirical and anecdotal, gives good reason to believe that transracial adoption was significantly hampered by the position statement of the NABSW.

Then, in the mid-1980s, the opposition to interracial adoption ran smack up against a major crisis sweeping through American inner cities.

The Epidemic

In the early 1980s, a huge glut of powdered cocaine caused a massive drop in price that dramatically reduced revenue in the cocaine industry. Few Americans would lament a loss of income for drug dealers, but price changes create market incentives for innovation, even when the markets are illegal and the innovations have awful consequences. Historically, cocaine powder was expensive and sold mainly to middle and upper-class drug users. In response to the price crash, the coke industry attempted to expand its consumer base. The solution came in the development of a new product that could be produced cheaply enough to be affordable to poor people, even when the price of cocaine powder recovered from its slump. Dissolved cocaine powder mixed with water and baking soda could be dried to form into small rocks that could be smoked instead of snorted. Because of the snapping and popping sound it made as it burned, the drug acquired the nickname "crack." As Fryer et al. describe it:

> Crack is an important technological innovation in many regards. First, crack can be smoked, which is an extremely effective means of delivering the drug psychopharmacologically. Second, because crack is composed primarily of air and baking soda, it is possible to sell in small units containing fractions of a gram of pure cocaine, opening up the market to consumers wishing to spend $10 at a time. Third, because the drug is extremely addictive and the high that comes from taking the drug is so short-lived, crack quickly generated a large following of users wishing to purchase at high rates of frequency.[53]

Crack first became popular in South-Central Los Angeles in 1984 and quickly spread to other major cities. Though most crack users were white, and many were middle class, the drug's most devastating effects were in the inner city. Levitt and Dubner state that "while crack was hardly a black-only phenomenon, it hit the black community hardest" proportionately.[54] In the mid-1980s, the black infant mortality rate, and the incidence of low-birthweight babies soared.

FIGURE 2. Children in foster care per 1,000, by race.

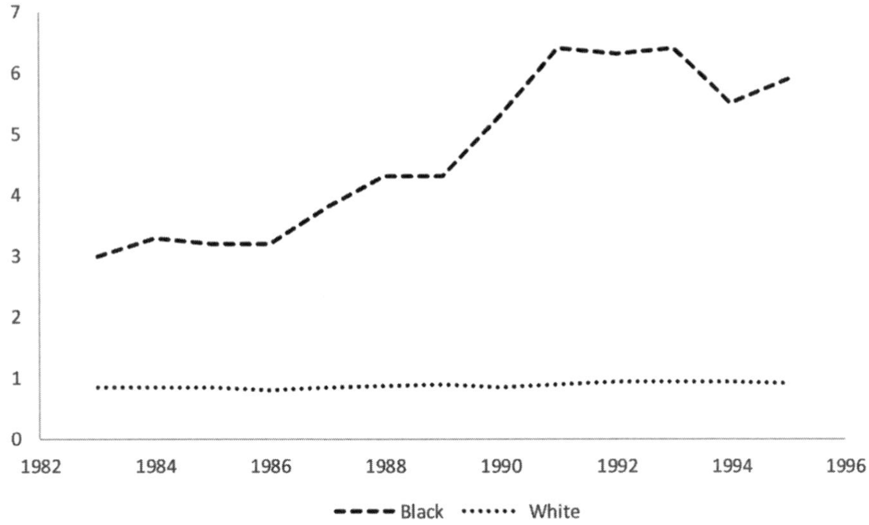

Source: Fryer et al., "Measuring Crack Cocaine and Its Impact," 2013.

The incarceration rate of black males tripled. In fact, "Crack was so dramatically destructive that if its effect is averaged for all black Americans, not just crack users and their families, you will see that the group's post war progress was not only stopped cold, but was often knocked as much as ten years backward."[55] Other numbers tell the same story. Using data for 144 cities, Fryer et al. calculated that after 1985 the cocaine death rate rose by a factor of seven and cocaine-related ER visits increased tenfold. Because so many foot soldiers in the drug trade were young boys, murder rates for males fourteen to seventeen more than doubled.

The typical crack user was male. But a 1991 report from the US General Accounting Office showed that crack appealed to women more than other hard drugs because of its relatively lower expense and because of users' perception that smoking a drug is more socially acceptable than injecting a drug.[56] This had important implications for adoption. As women also became victims of the epidemic, so, of course, did many of their children. Tens of thousands of children were either abandoned by their mothers or removed from their care. In 1987, the *New York Times* reported, "Hospital pediatric wards were suddenly swamped last year with crack addicts' newborn babies.... For weeks and sometimes months, hundreds of generally healthy babies lay, seldom held or nurtured, in hospital bassinets and cribs, waiting for the city to find them homes."[57] Medical staff invented a term to describe infants left in hospitals by crack addicts: boarder babies.[58]

Naturally, these additional children put a strain on the child welfare system. Starting in 1986, the number of children in foster care rose sharply and continued to rise until 1998, by which time it was more than twice as large.[59] The vast majority of these kids were black or Hispanic. As Figure 2, from Fryer et al. shows, the foster care placement rate for black children increased by a factor of two and a half, while the rate for whites remained stable.[60] This deluge of mostly minority children made the task of recruiting enough same-race families to absorb them even more difficult than it had already been. Thus, the unofficial policies against transracial adoption began to feel substantial push back.[61]

Interracial Adoption Begins to Revive

Most Americans would likely agree that the state of Texas is not seen as America's capital of liberalism and progressivity. By way of illustration: Texas has executed more prisoners since 1976 than the next seven states combined.[62] Not surprisingly, therefore, when we went to pick up our infant son, we found the state's adoption policies to be pretty consistent with its conservative image. In 1991, adoptions in Texas were closed, and the ability of birth mothers to change their minds was limited. In Texas, adoption laws were quick, decisive, and unsentimental.

Nevertheless, the supposedly hard hearts of Texans can apparently be melted by the suffering of children, especially when they see it on television. While we were processing Kurt's adoption, in another part of Texas the white foster parents of a black toddler were losing a court battle to keep him in their home. Young Christopher had started living with the Jenkins family five weeks after he was born (having experienced in-utero exposure to crack). Two half-brothers of Christopher's had been adopted by a black couple in Sweetwater. The Sweetwater couple thought Christopher would be better off in their family. The Texas Department of Protective Services had an official policy of preferring black families for black children, and they decided that Christopher should be moved to the home in Sweetwater.

> In the spring of 1992, state social workers began taking Christopher, then 3, for overnight visits to the black family in preparation for his adoption. By September, the visits were lasting a week at a time, and

Christopher grew frantic with each departure. "When the caseworkers came to get him, they would drag him away—with him screaming and crying," recalls Lana Jenkins. "It was just killing him. We could not stand to see what they were doing."[63]

The Jenkins videotaped one of these wrenching episodes of separation and sent the tape to Protective Services. Could they please be allowed to keep the boy? The agency would not budge. So, the privately recorded videotape made its way to a local TV station. There was a public outcry, enough to make the agency back down. The Jenkins family adopted Christopher in January of 1993. And by 1995, the state of Texas had passed legislation making it illegal for state officials to discriminate in adoption cases on the basis of the race/ethnicity of either the child or the adoptive parents.

At the same time, the use of race matching in adoption was also being challenged on the national level, and here again the impetus seemed to come through the TV screen. In 1992, the CBS show *60 Minutes* reported the story of a three-year-old African American boy named Reece who, in 1989, was living in Ohio with his white foster parents. When parental rights were terminated, the foster couple sought to adopt him, but the state welfare agency thought it better to have him adopted by a black family instead. He was subsequently murdered by his adopted parents.[64] The *60 Minutes* segment then went on to argue that the conventions against interracial placement for adoption have caused black children to languish in foster care much longer than their white counterparts (a fact which is, of course, unrelated to Reece's tragic case).[65] One person who was profoundly influenced by the story was Howard Metzenbaum, then a Democratic senator from Ohio. Metzenbaum pushed for the passage of the bill that (despite being signed after he left the Senate) is now associated with his name: The Metzenbaum Multiethnic Placement Act of 1994 (MEPA).[66]

MEPA was a federal act, and while the federal government could not dictate child welfare policy to the states, it *could*, as it so often does, threaten to cut funding to any agency that failed to comply with MEPA. The act and its subsequent amendments prohibit state agencies from considering the race of either the child or the prospective parents in a foster or adoptive arrangement. Placement could neither be denied nor delayed on the basis of race.

Of course, no one, not even the senator, was willing to claim that a white family should be chosen over a black family, all else being equal. So, to counterbalance its suppression of racial preference, the act also required state agencies to diligently recruit minority families to adopt minority children in foster care. Thus, MEPA simultaneously required state agencies to *do* something (vigorously recruit minority families) and to *not do* something (show racial preference in placement). The act would be enforced by the Department of Health and Human Services (HHS). It would turn out that HHS would not find these separate provisions of MEPA to be equally enforceable. After all, it is often easier to catch someone *doing* something they *aren't* supposed to do (like texting after bedtime) than to catch them *not doing* something they *are* supposed to do (like not brushing their teeth—"I already brushed my teeth."). MEPA was one of those cases. To be clear, we admire social services professionals; they do a vital and emotionally draining job for relatively low pay. But we cannot ignore the incentives created by MEPA. Relaxing the restrictions on interracial adoption made it easier to reduce caseloads; demanding more vigorous recruitment of minority families made a hard job even harder. The outcome was predictable.

Did MEPA Work?

In 2010, the US Civil Rights Commission published the result of congressional hearings on the effects of MEPA.[67] Testimony from adoption experts was solicited to answer questions such as, "Has enactment of MEPA removed barriers to permanency facing children involved in the child protection system?"; "Do transracial adoptions serve the children's best interest or do they have negative consequences for minority children?"; and, "How effectively has The Department of Health and Human Services (HHS) enforced MEPA?"

The report made clear that controversy over transracial adoption had not dissipated. Joan Ohl, commissioner for the Administration on Children, Youth and Family at HHS, said it was likely that MEPA was one of several factors that increased the percentage of African American children adopted into families with at least one non-black parent. (Even while the proportion of Hispanic adoptees into multiracial families fell.) Kay Brown, the acting director of the Education Workforce and Income Security Team at the Government Accountability Office affirmed that black children still entered foster care in higher proportions than other children and remained there on average nine months longer than white children.

J. Toni Oliver, co-chair of the Family Preservation Focus Group of the National Association of Black Social Workers, praised MEPA's provision to recruit minority families. But she argued that MEPA did little to ameliorate the fact that in the most populous states, minority children entered foster care at three to ten times the rate of white children. That, she said, was the problem that truly needed to be addressed. Similarly, Ruth G. McRoy, professor emerita at the University of Texas, explained that "transracial adoption is small compared to the difficulty of finding permanent families for the 129,000 children needing adoption."[68]

The executive director of the American Council on Adoptable Children testified, as we might have predicted, that HHS enforced the rule about removing barriers to transracial adoption more vigorously than the one about recruiting minority families. But well-known adoption advocate Elizabeth Bartholet praised MEPA. She argued that recruitment of minority adopters had succeeded, as evidenced by the fact that adoption rates among black and white families increased at equivalent rates. And Rita Simon of American University supplied favorable empirical evidence on the effects of transracial adoption on adopted children and their siblings.[69] According to the published report, her data "consistently portray a lack of difference between black and white children in these special, multiracial families, when differences have been and continue to be present between black and white children reared in the usual single-racial family. Something special seems to happen to both black and white children when they are reared together as siblings in the same family."[70]

That the controversy on interracial adoption is unsettled is apparent in how the commissioners voted on the report's recommendations. For example, on the seemingly innocuous statement, "It is in the best interest of the child to be placed in a safe and stable home," one of the eight commissioners abstained. Two abstained from affirming that "the U.S. Department of Health and Human Services should continue its vigorous enforcement of MEPA's antidiscrimination prohibitions."

The arguments advanced by the NABSW and supporters of the Indian Child Welfare Act are based on the assumption that interracial families deny a child the right to a birth culture and that this denial does long-term harm to the child and to the child's social group. But the opinions reported in this chapter (with the exception of Simon's results in the MEPA report, above) are those of adults, not the children themselves. Does interracial adoption ultimately harm children? That question cannot be answered by the rhetoric of adoption opponents or advocates. It requires empirical investigation of how these children fare in the families that adopt them. It requires actual conversations with the children and their adoptive families, and long-term follow-up to see how the kids actually fare in life. In the next chapter, we examine the empirical evidence about how transracial adoption affects adopted children.

An Unlikely Background for Raising Black Children

T he previous chapter was about the history of the interaction of race and adoption. In this part of Isata's story, we discuss the inspiring story of how the Sibleys' transracial adoptions emerged from a most unlikely pair of family histories.

"I grew up in California in the 1950's and 60's," Beckie says, "with the family moving around a lot. My mother married at age 14 and gave birth to me at age 16. My father was only two years older. Throughout my childhood, he was abusive, physically abusive to my younger brother and verbally abusive of the entire family."[1] Neither parent was a progressive thinker. "As a child, I had an African American friend named Kit. One day she called to ask if she could come over to the house to play." With Kit still on the phone, Beckie asked her mother. "She said loudly that she didn't want a colored girl in our house. Afterward she was quite angry at me for even asking." Colored people were dumb and they smelled, Beckie was told. She must never again invite one to their home. It was her father's opinion that "n*****s" should all be sent back to Africa, which was relatively enlightened compared to his attitude toward "queers"—he thought they should all be shot. Early in her life, Beckie started thinking about adoption—her own. "I always wished I could be adopted into a loving, supportive family with a sense of purpose." As a teenager, in bed at night, Beckie would recite to herself the mantra, "I will not be like them, I will not be like them."

On September 20, 1975, shortly after graduating from high school, Beckie married Jason Sibley. She was eighteen and he was nineteen. In terms of celebrating America's racial diversity, Jason's upbringing was not qualitatively different from Beckie's. In the late 1960s, most of the two hundred residents in his hometown of London, Oregon, were shocked when a local lad brought home an army buddy who happened to be a "Negro." Jason remembers how discombobulated his mother became when the black man entered their family store. Many years later, however, Jason's mother would exemplify how interracial adoption can body-slam an old prejudice—she was brought to tears when young Sia uttered a single word to her: "Grandma."

A daughter was born to the Sibleys in 1977 and a son in 1979. "We thought we had entered the decade of the 1980's with our family complete," Beckie said. But in 1996, a relative had a child she was not able to care for, and they adopted the boy, Carlin, a year later.

"We learned about the civil war ravaging Sierra Leone and Liberia through a young couple at church who were adopting a girl from Liberia. We started the process of adopting from Sierra Leone in November of 2000." It took three iterations to get to an agency they felt comfortable working with. "We began our journey with PLAN Adoption Agency but soon learned of serious corruption amongst its in-country staff, so began working with a small organization called Cherith International, which also proved to be involved in less than honorable practices." They lost $3,000 in their dealing with Cherith, which was "everything [they] had."

Eventually the Sibleys connected with The Children's Home (TCH), the agency through which we (the authors) would get our son GB. They began the process of adopting four-year-old Sia. Diane, director of TCH, told them that Sia was GB's sister, but that GB was already being adopted. She also asked if the Sibleys could take another child, an eight-year-old orphan named Isata, who had been living at the home for almost a year, having been brought there by her aunt and uncle. Beckie and Jason agreed. Waiting for the adoptions to be approved, "We lived on beans and rice and sent what was saved on groceries to TCH as monthly expenses for Sia and Isata. Towards the end, several people organized a fundraiser on our behalf to raise the remaining funds, including airfare." On Monday, July 29, 2002, Jason left for Senegal to pick up the two girls. By the time he returned with the girls the following Friday, he and Isata had contracted typhoid fever (caused by fecal contamination of food).

Not long after Isata and Sia joined their family, Beckie learned through a blog about two Leonean siblings, a girl and a boy, whose adoptive mother was apparently having serious difficulty with them. The mother argued that the children were uncontrollable. "I sensed that this adoption was going to disrupt even before the children arrived because of the way she had discussed adoption and parenting," Beckie said. "And the way the mother talked it seemed to me the fault was mostly hers. So I said that if the adoptions fail I want those kids." So, despite the pressure of two more children on a financially struggling family, Beckie and Jason adopted Shauna, who was Isata's age, and Steven, who was a year younger.[2] To save costs, the Sibleys processed the adoption without an agency or the help of a lawyer. Their instincts were right; Steven and Shauna fit into their family with only minor adjustment issues.

The fact that the Sibleys could adopt four African children illustrates the possibility of overcoming a family legacy of intense racism. More importantly, in our opinion, it illustrates the possibility of true love crossing racial barriers. Not "true love" in the romantic sense, which is how our culture normally thinks of it. Divorce rates illustrate how transitory and fragile that kind of love can be. But the permanent love of a parent for a child. This love is all the more inspiring as it involves intense financial sacrifice for a family of limited income. To us, the Sibleys are a genuinely model family.

CHAPTER 4

Walking While Black (WWB)

"One of the interesting things from when I was younger is when you grow up with white parents, white neighborhood, white church, your default identity is a white kid. Blackness comes later. People always reminded me I was black."

Chad Goller-Sojourner, author of *Riding in Cars with Black People and Other Newly Dangerous Acts*, 2012

Before we examine the empirical evidence about the effects of transracial adoption on children, we look at the not-so-empirical evidence about how we experienced transracial adoption within our family. As this experience is based on a not-even-close-to-random sample with only two observations, our "results" will not meet the standards of statistical rigor that would satisfy, say, the Econometric Society. Moreover, we don't even know what our results *are*. Did we do an OK job or a bad job of equipping two young black men to make their way in America? We don't know. We, their parents, may never know. But in the interest of honesty and disclosure, we will just report what happened and let the reader form her own impression. Both sons, now adults, have explicitly given us permission to tell their stories in this book.

By the time we brought Kurt home from Texas, in November of 1991, Tinker had already created a collage of African American heroes, framed it behind glass, and hung it in his bedroom. While applauding this effort in principle, Mark pointed out that as Kurt was only a few days old, it might be a while before the effects of the collage started to kick in. Tinker didn't care; it would be hanging there when he needed it. From the very start, we read Kurt and Mary (our first-born, and birth, child) tales from African American children's literature and stories of famous black Americans, but otherwise race remained pretty much in the background.[1] Although we openly mentioned skin color by saying, for example, how beautiful Kurt's brown skin was, our basic strategy was to avoid emphasizing the differences in gender, appearance, and "markers of race" between Mary and Kurt when he was very young. We would wait until he indicated a need to discuss it. Whether this was a good idea or a bad one we are unprepared to say, though many scholars in this field would opine without hesitation.

These many years later we can't recall how we figured the issue of race would play out in real time. Exactly how casually did we expect racial differences could be slipped into the family saga? Did we imagine that one day Kurt would stroll into the living room and ask, "Hey Mom and Dad, how come I'm black and you're white?" To which we would frown thoughtfully for a few seconds before replying, "Oh, yeah, I remember now, you're adopted!" As if it made so little difference we had practically forgotten?[2]

The tension of wondering when Kurt would raise the subject grew. And what would we say when he brought it up? One day, when he was two or three and had learned the names of the various colors, the fateful moment seemed to arrive. We were loading him into his car seat when suddenly he pointed at his mom. "You're white," he said, big smile on his face, "I'm black!" We looked at each other, wide-eyed.

It's happened! He's noticed. *Battle stations! This is not a drill.*

Should we explain it to him, right now, right here, out in the front yard? Is it time to tell him that yes, he came from a different place than Mary, that he actually had *another* mommy and daddy, but that we loved them both just as much...

We both noticed, at the very same moment, the color of the outfits he and his mother were wearing. Do you mean the shirts, we asked him? He did.[3] *Stand down from general quarters.*

If there was some moment when we first talked with Kurt about why he was of a different race, and about his adoption, we no longer recall when that was. But the night it first became an issue is one we both remember pretty clearly. Kurt was about five. It was bedtime and Mark was reading him a new children's book, recently discovered by Tinker, that was an allegory about race, family, and adoption. The story was about a young cheetah who had a tiger mom, not in the sense that his mom made him practice violin three hours per day, but in that she was an actual tiger. His dad was a tiger too—he'd been adopted into a tiger family. It worried this young cheetah that his mom and dad and all his aunts, uncles, and cousins had striped fur while his was covered with spots. Why didn't he look like the rest of his family? This difference began to bother him a lot. So, one day, the cheetah left the house looking for some other family whose fur was like his. Wandering in the city park, he noticed (not to say spotted) a family of cheetahs having a picnic. The cheetah family was very friendly, and he spent the afternoon playing with them and having a great time. But as the day ended and his new friends packed up to go home, the little cheetah suddenly felt very tired and hungry. He started to miss *his* mom and dad—his tiger mom and dad! As it happens, they had been looking everywhere for their little cheetah, and, with uncanny timing, they entered the park at the very moment he realized how much he wanted them. Putting her son to bed that night, the tiger mom tells him just why they chose him to be part of their family: they loved his spots!

After Mark closed the book and kissed him on the forehead, Kurt looked up and said, "I think I should go back with my African American family."

Huh? What?

"My African American family has money now and they can take care of me," Kurt said, sort of referring to one part of our explanation of why he'd been placed for adoption. "I should go back with them." As Kurt was clearly missing the point of the story, Mark offered him a CliffsNotes review of its key points: while the cheetah's parents might *look* different from him, *emotionally* they were the people (or big cats, in this case) who mattered to him most. To this recap Kurt responded, "I think I should go back with my African American family."

Why wasn't he getting this? Silently and unfairly cursing Tinker for having bought this book, Mark explained to Kurt that he was now *our* son and would be for the duration of his life plus six months. Kurt replied that unless he went back to his African American family, we (Mark and Tinker) might get in trouble with the police. Boy, this conversation kept getting worse—was he threatening to have us arrested for kidnapping?

Mark must have called for backup, because the next thing he knew Tinker was standing in the room. In a preternaturally calm and steady voice, she said, "Kurt, you're in our family now, and you always will be." After a little more back and forth, we kissed him goodnight and left his room. Outside the door, Tinker turned to Mark and said, "Do we cry now?"

There was no mention of this the next day. At bedtime, there was the usual reading of a story (no cheetahs tonight, thank you), the requested singing of Kurt's favorite, though politically incorrect, "Ol' Man River," and the nice hugs and goodnight kisses. But five minutes after Mark left the room, Kurt strolled out of his bedroom, came into ours and stood next to the bed. "I think I should go back with my African American family." Again, with simulated calmness, we reiterated the highlights of last night's conversation: we are your Mommy and Daddy, you are our son, and neither of these conditions is the least bit negotiable. When he was grown, if he wanted to, we would help him find his African American parents. We kissed him again and said goodnight. Next day, no mention, even at bedtime. But as Mark was leaving, almost as an after-thought he said, "I think I should go back with my African American family."

Pause, moment of reflection, sudden realization. Two days before, the cheetah story had aroused genuine feelings of loss in Kurt, but by now he had figured something out: mention going back to your African American family at bedtime and your parents will extend bedtime by talking to you. "Good night, Kurtie." That was the last we heard about it.

There was little more mention of race until one evening when Kurt was about eight and we had just watched *Amistad*, the movie about the slave ship that was commandeered by its inmates and sailed to America, where they were imprisoned. The film recounts the court battle by which they were eventu-ally freed. That night, midway through the ritual we call "Climbing Mount Bedtime," Mark was reminding Kurt that brushing one's teeth should take less time than, say, building the Brooklyn Bridge. Kurt looked up at him and said, "Dad, you're just a white man trying to treat me like a slave." Hmm.

When Kurt was about ten, Tinker took him to see one in a string of kid-friendly movies with African American themes. In one film, Keanu Reeves, sentenced to community service, unwillingly coaches a Little League team in a poor neighborhood, only to have his cynical heart predictably melted as he starts to care about his young charges. Near the end of the movie, when one of the kids is accidentally killed in a drug shooting, Tinker saw tears trickling down Kurt's cheeks. They both started to rethink their movie-going strategy. A while later, when Tinker proposed they see another film in this genre, Kurt demurred.

"You want to take me to every movie with African Americans," he said, "We don't have to do that."

"But this isn't like the Keanu Reeves movie. It's not just about poor black children, and it won't have one get killed just to make us cry."

"I know," Kurt said, "but we don't have to go to *all* of them."

Lessons Learned from Our Experience Raising Kurt

The training that adoption agencies now provide in raising children of different race or ethnicity is an improvement over the old days when the issue was more or less ignored. But even now this training could be better at preparing white parents to raise, for example, black children. Most efforts at "culture keeping," as Heather Jacobson terms it, tend to focus on activities when kids are young and focus on relatively superficial (though not unimportant) activities like hair and skin care, ethnic crafts, holiday celebrations and culture camps, or things like the poster of African American heroes we hung on Kurt's wall.[4] (See Barbara Katz Rothman for an excellent discussion of this.[5]) Advice about hair and skin care was by far the most common comment we got from black strangers when we were in public with young Kurt. But these black kids need advice on how to answer tough questions when they are younger and how to respond to situations they may face in school. Even more importantly, from the perspective of having twenty-five- and twenty-one-year-old black sons, it seems the most important time for white parents to have the knowledge to help their black kids is when they are teens and young adults. That is when identity issues are heightened for transracial adoptees, and that is when the dangers they face in their environment and by their own decisions are greatest as well. Fortunately, adoption advocacy websites increasingly provide support and education for white parents to prepare their black adolescents or young adults to face the world.

Kurt, in particular, was slow to see racism in anyone, just as he was generally reluctant to see bad in people. He said to us once, when still young, that racism had happened in the past but didn't happen anymore. He was adamant even as we tried gently to disabuse him of this notion. But as an older teen and now as a young man, he is very aware of and knowledgeable about current racism in American society, mostly from the media, but also from personal experience. We have had many discussions about it, including how to behave with the police when they stop you for being black, as he has been. Not everything has gone smoothly for him.

Gibrila (GB)

GB's experience of being a black child entering a white family was qualitatively different from the one Kurt had. On Thursday, April 15, 2002, six-year-old GB lived in an all-black orphanage in an all-black country; the following Monday, he was taking golf lessons at an Iowa country club of which he personally constituted a quarter of the black membership. Was it immoral of us to do this to a six-year-old child? We had certainly considered the possibility. But Sierra Leone was just emerging from a civil war in which the hands of innocent villagers had been hacked off by drug-addled child soldiers. It was the world's poorest country. Even overwhelmingly white Iowa couldn't be worse than that, could it?

When we started writing this book, we believed the official version of GB's backstory, sworn to in a Leonean court, that his birth parents had been murdered by the RUF as they fled from Makeni to evade the rebels. He had been raised by an aunt named S., who placed him and her daughter Sia for adoption. Isata's birth family, the M.'s, tracked down S., who had moved from the neighborhood but still lived in Freetown. She explained (via an interview with Isata's brother Shaun M.) that she was in fact GB's birth mother and that GB's birth father was gone by the time GB was born.[6] We believe her, but this story could just as easily be untrue, because, having connected with us, she has incentive to emphasize consanguinity; it might increase our willingness to help her financially. We have done so, but we would have anyway once we found her. In any case, as a family we now regard S. as GB's birth mother and Sia as his sister (technically his birth half-sister), not a cousin.

Few Americans would see our son GB as African instead of African American, and fewer still would know that he is West African rather than, say, Ethiopian. And he knows this. So, he has an identity as an African and as an African American, if he wants both. But while GB's accent and Krio vocabulary are long gone, he is still probably the most darkly complected permanent resident of our little Iowa town. The reactions of local people occasionally remind us of this.

For example: Surviving a singularly brutal civil war, even if he hardly remembers it, might make GB understandably afraid of men with guns. Moreover, opposing sides in the Sierra Leone war tended not to be easily divisible into the "good guys" and the "bad guys," so it might not much matter who the men with guns were. They might even be the local police. One calm summer evening when GB was about eleven, our local police appeared at the front door asking his whereabouts. We replied that he was staying overnight at a friend's house. No, he wasn't, they said, he had just been spotted running away from a police car that had been called to the scene of a loud public argument that some older teenagers were having. GB had done nothing wrong—except to run from the police.[7] They hadn't caught him (he's really fast) but no detective work was required to identify the preteen African seen sprinting into the bushes in Grinnell's Central Park. Who else could it be? When we asked him later what he had been thinking to run from the cops, he admitted that thinking was not part of the process. He had just panicked.

Occasionally GB's racial distinctiveness has some advantage. A few years ago, he walked into the bank downtown and asked to get money from his account, though he had no checks, no debit card, nor any form of personal identification. Sure, the teller told him, just sign this slip of paper. Needless to say, sometimes his race is a disadvantage. Most African Americans will tell you that they have been pulled over for DWB, driving while black; GB got stopped for WWB—walking while black. Coming home from a friend's house one night, again when he was eleven or twelve, he was playing around with a new flashlight and made the mistake of shining it into a parked car. A local policeman had been watching him in his rearview mirror and, seeing the light flash in the parked car, he assumed that GB had opened the car door. The cop drove around the block, apprehended GB now walking up the street, frisked him, locked him in the back of the police car, and then woke up the elderly couple who owned the car to see what was missing from it. Nothing was—he'd just been playing with his new flashlight. This is when he got his first taste of what it was to be a young black male.

Still, GB feels life in America has been pretty kind to him. While more willing to accept that racism exists than his older brother, he also has seemed less bothered by some of its manifestations, perhaps partly because he always tries to see the humor in any situation. For example, a friend of ours was walking out of the high school one day behind GB and a black friend of his. It was MLK day, but they had school because there had been so many snow days already that they had lost several of their holidays off (Presidents Day, etc.). GB and his friend were saying that they were going to go to the principal and stage a protest because they, as African Americans, shouldn't have to go to school on Martin Luther King's birthday. They were joking, saying it was just racism by the white administrators to make black kids attend school on MLK's birthday. On the other hand, we've had serious discussions in our living room with these same kids about racism—after the shooting of Trayvon Martin, for example.

Growing up, both Kurt and GB had white and black friends. Because the number of black kids is small in this Iowa town, it can be said that they were friends with nearly all the black kids in their cohort. We used to joke that on any given day, a large fraction of the young black male community in Grinnell, Iowa, could be found on the third floor of our house, as well as many white friends. As for dating, Kurt has demonstrated in word and deed that he is interested in both women of color and white Anglo women. GB also has dated women of color and Anglo women, including one friend adopted from Sierra Leone. Both sons identify themselves as black men and always have.

The point of relating these stories about our sons is to acknowledge that we have not only adopted transracially, but have raised two black boys in an über-Caucasian part of the country. We had two tenured academic jobs that we loved in a small town in Iowa, and, unlike many white parents of black children, we chose not to move to a mixed-race community. Kurt has loved growing up here, although he realizes that his experiences have been limited and may move someday for that reason. He, especially, has worked on identity issues, including racial identity, and the latter has added somewhat to the pain he has experienced in "finding himself," a process already difficult for teens and young adults. GB has enjoyed growing up in Grinnell, except for the cold winters, and will likely move to a warmer state in the US as soon as possible. He seems to have a firmer sense of self, racially and otherwise, at least so far.

Empirical Evidence on the Effect of Transracial Adoption

Is transracial adoption bad for children? That question has a simple answer: "Bad compared to what?" To what can we reasonably compare transracial adoption? Adoption within families of the same race? Foster care? Institutionalization? Remaining with parents who are abusive or neglectful (in the domestic case), or too poor to feed the child (in the international case)? What is the "counterfactual" experience of the child, as social scientists would put it? Not all children, of course, face the same set of counterfactuals. Moreover, the counterfactual is unobservable, because we never know what might have happened to an adopted child had she not been taken in by the adopting family.

Luckily, there is an easily implemented, scientifically valid method of determining whether transracial adoption is in the best interest of the child. We need only add one tiny step to the current adoption procedure. It works like this: When the long and exhausting adoption process is finally complete and the parents are climbing into a taxi with their new bundle, ready to head off to the airport, a man in a white lab coat suddenly appears. "Hi, there," says the man in the lab coat, "watch this." He tosses a coin in the air. It lands on the sidewalk beside the taxi. If the coin comes up heads, he says to the frowning parents, "Congratulations on your successful adoption. Please have a safe and pleasant journey home." If it comes up tails he says, "Sorry to tell you this, but your child is in the control group." Whereupon he snatches the kid from the mother's arms and disappears into the crowd before the screaming couple can scramble from the taxi and chase him down. The child is then returned from whence he came. Ridiculous? Keep reading.

Having replicated the above procedure a few hundred times, we then wait about twenty years, after which we survey the two sets of children, the Heads group and the Tails group. If the Heads group has outcomes like, say, higher income, more education, and better health than the Tails group, we can attribute these improvements to having been adopted. If, on the other hand, they suffer outcomes like more relationship problems and a propensity for depression, those too we can blame on the adoption. It's a simple and scientifically valid approach. There are no systematic differences between the "treatment" and control groups to explain the differences in outcomes, only random differences, because assignment to either group was decided by a coin toss; therefore, any observed differences can be expected to result from adoption, the "treatment" in this experiment.

Despite its statistical advantages, we hesitate to propose this methodology, however, on the grounds that it is entirely infeasible, spectacularly illegal, and monstrously cruel. So why mention it if it's such a horrible idea? We are attempting to illustrate that it's well-nigh impossible to study adoption in a crisp, clean, scientific way. We can observe various outcomes for adopted children and compare them with other children, but whether any differences will be the result of the adoption will be hard to discern.

To illustrate the problem, consider the assertion by the NABSW that white parents can't teach black children how to resist the implied message of inferiority constantly blared at them by a racist society—only black parents can do that. How might we test this hypothesis? Intuitively it makes sense to compare the self-esteem of black adoptees in white homes with that of black adoptees in black homes. If the kids in black homes have higher self-esteem than kids in white homes, does this confirm that the NABSW was right? Not necessarily. It could be, for example, that white families tend to adopt higher proportions of special needs children, or to live in school districts that are more academically competitive, factors that can lower *any* child's self-esteem. Consequently, we might observe lower self-esteem in the white households even if those parents were doing every bit as good a job of conveying self-worth as black parents would do *with the same special needs children*. Or the converse could be true. Maybe the emotional cost of feeling like an outsider within one's family is masked by the higher social status of white households, so that transracial adoption is even *harder* on a black child's ego than the data seem to imply. So, not only do we expect bias, we don't even know the direction of the bias. That is, transracial adoption could be better or worse for the adoptee than it appears to be.

We offer one more hypothetical example. Suppose we were to observe that children adopted from Korea by white parents have lower average SAT scores than the children born into Korean American families. Can this be interpreted as an effect of adoption? Again, not necessarily. The two groups of children will differ in ways unrelated to the parents' race (or their income, or anything else). It *may* be that "being different" within the family or the neighborhood affects academic performance, but it could also be that Korean birth mothers of adopted kids got inferior prenatal health care or had poor nutrition while pregnant, factors that might affect academic performance. These explanations are speculative, of course, but that is the point. Absent some rigorous randomization process, comparison between groups is always haunted by unobserved factors that might matter. There are nifty statistical techniques to address this problem, which help somewhat, but the problem cannot be made to go away. In reading the empirical studies on transracial adoption, we were surprised to find almost no discussion of potential biases in the findings. It is useful to keep that in mind as we review that body of work.

Studies of the Effects of Transracial Adoption

Just as twentieth-century fiction can be seen as having two periods, the modernist and the postmodernist, the literature on transracial adoption can be similarly divided: studies published *before* we adopted Kurt and studies published *after* we adopted Kurt. Other scholars of adoption have been slow to embrace this dichotomy, but it seems pretty darned obvious to us. Back in 1991, when we were contemplating adoption of a black or biracial child, we knew there was controversy surrounding interracial adoption, so, we started reading up on the subject.[8] We did not, after all, want to be harming a child instead of helping one. So, we reviewed the pre-Kurt literature on transracial adoption.

The earliest formal analysis of transracial adoption was the follow-up study to the Indian Adoption Project, already described. Daniel Fanshel concluded that after five years, eight out of ten children were doing "quite well," and only one in ten showed problems that "make his future adjustment seem uncertain."[9] The children in the study, however, were all Native Americans adopted into white families; in this case, there was *no* comparison group. So, while Fanshel's results are reassuring, they don't tell us whether the children would have ultimately fared better in Native American adoptive families, or even with their birth families on the reservation.

One of the first studies to compare black adoptees in white families with those in black families was by Ruth McRoy and Louis Zurcher.[10] Their sample included sixty black adoptees, average age about fourteen, half of whom were in white families, half in black. They found no statistically significant differences between the two groups in terms of self-esteem, self-concept, or family integration and cohesion. Nor were there significant differences in academic progress or in the incidence of behavioral problems.

Where the color of the adoptive family *did* matter, McRoy and Zurcher found, was in the formation of racial identity. Most of the kids in black homes self-identified as black, compared to less than a third in the white homes, where they more often considered themselves *mixed* (56 percent) or *white* (10 percent).[11] Critics of transracial adoption tend to view this as identity confusion. Again, however, we need to interpret this finding cautiously. The race of the adoptive family was not chosen at random. At least partly as a result of placement practices by welfare agencies, white couples are less likely to adopt a child with two black parents instead of one than are black couples. This was especially true in the early years of transracial adoption, when the study was conducted. Consequently, we would expect the population of transracial adoptees to not just *believe* themselves more biracial, but to actually *have* a higher proportion of mixed-race children. Some analysts might argue that these kids need to consider themselves black because society will consider them black. Fair enough. But the point is that we still don't know how to interpret the outcome.

A study similar to that of McRoy and Zurcher was published by Joan Shireman and Penny Johnson, who compared outcomes for thirty-six black children adopted by white couples with nineteen black children adopted by black couples.[12] Their average age was thirteen. Unlike McRoy and Zurcher, Shireman and Johnson found that the racial identification of back adoptees in white families did not differ from those in black families. Neither did their answers to the question, "Would you want to be of a different race?"[13] No significant difference was observed in overall adjustment or in the strength of family relationships. Shireman did, however, find more serious academic and/or behavior problems among the transracial group: 33 percent versus 21 percent. But they noted that this likely resulted from an unusually high number of boys in the white families who had preplacement learning disabilities. Indeed, both these studies had relatively small samples.

But at the time we did the research for our first adoption, the most cited empirical study was that of Rita Simon and Howard Altstein, who studied a group of adoptees in their mid-late teens.[14] They had been following this group since 1972, when the children were between three and eight years old. The sample size was larger than in previous studies—366 to begin with, 218 by the time of publication—and the children were older on average.[15] Also, the sample included some children of color who were not black. The non-white children in the sample were all in white families that had *also* adopted white children. Thus, each household had adopted both children of color and white children, and sometimes also had (white) birth children.

Simon and Altstein's results were generally quite favorable to transracial adoption. They found that "transracial adoptees [were] as integrated into their [white] families as the children who had been born into them."[16] Also, the transracial adoptees had as much self-esteem as their white siblings, whether those siblings were adopted or genetically related children. School performance was almost as high: B-minus average for the children of color, B average for the white children. Finally, there were no differences between the groups in terms of behavioral problems or academic difficulties. The transracial adoptees were somewhat less likely to aspire to a college education: 75 percent versus 94 percent for the birth children.

In terms of racial identity, Simon and Altstein found that 72 percent of black or biracial adopted children said they were proud to be black, 82 percent of the nonblack transracial adoptees said they were proud to be Korean, Latin American, etc., and 82 percent of the white birth children said they were proud to be white. Interestingly, 11 percent of the black adoptees said they would prefer to be white, and 7 percent of the white birth children said they would prefer to be black.

It is worth reminding ourselves that Simon and Altstein chose for their study only families that had adopted both white kids and children of color. This had a significant advantage: it allowed them to control for the socioeconomic status of the family—a confounding factor in previous adoption studies. It also had a disadvantage: the study group was not representative of the whole population of adoptive households.

To summarize the pre-Kurt literature on transracial adoption: empirical studies tended to conclude that for black adoptees, the race of the parents had only a small, if any, effect on objective outcomes such as school performance and behavioral problems. Black adoptees tended to be as well integrated into white families as into black families and as well integrated as white adoptees and even birth children. There was very slight, and somewhat questionable, evidence that racial identity might be more of an issue for transracial adoptees.

The Post-Kurt Literature on Adoption

The post-1992 studies on transracial adoption tended to have an increased focus on subjective experiences such as adoptee self-esteem or ethnic-identity formation. This literature is vast. So vast, in fact, that Femmie Juffer and Marinus H. van IJzendoorn could publish a study called "Adoptees Do Not Lack Self-Esteem: A Meta-Analysis of Studies on Self-Esteem of Transracial, International and Domestic Adoptees."[17] For readers outside of academe, a meta-study is a statistical analysis in which the data points are not, say, adoptees or families, but *studies* of adoptees or families. So the "sample" is a group of studies of self-esteem, each of which has its own sample of adoptees whose self-esteem is being examined. This is an increasingly popular way of analyzing the outcomes of an entire literature in one go. The authors found "no difference in self-esteem between adoptees (N=10,977) and nonadopted comparisons (N=33,862) across 88 studies." Moreover, "This was equally true for international, transracial and domestic adoptees."[18] A meta-analysis of behavioral problems and mental health referrals by the same authors concluded that "international adoptees present fewer behavior problems and are less often referred to mental health services than domestic adoptees."[19]

Another comprehensive literature survey appears in a 2009 study by the Evan B. Donaldson Adoption Institute. "In general these [empirical] studies [of ethnic identity among international adoptees] have found that children adopted transracially had overall adjustment outcomes similar to children placed in same-race families, particularly when they were adopted early in life," states the report.[20] Regarding other work on emotional problems, the report says that "taken in total, this body of research suggests that approximately 70–80 percent of transracial adoptees had few serious behavioral problems—a rate similar to samples of same-race adoptees—and they do not differ significantly in levels of self-esteem or social adjustment."[21] To be sure, as the report shows, there are definitely better and worse practices that parents can engage in to help transracial adoptees to cope with the challenges they will face.[22] But the overwhelming conclusion of studies of transracial adoption is that it is not bad for children. This greatly weakens the case of the opponents of transracial and transnational adoption on the grounds that it harms children.

Moreover, Rebecca Compton also reviews the studies on cross-race and cross-cultural adoption and concludes:

> In summary, then, given the evidence to date, does international adoption serve the child's best interest when we broaden our consideration of outcomes to include identity development? While the evidence related to identity development is not as straightforward as evidence related to physical or cognitive outcomes, [it] does not amount to a persuasive argument against international adoption. Children adopted across cultural, racial, and national lines appear to generally fare well, notwithstanding the considerable work in constructing a complex sense of identity that incorporates both birth and adoptive families and ethnicities.[23]

Nevertheless, it must be acknowledged that, as Tobias Hubinette says, "Recently a multidisciplinary field of critical adoption studies has emerged, inspired, in part, by critical race and whiteness studies and gender and queer studies."[24] He summarizes a body of literature that focuses on interviews with adult transracial adoptees. "What is striking in the empirical results is the always-present feeling of profound bodily alienation and racial isolation." The isolation comes from "almost always being the only non-white person in the close environment, such as among family and kin, in neighborhood and school, and at the workplace."[25] As children, Hubinette says, the adoptees tend to be protected by the company of adoptive parents, but from adolescence to adulthood, they lose that security. The adoptees are "constantly racialized in their everyday life."[26] Hubinette is Korean-born and was adopted in Sweden, and we might expect that *any* Korean child living in Sweden, whether adopted or not, might feel considerably out of place in terms of race. But no one proposes that Korean families be banned from moving to Sweden. Hubinette acknowledges this. "This is of course similar to the migrant experience in most Western countries, but the main difference is that contrary to the majority of migrants who at least have their own families, friends, neighborhoods and communities, adoptees are often more or less isolated. They have no safe space where they can be left alone, and no significant others whom they can fully trust to defend or at least understand and empathize with them."[27]

We have three comments to make with respect to Hubinette's arguments about the racial isolation experienced by teens and adults who were adopted transracially. First, it is a reasonable hypothesis that adoptees face greater challenges in dealing with racial differences than children of migrants in a racial minority. However, we are not aware of anyone having studied this. It would be useful for someone to compare these two groups to get an empirical sense of how the experiences of the two groups differs. Until then, we have no evidence regarding this hypothesis. Our second comment is that postplacement transcultural training seems to be especially important for the teen years. The Ethiopian summer culture camp we attended, at the suggestion of Melissa Faye Greene, author and adoptive parent, had the children of Ethiopian migrants as well as adopted kids. But there weren't many teens there because they have generally "outgrown" their willingness to attend. Our third comment goes back to the question asked at the beginning of this section. Is transracial adoption bad for children? Bad compared to what? We do not know the counterfactual for the adult adoptees: what would have happened had they not been adopted. Do any difficulties they face from racial isolation mean that they would have been *better off* had they not been adopted? Ultimately, that is the most important question in judging adoption, but it is also the hardest question to answer, unless, perhaps, the comparison group is the hundreds who would no longer be alive, as noted above.

Compton makes a similar point. She grants that minority-race adoptees face discrimination, and that it might be, as the qualitative studies suggest, greater than "realized or acknowledged by adoptive parents." "But," she says, "that by itself seems an odd reason to oppose international adoption. By analogy, we should not oppose immigration simply because immigrants will experience discrimination, nor should we oppose interracial marriage simply because biracial children will experience discrimination."[28] And, we should not oppose international adoption any more than we should oppose immigration and interracial marriage because international adoptees experience the same difficulties of adjustment and identity development with two cultures that biracial children and second-generation immigration children do, especially in the teen years.

From an All-Black to an All-White World

The previous chapter described, among other things, the experience our two sons had growing up black in a very Caucasian part of America. Isata was in a similar situation, as shown here. In this part, we also describe how the Sibleys took their children on a journey that was most decidedly, in the words of the Donaldson report on adoption, "Beyond Culture Camp."

With the civil war, the M. family had sound motivation for placing Isata in The Children's Home and allowing her to go to another family in America, but at age eight she could hardly be expected to understand them. As Beckie would write ten years later in an e-mail letter to the M.'s, "[Isata] never understood why, out of all six of your children, she was the only one who could no longer live with the family."[1] Isata confirmed Beckie's account. "My mom told me, 'You will go to America and get a good education, and then come back to help your family.'"[2] When she first went to TCH, she remained aloof from the other children. "She lived every single day with the hope that you would return to take her home," Beckie wrote. "She was terrified. Every time the family visited TCH then left without her, she felt abandoned."

She had very little experience with white people. There was one Caucasian at TCH, the director, Diane. Once, when another white woman visited, Isata said, "I was afraid of her, thinking that her pale skin made her ghost-like."[3] We asked Isata what it was like living in Redmond where she was one of a very few black residents. "At first I was afraid of all the white people in America, even the kids in the neighborhood. Some had never seen a black person before, they wanted to touch my skin. I was terrified and wanted to get away from them." But that didn't last. "Everyone in Redmond has been very kind and supportive of us, even in the high school" (where she went for her last year of schooling). "Mom taught us to be proud of ourselves, in who we are. That gave me the confidence I would need if anyone verbally attacked me." How was her one year in high school? "It was hard because I was older than the other kids, and maybe because I had more experiences. They cared about things that didn't interest me."

Zambian Cultural Interlude, 2006–2010

Recall that by the mid-2000s, the Sibley's had four African and one American child living at home. Partly as a means of giving their children an African cultural experience and partly motivated to do missionary work, in February of 2006, Jason and Beckie visited Zambia to investigate the prospect of moving there with their kids for a couple of years. The plan was for Jason to train pastors and Beckie to help run a local orphanage she had visited. Beckie explained, "On our first visit in 2006 I went to an orphanage that I was supposed to work in when I got back, helping with hygiene and other things. The place was filled with kids and I played with them and talked to the staff about what I would do when I returned to Zambia. The kids sang group songs for me and said prayers."[4] So, Jason and Beckie sold everything they had and packed up the five kids to spend two years in Zambia. Of course, their children wouldn't experience Sierra Leone, but at least they would live in Africa. Moreover, Sierra Leone was out of the question as the new kids, Shauna and Steven, who had been abused by their birth parents, refused to go back there. Indeed, they had to be convinced, via an actual map, that Zambia was thousands of miles from Sierra Leone before they would consent to return to Africa at all.

So, in February 2007, they all arrived in Zambia. What they encountered there caused a bit of culture shock. As Beckie said,

> When I returned in 2007 the orphanage was gone. The building was empty. There were no kids or staff at all. When I asked about this I was told that there had never been an orphanage. The whole thing was a show staged for my "benefit." Local kids had been recruited with the promise of a meal to come and pretend to live there. Why, I asked, would they do a thing like that? I was told matter-of-factly that they wanted me to come and bring money and they figured that I would be more likely to come back if I thought there was an orphanage I could work in.

Beckie and Jason asked (subtly, they hoped) the pastor who was involved with the "orphanage" story, whether there wasn't something morally unacceptable in this charade. He didn't think so. "Their view was, 'No, there is no orphanage. But, you can start one. Make a name for yourself.'" Also, while the Sibleys had adopted Africans, they did not realize you could inadvertently adopt a grown man and his entire family simply by allowing him to live on your property. A caretaker who had lived at their first house sued to go with them to their second house, even though they had no desire to continue his employment. Moreover, he told the court that because the Sibleys treated him as family, they were obligated to continue treating him as family—and so they should help him build his house. Plus, there was the minor matter of discovering that when you rent a house in Zambia, you automatically assume the unpaid taxes owed by the landlord. (Or, at least, if you're a "rich" westerner you do.) Suffice it to say, it was a rough two years for the Sibleys in Zambia. But, Beckie told us, because of what they faced together, when they came home from Zambia, they were truly a family.

We should note that a reader of the manuscript of this book questioned the rationale for including the story about Zambia. Did we want to make African culture look inferior to the Western culture that these children ended up in? That is not the point, at all. Africans function under much more severe resource constraints than westerners, and it would be absurd to judge the economic behavior of people operating in such hugely different circumstances. As for the fake orphanage, for example, false advertising was hardly invented by Africans, though this is admittedly an extreme case. The African pastor decided that getting additional resources for his impoverished congregation was worth deceiving people he thought (incorrectly) were rich Americans. We think that the morality of that decision is not absolutely straightforward, unless you do indeed have a Western bias. In any event, we consider it important to report this Zambian episode to give a full account of Isata's adoption experience with the Sibley family. We want to note, by the way, that the Sibley children learned far more about living in Africa from their trip to Zambia than they might have in an African heritage festival or a summer culture camp, as valuable as these latter experiences can be.

What was it like, we asked Isata, going to Zambia, returning to an all-black world for the first time in years? "That was not very welcoming," she said. "There we felt discrimination. The locals didn't pay much attention to us African kids. They were more interested in Mom, Dad and Carlin, who were white. We learned to appreciate the things available to us in America like electricity, good food, clean water, and our friends."

Overall, Isata has fared well in her adoptive environment. The evidence suggests that she is happy and well-grounded in her family. Her transition, and her life, were not without some racial issues, but she seems to have handled them well. It is worth remembering, however, that she had four siblings who were also African. We cannot rule out the possibility that she would have had a different experience had she been the only black adoptee—indeed, avoiding that was one motivation the Sibleys had for adopting two children for their first African adoption.

CHAPTER 5

Trafficking Jam

Celebrity accessories come and go. Once upon a time, it was expensive designer handbags. Then, it was miniature doggies—which were often carried in those handbags. These days, it's children from Africa.

Lola Adesioye, The Guardian[1]

There has been much coverage of Madonna's difficulties adopting two children from Malawi: a one-year-old boy, David, in 2006 and a four-year-old girl, Mercy, in 2009. No fewer than sixty-seven human rights groups filed amicus briefs in court opposing the first adoption, and a consortium of eighty-five organizations protested the second.[2] During David's adoption, a group called Eye of the Child complained, "It's not like selling property.... It is about safeguarding the future of a human being who, because of age, cannot express an opinion."[3] In any case, the specific complaint was that a court allowed Madonna and her husband to bypass the usual eighteen-month residency requirement. Some people believed that the waiver might possibly have been expedited by Madonna's celebrity, wealth, and massive donations to Malawi charities. David's adoption withstood the challenge, and David came home with the couple.

For the adoption of Mercy in 2009, the star was not so lucky. A court ruled that Madonna could not bypass the residency requirement. The judge said that "by removing the very safeguard that is supposed to protect our children the courts by their pronouncements could actually facilitate trafficking of children by some unscrupulous individuals who would take advantage of the weakness of the law of the land."[4] Relaxing the residency requirement, the court said, would open the floodgates to child trafficking.

Madonna appealed, and the Supreme Court of Malawi reversed the decision. A three-judge panel ruled that the lower court judge erred by "basing her decision on some imaginary unscrupulous individuals allegedly involving themselves in child trafficking. These unscrupulous individuals were not before the court.... The court ought to have based its decision on the particular appellant and the particular infant that were before the court."[5] Mercy was cleared for immediate adoption, and she went home with her new mother.

Was the court's decision an example of responsible jurisprudence based on a sound interpretation of Malawi's constitutional law? We don't know Malawi's constitutional law, but it isn't the important point for us. What matters most from our perspective is the lower court judge's view that child traffickers waited right outside the boundary of the law, like dingoes circling in the dark.

What Constitutes "Child Trafficking"?

There is wide agreement that "trafficking" exists in international adoption, but much less agreement on what that means and how often it occurs. The term itself is controversial. The definition of human trafficking used by the United Nations in the Palermo Protocol of 2003 would not count fraud or even kidnapping for international adoption because its purpose is not exploitation. Of course, no protocol is required to deem kidnapping a crime. "Child selling," that is, receiving compensation for surrendering parental rights, would not be considered trafficking as long as the adoptive child was not to be exploited. Exploitation is defined by the UN as "at a minimum" things like forced labor, prostitution, sexual abuse, or forced commission of crimes. The US State Department agrees. The State Department's 2010 *Trafficking in Persons Report* states that "kidnapping or unlawful buying/selling of an infant or child for the purposes of offering that child for adoption represents a serious criminal offense, but it is not a form of child trafficking."[6] E. J. Graff, a well-known commentator on human rights writing in *The American Prospect*, takes strong exception. "When a child is bought, defrauded, coerced, or abducted away from its birth family to be sold into adoption, *call it trafficking*. And deal with it accordingly" (emphasis original).[7]

In some countries, such as China, Vietnam, Liberia, and Sri Lanka, legislation deems illegal adoptions to constitute human trafficking. The Australia government is willing to regard some adoption activities as trafficking as well, even when no apparent exploitation takes place.[8] UNICEF also considers fraudulent adoption to be human trafficking, as evidenced by the fact that it is included on the list of why children are being trafficked in Asia.[9]

To avoid some of these issues of legal terminology, David Smolin prefers to use the term "child laundering" to encompass the various forms of fraud and abuse in international adoption.[10] Below we give examples of recent abuses, roughly following the taxonomy of Smolin. These are listed in declining order of maleficence, at least as judged by public reaction to them, somewhat tempered with our own judgement. This will help parse out the various abuses that can occur in international adoption and decide whether they are all apiece and, if not, how and why they differ.

Child Theft

Sometimes children have been stolen or kidnapped from their parents, in various ways, for the purposes of international adoption. Clearly this is the worst abuse in adoption, the most harmful to birth families, and the type we all would like to avoid if only for the sake of the birth parents. Once discovered, and possibly at the time of the theft if the child is old enough, the child and adoptive parents also suffer. Here we provide examples of how it can happen.

Kidnapping

In March of 2010, a Chinese construction worker named Liu Liquin was on a job when his wife called to tell him that their two-year-old son, Jingjun, was missing. Liu and his wife began a frantic search for the boy, phoning relatives and canvassing their neighborhood calling his name and asking passersby if they had seen the child.[11] The local police would not help because twenty-four hours had not passed since the boy disappeared. That evening, it occurred to Lui to look at the footage from a surveillance camera for a building on the street where they lived. "Sure enough, when the video footage was queued up, in a small corner of the frame, Lui could see a man, face obscured, carrying little Jingjun down the narrow alley where the Liu family live[d]."[12] They never found their son.

China has an enormous child kidnapping problem relative to other counties. The *China Daily*, a state-run newspaper, claims that as many as seventy thousand children are abducted each year. Compare this to America, where about one hundred children are abducted by strangers each year, making the Chinese abduction rate about .03 percent of children per year versus .0002 percent for the United States, both small but still more than a hundredfold difference.[13] Why are these children being stolen? One, though not the only, factor is surely the "one-child policy," a stringent attempt to reduce the country's fertility rate. Recently relaxed, the policy was launched formally in 1979, when the country's population reached 1 billion, with an initial goal to stabilize population at 1.2 billion, later revised to 1.4 billion, by 2010. The policy permitted urban couples to have only one child and rural couples to have two. It was enforced unevenly by geography, time, and ethnicity.[14] The policy was enforced by the National Population and Family Planning Commission, which employed three hundred thousand full-time, paid family-planning workers and eighty million volunteers. "Parents with extra children can be fined, depending on the region, from $370 to $12,800, many times the average annual income for ordinary Chinese. If the fine is not paid sometimes the couple's land is taken away, their house is destroyed, they lose their jobs or the child is not allowed to attend school. Government employees risk losing their jobs if they do not adhere to the policy."[15] Adopted children, however, do not count against the one-child policy; there is no penalty for expanding one's family through adoption.

But most children adopted and kidnapped for adoption within China are boys. While Chinese parents' desire to have girls has increased over time, two forces conspire to create a preference for boys in practice.[16] One is the strong patrilineal need for a son to carry on the family name. The other is an even stronger need for financial security provided by sons in the absence of wide-spread government old-age support, especially in rural areas. Thus, many families without boys are willing to adopt one. Consequently, most of the children kidnapped for domestic adoption purposes are boys.

The kidnapping of boys is not directly an issue for international adoption; almost all healthy Chinese children sent abroad are girls. The effect of the one-child policy on international adoption is to make tens of thousands of baby girls available through abandonment. Nevertheless, because adoption is a large source of revenue for orphanages, who will pay substantial prices, abduction of girls does occur. A 2005 report from the New China News Agency, for example, said that thirty-one babies were kidnapped from the southern province of Guangdong and sold to welfare institutions in Hunan province.[17] Sixteen people were prosecuted for those crimes.

In the case of international adoption, it is difficult to assess the size of the stranger-abduction problem, as most writers about child trafficking lump child sale by birth parents and child sale by kidnappers into the same category, even though the harm affects different groups in different ways. Much more is known, however, about another type of abduction that has the same motivation but is in some ways even more appalling. In 2005, in Longhui County, China, a nineteen-year-old father named Yuan Xinquan experienced what could reasonably be described as a kidnapping of his daughter. Yet the obvious recourse, to report the incident to local authorities, was not likely to be much help in this case—it was local authorities who did the kidnapping. He was holding his seven-week-old daughter when "a half dozen men sprang from a government van and demanded his marriage certificate" and birth certificate.[18] He did not have a birth certificate for the baby, as he and the child's mother had married below the age of legal consent, making their child illegal as well as their marriage The officials, who were from the family planning authorities, demanded he pay a fine equivalent to $745 or they would take the baby. He could not pay. "He was left with a plastic bag holding her baby clothes and some infant formula."[19]

Between 1999 and 2006, officials seized sixteen babies in Longhui County, and, if parents could not pay the fines, the children were turned over to orphanages. A 2009 article in the *Los Angeles Times* describes how the policy of official abduction was explained to one hapless birth mother: "'I'm going to sell the baby for foreign adoption. I can get a lot of money for her,' [the family planning official] told the sobbing mother as he drove to an orphanage [in a nearby city]. In return he promised that the family wouldn't have to pay fines for violating China's one-child policy."[20] In the case of Longhui County, all foreign adoptions from the local orphanage required a $5,400 donation from the adoptive parents, obviously a significant source of revenue for the institution itself. According to Brian H. Stuy, a noted expert on Chinese adoption, official confiscations of children sometimes involve over-quota children who have been hidden from authorities, but "just as often they involve children who were simply not registered with the Residence Committee in the family's town or village."[21] In other words, authorities used weak excuses to take away children because they profited by turning them over to orphanages.[22]

Tricking a Mother Out of Her Children

Child abduction is not always as abrupt and violent as in the cases in China. But, in these cases, the child is essentially stolen from the birth parent, and the effects are similar. In *Finding Fernanda*, Erin Siegal presents a fascinating real-life mystery about a Guatemalan woman whose beautiful two-year-old daughter, Fernanda, vanished into the international adoption network.[23] At age twenty-eight, Mildred Alvarado, pregnant, husbandless, and with three hungry children, accepted the kind offer of the friend of a friend, a self-described "Christian" and "good Samaritan of sorts" named Sabrina, to let Mildred and her children stay in her home for free. Soon, a cousin of Sabrina's boyfriend began dropping by and snapping photos of Fernanda, completely ignoring the other two children. Eventually, Sabrina badgered Mildred into placing Fernanda in the care of one Doña Coni, who was also "a good Christian."

Filled with doubt, Mildred let Fernanda go with Coni, who, upon collecting the child, "handed Mildred a small stack of 12 blank papers and coolly told her to sign each one." When Mildred balked at letting the child go she was told, "Don't be stupid, if you make a stink here, the police will come and they'll drag everyone to jail. Including you."[24]

Still living with Sabrina, Mildred began hemorrhaging a few weeks before her new baby was due. Taken to a run-down clinic in a poor neighborhood, she was given injections "for the pain," only to wake up in a hospital the next day and be told she'd been given an emergency C-section. "Where is my baby?" she asked. "Safe with Coni," she was told. Now she had lost two children to the good Samaritans.[25]

Shortly after Fernanda had moved in with Coni, Coni's son Marvin sent an e-mail to an American adoption agency called Celebrate Children International (CCI), run by one Sue Hedberg. "I'm sending you photos of Maria Fernanda Alverado.... I hope you can find a family soon."[26] Both Hedberg and CCI would become notorious among the adoptive parents they worked with.

One prospective family for Fernanda was that of Betsy Emmanuel, a deeply religious woman from Tennessee who, with her husband, Leslie, had three birth children and four adopted children (from Korea and China). Betsy was smitten by the online picture of Fernanda on the CCI website, but Sue Hedberg informed Betsy that Fernanda had a little sister, Anna Christa, whom they would also need to adopt, at full cost, which they could not afford. Still, Betsy would play a key role in the recovery of Mildred's children.

Meanwhile, Mildred went to the authorities to make complaints about her missing children, but though they investigated for a long time, little was accomplished. Eventually, Coni and Sabrina were arrested, but Mildred still didn't know where her children were. Moreover, the government prosecutor said that handling a case like Mildred's made him nervous because "it wasn't uncommon for Ministirio Público staff to be murdered by those they were trying to investigate."[27]

The break in the case came when, in 2008, Betsy Emmanuel came across an online article from Guatemala's *Prensa Libre* about a missing child named Fernanda and the mother, Mildred Alvaredo, who had lost her to kidnappers in 2006. Upon reading this, Betsy realized "she'd been adopting a stolen child."[28] It took a number of phone calls to Guatemala to straighten the matter out. Mildred's case became a minor media sensation and was one of a handful of similar cases that had been discovered. A court finally ordered the children returned to Mildred in February of 2008. The mothers in the other cases had not found their children.

Meanwhile, Celebrate Children International, the agency that had accepted the referral of Fernanda, was denied State Department certification under the Hague Convention, certification which was necessary after 2008, in part because of "willingness to work with unscrupulous facilitators," as well as agency head Sue Hedberg's behavior, which was seen as "unfriendly and not transparent."[29]

How Serious a Problem Was Child Theft?

Stealing someone's child or kidnapping is a high crime in anyone's reckoning. It is a good justification for hostility to international adoption, at least as IA is currently practiced. So, how prevalent was actual stealing or kidnapping? The

Guatemalan families involved in international adoption were less likely to lose a child to the United States through "trafficking" than the average American family was to have a child removed by local authorities, and much less likely than an American family that happened to be poor. In 2006, Guatemala had about four thousand adoptions to the United States, one hundred of which involved allegations of child theft, with only five of those eventually confirmed.[30] That's about 1.2 children taken illegally per thousand adoptions, many times fewer children than the number taken for adoption to the US per thousand children in the population. In 2008, authorities removed American children from poor families at a rate of 20.2 per thousand.[31] Child theft and child removal are not the same thing, but in both cases poor families lose children against their will.[32] The comparison gives us some concept of scale.

The Guatemalan press was eager to believe that kidnapping was routine among those facilitating adoptions to America. In a 1989 cable to the State Department, the staff of the US embassy in Guatemala City said that "newspapers report more than fifty lost or stolen children per year" to America. The embassy described a typical incident: "Periodically the police raid... the nurseries where attorneys handling adoption keep the children pending approval of the adoption. These raids receive headline newspaper and television coverage.... Usually the children are quietly returned to their birth mothers a few weeks later who in turn return them to the attorneys and the adoptions go forward."[33] Obviously, these children were not kidnapped, though media coverage implied that they were.

Kidnapping or stealing a child is clearly the worst offense related to international adoption. Why does it occur? Most commentators on international adoption argue that it happens because babies are worth a lot of money to parents in Western countries, so there is a large incentive to commit this crime.[34] They argue that this problem is endemic to international adoption and therefore that IA is not a viable option. Some argue that, because of this, IA should be shut down. Others argue that it should be heavily regulated in a way that means few children are adopted across country borders. But healthy white infants born in America have an even higher value in the domestic baby "market," yet kidnapping for adoption is rare in this country. Why the difference? This is a subject at the heart of the next chapters.

Children Adopted from Orphanages
Without Parental Knowledge

In January of 2013, we met with Sierra Leone's minister of Social Welfare, Gender and Children's Affairs. When he heard about our interest in adoption, he immediately shuffled us to an assistant minister who handled such matters. Before we could even state our interests, the assistant said, "So, you want to know about the HANCI case, right?" The adoption scandal that became known as the HANCI case, after a local NGO called Help a Needy Child International (HANCI), was an international embarrassment to the Leonean government and gave more ammunition to the opponents of international adoption.

E. J. Graff describes the experience of one American mother confronting the circumstances of her HANCI child's adoption. In 2010, Judith Mosley was reading a Facebook post by *Ethica*, a nonprofit organization that promoted ethical adoption, when she saw something that "made everything go silent," as if she'd "been pulled underwater." The post reported the lament of a father from Sierra Leone who in 1998 had placed two children in an orphanage only to discover later that they were adopted by Americans. He had not seen or heard from his son or daughter in fourteen years. When he gave the children's names in the post, Judith was thunderstruck—one of those children was her adopted son, Samuel. "We want our children who were sold to these white people," the father said. "We want to know whether they are alive or dead."[35]

Mosely's anguish at this discovery was surely compounded by the fact that it was not her first encounter with adoption fraud. Ten years prior, she had adopted a girl, age nine, from Cambodia who, upon learning English, began talking of an extended birth family. The adoption papers had made no mention of this family; Mosely was assured the child was an orphan.[36] In 2005, Mosley gave a number of press interviews that openly discussed her daughter's painful revelations. Now here she was going through it all over again with Samuel. The deception was part of what is now a rather famous incident.

The Leonean birth father of Judith's son Samuel was among the parents of twenty-nine children from Makeni who tried to protect their children from the horrific civil war by placing them in the custody of the group called HANCI. HANCI had placed them for adoption in America, allegedly without informing the parents. One of those children, Michaela DePrince, is one of the very few internationally acknowledged black ballerinas.[37]

What happened after the children were placed in the Makeni orphanage gets pretty murky. Like many poverty-stricken families in developing countries, most of them had placed their kids in an orphanage, the HANCI center, so that they would be fed, educated, and, during wartime, kept safe. In 1998, the rebels entered Makeni, taking it over as their headquarters city, killing, amputating limbs, burning and stealing food and supplies. According to the HANCI families, as the rebels overran the town, they called, by phone primarily, to collect their children, but the HANCI workers would not allow them to have their children back. Is this true? Accounts vary, particularly between the birth parents and the HANCI workers. What is clear is that twenty-nine children left the country and were placed for adoption. The birth parents claim they were not informed that this would happen. HANCI claims that they were fully informed and that some of the parents falsified their statements, claiming the children were really nephews and nieces and that the parents had been killed in the war. These falsifications were presumably to improve the chances that the children, as ostensible orphans, would find adoptive families. Do the birth parents now have any incentive to lie about their alleged confusion? Alas, yes, as they might expect to get money from the American families who have their children, especially, perhaps, if they win the court case. Contact information would facilitate this. By one not entirely trustworthy account (a Freetown blogger), the HANCI workers, all from Sierra Leone themselves and thus potential victims of the rebels, fled with the children to Guinea or Ghana. All we know for sure is that with or without the parent's knowledge or understanding, the children were placed for adoption with American parents.

Whatever the truth, in 2010, the birth parents demanded government action against HANCI. President Ernest Koroma appointed a commission to investigate HANCI's handling of these twenty-nine adoptions.[38] In April of 2012, the commission appointed to review the case issued a white paper calling for the police to conduct a criminal investigation of the charges brought by the parents, which itself suggested that the criminal charges should be referred to the High Court. It also recommended that the government shut down all HANCI activities in the country—not just adoption—pending a review of the organization's financial records. This triggered a protest march by HANCI supporters. HANCI provided aid to thousands of Leoneans in ways ranging from integrating street children back into their communities to teacher education programs. An article in the local *Awareness Times Newspaper* reported, "An eight year-old beneficiary Solomon Stevens told this reporter that he is an orphan, with all his hopes for prosperity on HANCI. He said without HANCI, he will drop out of school and might also become a beggar as there will be no one to cater for his welfare as HANCI has been doing."[39]

In February of 2014, after our trip to Sierra Leone, the Freetown *Concord News* reported, "[High Court] Magistrate Kamanda said the evidences before his court proved that the accused persons observed the legal procedures and that all the court orders presented were issued and stamped by the Sierra Leone court, including the High Court." He ruled that "the HANCI parents were cognizance [*sic*] of the process and that after 15 years, they decided to take another action."[40] In other words, he ruled against the parents.

The key question isn't what the truth of this particular case is, or what the court determined. The truth is as clouded as it is in most cases of disputed birth parent knowledge of adoption placement, which is the point. If a child is placed for adoption from an orphanage without the parents' knowledge and consent, that must surely be classified as theft. But the difference between these cases and outright kidnapping is that the circumstances in these cases are often murky: Has the child actually been abandoned? Did the parents give permission for adoption? The HANCI case is a well-publicized and detailed example of what may or may not be a serious transgression against parental rights, and it is certainly not unique, as we show in Isata's story as well.

Other cases, from Vietnam, for example, appear to be more straightforward cases of abuse. In 2008, the US embassy in Hanoi published details of ten adoption cases for which it had denied entry visas to the children in question. Two of those cases involved women who had placed their young children in local centers without the intention that they be adopted. But the children were nevertheless matched with prospective adoptive parents without the mothers consenting, or even being aware of it. The US consular office denied the visas after the mothers and other witnesses told their stories to embassy investigators. But this was not the end of it. Cables to the State Department describe how Vietnamese government officials, both local and national, pressured mothers and witnesses to recant their testimony, threatening them with large financial charges if they didn't.[41] Said officials even went so far as to provide alternative statements for mothers and witnesses to give to the Americans. Birth mothers were then given relinquishment papers to sign. From the perspective of this book, the point of these stories about children adopted from orphanages without parental permission is that the current system encourages deception. Multiple forms of deception. Orphanage directors who can gain adoption fees have the incentive to claim children in the institution were relinquished for adoption by their birth mother even if they weren't. If the parents never intended for the kids to be adopted, then these cases amount to child theft. But the birth parents of children adopted in the West also have incentive to later claim that they were deceived and that they deserve compensation, either from the orphanage or from the relatively wealthy adoptive parents. We don't begrudge birth parents for needing financial support, and we will argue that this sort of problem would be avoided if birth and adoptive parents could directly negotiate the arrangements of an adoption. But the Hague Convention regulations specifically forbid this.

Birth Parents Selling Parental Rights

Here we consider cases where the birth parents accepted compensation for placing their children for adoption. Many critics of intercountry adoption consider parent selling of children for adoption as heinous, or as equal to child theft, and consider both as child trafficking. Certainly, when children are kidnapped, the middlemen who kidnap will then sell them to orphanages or adoption facilitators or adoptive parents. So kidnapping and selling by facilitators are inextricably linked. But we rank birth parents selling their children as typically different than child theft, with different effects and harm depending on the circumstances.

A Baby-Selling Business

In January of 2010, Barbara Demick of the *Los Angeles Times* interviewed members of the Duan family, uneducated rice farmers who became first rich, then notorious, in China for selling babies to orphanages for as much as six hundred dollars each.[42] "They [the orphanages] couldn't get enough babies," thirty-eight-year-old Yuelin Duan told Demick. The story began in 1993, when Yuelin's mother and sisters took care of babies for a local orphanage, being paid one dollar per day. The Duans found abandoned infant girls "all over," often wrapped in filthy rags, sometimes crawling with ants. At first, the short-staffed orphanages might refuse to take the children, but by 1997, the institutions began placing these girls for international adoption, collecting a three-thousand-dollar fee per child. "Now, instead of rejecting the babies the orphan director was begging Chen to bring as many as she could, even offering to pay her expenses and then some." Suddenly, five other orphanages sprang up nearby. Finder's fees that were originally six to twelve dollars per baby increased eightfold and kept rising.

The Duans located another woman in Wuchan Province who found and cared for lots and lots of abandoned children and recruited her into their burgeoning supply chain. While many of the babies located by the Duans and others were found abandoned, some were placed directly by their mothers, and it seems highly likely that some of these mothers were compensated.

The baby selling business ran quite profitably until one Friday afternoon in November 2005. On that day, two Duan sisters emerged from the Hengyang County railway station with three infant girls, having arranged to meet high officials from a local orphanage, the Hengyang Social Welfare Institute, who planned to buy the babies.[43] The Qidong County police, who had been tipped off about the sale, appeared and started making arrests. The story of the Duans' apprehension was national news in China and quickly went international, where the Western press dubbed it the "Hunan baby trafficking scandal."[44] On November 24, Reuters quoted the *People's Daily* website as reporting that twenty-seven people were arrested, including the head of an orphanage.[45]

Why were the Duans arrested? That may seem a silly question, but selling babies to other families had a long history among Chinese peasants. It was, nevertheless, illegal, and a 1991 law strengthened the proscription against the "buying, selling, transfer and transit of children for the purpose of sale."[46] So the Duans were clearly breaking the law, and the police were dutifully enforcing the law. Obviously. But in a 2014 article in the *Cumberland Law Review*, Brian Stuy lays out a much more complicated story.

Duan family members had been arrested before, in or around 1999, 2002, and 2003. But they had always been able to explain to the police that they simply were delivering babies to the orphanage, and the director had backed them up. Eventually, however, the orphanage directors "grew tired of paying the Duans for the children and began working to make arrangements directly with the Duans' Wuchan contact," a Ms. Liang.[47] When Ms. Liang refused to do business with anyone but the Duans, the director of the Hengyang County facility hatched a plan to arrange for the police to arrest the Duan sisters.

But the plan and subsequent rounds of greedy intervention and political machinations from the level of the local police up to the national government created a firestorm of international media attention. The Duan family members were the biggest losers out of the many who were implicated in the scandal—they were sentenced to fifteen years in prison. Media coverage posed a genuine threat to China's lucrative international adoption system. The China Center for Adoption Affairs (CCAA), the country's central adoption authority, "investigated" all the Hengyang adoptions and announced that all of those adopted by Americans were "legitimately orphaned or abandoned and that there [were] no biological parents searching for them."[48]

When the scandal died down, the CCAA faced the problem of ensuring this embarrassment did not repeat itself. Ground rules for orphanages had to be set. A February 2006 meeting of orphanage directors was held in Tianjin. As Stuy reported, "According to one orphanage director present at the meeting, the 'CCAA gave us an exact figure we can pay: 500–1000 yuan. They said if we crossed that line and got caught we must deal with it ourselves.' However, the CCAA emphasized that they needed as many children as possible and not to get caught paying more than 1000 yuan or the directors would be on their own."[49] The Hunan baby trafficking scandal, with its deception, hypocrisy, official corruption, and punishment of mainly minor operatives, is a near textbook example of how black markets operate, but to the extent the babies were sold by birth mothers, or even abandoned, the harm done is different than with theft; when the birth mother sells her baby, she is getting compensation and has chosen to do so, however much her circumstances have forced her to that horrible decision. She has done neither in the case of child theft, making that experience much worse. The compensation can be used to help her other children perhaps. Again, with abandonment there is choice involved, though no compensation. A terrible choice, for sure, but with child theft, a shocking loss of a child occurs through no choice of your own and with no knowledge of the outcome.

Having Babies Just to Sell Them

As with the case of baby abduction, Guatemalan incidents of baby buying were subtler and on a smaller scale that in China. Like *Finding Fernanda*, Jacob Wheeler's book *Between Light and Shadow: A Guatemalan Girl's Journey through Adoption* is the story of two mothers linked by an adopted child. And, as with Mildred's search for Fernanda, it seemed to be the story of a Guatemalan woman tricked or coerced into giving her daughter up to adoption facilitators.[50] But to the surprise of Wheeler, the story did not ultimately unfold that way. The books are painfully similar at the start: having found a new woman, Antonia's husband kicked her and her four children, three sons and a daughter, out of Antonia's own house. Like Mildred, Antonia was pregnant at the time. With no help from her husband, Antonia occasionally resorted to desperate measures to feed her family. The daughter, Bernice, would sometimes come home to find her mother "lying on a dirty mattress in the dark room, the sweat still glistening on her naked body and the unmistakable look of guilt filling her eyes like tears."[51] Bernice was then six years old.

An acquaintance from the marketplace told Antonia something akin to what Mildred had been told, "that [Antonia] was dirt poor, that her work was despicable and evil, that her kids were malnourished and small, and that the little girl [Bernice] would have a better life elsewhere."[52] As Wheeler puts it "UNICEF calls women like [this acquaintance] *jaladoras*, from the Spanish word *jalar*, to grab."[53] According to Antonia, she was pressured to place Bernice, by then eight years old, for adoption. Antonia gave in. Bernice was delivered to a *hogar* (orphanage or children's home), where she would wait six months, crying every night, for a family to come and make her their daughter.

The family that came, after some initial reservations, was that of Judy Barret, her husband, Bob Walters, and their twin daughters, from Michigan. Eventually Bernice became a typical American teenager. But the transition was not without some real pain for the child. Why had her mother abandoned her, she asked Judy? Judy began to wonder about this birth mother. Bernice had burn marks on her arms and legs and drew artistically adept, but disturbing, pictures of men with large, engorged penises. Had the little girl been abused? When Judy met Wheeler, who was writing a book about Guatemalan adoption, she asked him if he could find Antonia. Against long odds he managed to locate her—Judy flew down to meet the birth mother.

Antonia's story was as sad a tale as Judy had expected—men who were abusive and/or neglectful, Antonia being evicted from the house she paid for, hunger and desperation. With great emotion, Antonia confesses something that explains the burn marks: her harshness toward her daughter.

> "She always wanted to be with me. Todo todo. But when I became pregnant with another I grew tired of handling her all the time, and I beat her often."
>
> Why?
>
> "Because she was very loving, my nina." Antonia is sobbing uncontrollably and her words fly out of her mouth along with drops of saliva. "But I had another in my belly, and I didn't want her. I beat her, and after I regretted it, but it was already too late."[54]

Judy is understanding. They agree to meet again to continue the discussions. It is at the second meeting that Judy hears something about Antonia's past she seems not quite able to process. Wheeler describes the scene.

> "She tells me she's given up five of her children for adoption," Judy blurts out.... "[Bernice] is the last of the five." My jaw drops. This is the information I have been dying to ask about. It's also the reason so many Guatemalans give for wanting to shut down adoption—what they call an "industry," though organizations like UNICEF have been hard pressed to document a single case of a woman being paid to give up her baby.[55]

Moreover, Antonia is angry that she got no money for Bernice. "That's how I built the house where we lived with [Bernice's father]," she tells them, "with my own money." With the money she got from selling tortillas? Wheeler asks, incredulous. "No, from the others I gave up." She isn't sure why there was no money for Bernice. "I just waited and waited for them to give me money. But they never gave me anything. They never gave me a single cent."[56]

When, later, Judy asks, "Are some people having babies just to sell them?" Antonia says, "Hay muchas."[57]

It is hard to prove, as no one will admit to it, but it is widely believed that baby selling was common not only in China and Guatemala, but in Cambodia, Vietnam, Romania, and Ethiopia as well, although the evidence is stronger for some countries than others.[58] And as baby selling is generally illegal, or at least highly illegitimate, it was a major factor in essentially shutting down adoption in all of those places.[59] The US State Department would not approve travel visas for adopted children who they found through investigation had been sold. Yet, is this trafficking in any meaningful sense? Can we consider "child selling" by birth families a crime like kidnapping, as in *Finding Fernanda* or in some cases in China, or like exploitation of birth families, as in Vietnam or like the HANCI case, if true? Most importantly, can transactions between two willing parties, the birth and adoptive parents, justify denying homes to thousands of children in desperate circumstances? The matriarch of the Duan family from the Hunan baby trafficking scandal said, "Many of those babies would have died if nobody took them in. I took good care of the babies. You can be the judge—am I a bad person for what I did?"[60] This question needs more careful consideration than it has so far received. Does the monetary motive for exchanging parental rights mean that the objects of the exchange, the adopted children, are necessarily abused or exploited? Also, payment to a birth parent for parental rights is not the same as payment to a child finder—this fact needs to be considered.

Document Falsification, Incomplete Information

False documentation is a problem in its own right as a symptom of the larger problems we've already discussed, such as baby theft, illegal baby buying, or duplicity in the soliciting of babies for adoption. The child laundering that Smolin talks about typically involves falsification of the paperwork that authorizes the adoption. Cambodia in 2001 illustrates this well. In a June 2002 *New York Times Magazine* article, "Where Do Babies Come From?" Sarah Corbet describes what happened there. "On Dec. 21, James Ziglar, commissioner of the Immigration and Naturalization Service, formally suspended new visa processing for adopted children in Cambodia, citing suspicions that they were being bought or stolen from their parents and put into orphanages with false paperwork in order to feed the growing American demand for babies." Supposed abandonment of certain children, which would make them adoption eligible, could not be verified. "Documents didn't match up; signatures were forged," INS spokesman Bill Strassberger was quoted as saying in the article. "The paper work would say babies had been abandoned in a certain village, and then an investigation would show that no babies had been abandoned in that place for years.'" In Vietnam, the US embassy uncovered cases of hospitals fraudulently documenting children as deserted when their birth parents failed to pay their outstanding bills.[61] The US embassy cables from Guatemala even report a number of instances where American parents had themselves listed on false birth certificates so they could take the children without needing to adopt.[62] Some of these frauds were egregiously obvious.

But false documentation can be a symptom of simple error or have more benign motivation than to cover up kidnapping or even buying a child. Required documents like birth certificates for children or death certificates for parents to verify orphan status are not always routinely issued in very poor countries, especially in the chaos of war.[63] When GB's adoption dossier arrived, for example, the death certificates of his parents looked a bit fishy: too recently filed for them to have died years before. But we were not unduly alarmed by this, as they were purportedly killed in a bloody civil war in the world's poorest country—official documents could hardly be expected to be up to date. It would turn out, of course, that his parents weren't dead. One possible explanation for this fraud is that GB's mother (as she later told us) had no idea where his birth father was. If she needed the latter's signature to release Gibrila, as is true in Guatemala, Sierra Leone, and many other countries, then the adoption could not proceed. Falsified death certificates may have been an expedient to overcome that problem.

Inaccurate documents would be an impediment to adoption in many countries. In one case in Vietnam, the place of birth was listed as the hospital to which the newborn infant had been transferred due to a health problem—a common practice in Vietnam. But the US embassy deemed this to be fraud.[64] Missing documents are an even bigger problem.[65] Roby and Maskew point out, for example, that in Cambodia births often go unrecorded.[66] We have been told that this is also true in Ethiopia, Haiti, Sierra Leone, the Congo, and many other poor countries. So, some adoption "fraud" occurs when nothing irregular happens—no kidnapping, no selling, no trickery—except that the birth parents are unable to produce the appropriate documentation. But, sometimes they can pay to get false documents or legitimately obtain papers from the attending midwife. In the former case, they can produce documents, but deeper investigation might show them to be false. In the latter case, the midwife papers accurately show the birth, perhaps the local court accepts the documentation, but then the US State Department does not; or, the local US State Department office may understand the importance of the midwife registry system, but to anyone else at the State Department or to any investigator outside the system, the documents look false. Finally, given all the stages and people filling out paperwork for an adoption, simple human error can occur. All of this is what could lead a top administrator in charge of child welfare to declare that every adoption packet coming from Ethiopia had something false in it.

Some adoption researchers list misinformation, or lack of information, as adoption fraud or even child trafficking. For example, it is not unusual for birth parents or adoption facilitators to say a child is younger than she is. (This was probably the case with GB.) Adoptive parents generally prefer younger children, and the children can often be "passed" as younger because malnutrition makes them small for their age. So, by lying about the child's age, the birth family, or the orphanage, increases the likelihood that he or she will be adopted. Also, sometimes health information is not accurate or is missing. In any case, even when false documentation does not mask child theft or child selling, the misinformation can cause much anguish for the adopted child and the adoptive parents. We saw this in Isata's case when, because of having been misled, her adopted family told her that the parents she *knew* she had were not her parents but were really an aunt and uncle. This caused her much anxiety and frustration. Better information about the mental health of the Russian boy, Artem Saveliev, might have averted the fiasco of his adoptive mother literally shipping him back to Moscow.

Another form of misinformation may be unintentional, or not, but still causes lots of heartache. One point that IA critics make, particularly when they provide examples of so-called trafficking, is that other cultures don't have a Western understanding of "adoption," either as a word or a concept. Thus, goes this argument, when an adoption facilitator speaks of adoption, and having a child go live in the United States, for example, the birth family does not understand that signing the relinquishment document means that they give up parental rights *forever*. This argument sometimes proves to have merit. In the late 1990s, a number of children were adopted to America from the Marshall Islands. Children adopted in the Marshall Islands do not require a visa to travel to the United States, and it became clear that most of these children traveled without typical documentation, especially without the usual consent documentation from birth mothers. One study indicated that as many as 83 percent of the birth mothers surveyed did not understand that the adoptions meant a permanent transfer of parental rights.[67]

Still, it is worth pointing out that in some parts of Africa, for example, sending children to another family is far more a cultural norm than it is in the West.[68] In *Cross-Cultural Practices in Adoption*, Fiona Bowie says, "It is so self-evident to most people in Euro-American society that children should be raised by their 'natural' parents that it might come as a surprise to learn that this is not always and everywhere the case."[69] Erdmute Alber says that among the rural Baatombu in Northern Benin, "people think that biological parents are less able than foster parents to provide a good education for their children. The Baatombu therefore find it very reasonable to give their children to other persons to be fostered."[70] Esther Goody found that social parenting was also common in Ghana.[71] Research by Hillary Page similarly found that among the Ivory Coast groups she studied, about 50 percent of children were not being raised by their biological parents.[72] And in East Cameroon, says Catrien Notermans, 30 percent of children ten to fourteen years old live with someone other than their genetic mother.[73] Among the Maasai of East Africa there are even occasions of baby buying. Aud Talle has reported that a childless woman will sometimes approach a pregnant co-wife or sister-in-law and ask for custody of the baby, for which she will pay some price, like a heifer. After a formalizing ritual, the baby is considered hers in all ways, and she is considered by everyone to be the mother.[74]

By way of illustrating this tradition in Africa, Gesue Gebrier Roberts tells of many routine separations of children from parents, including his own, growing up in Liberia.[75] He recounts how, when he was about a year old, he and his siblings accompanied his mother and grandparents back to Zammie Town, where the family had originally lived. He never saw his birth father again. Over the next seven years in Zammie Town, he did not live with his birth mother and rarely even saw her. He stayed with his grandparents while his mother lived on a farm further into the country. Later, his mother remarried, but Gesue did not go to live with her and his new stepfather. When he did visit his birth mother, Gesue would be fed less than the other children in the household because, as his grandmother told him, his mother's husband was only his stepfather. When his Aunt Krayonor moved relatively far away, to Zwedu, for her second marriage, Gesue cried. "Aunt Krayonor loved me... because my mother had given me to her as her son," he said, "while [my sister] Teetee was given to Uncle Brown as his daughter." In Africa, Roberts says, "it is common for a woman with many children to 'share' them as an 'altruistic' act."[76] After a couple of years, his aunt came back and took him with her to Zwedu so "he could get an education." The trek took them about a week through sometimes dangerous terrain, so the boy understood that it might not be possible to ever visit his original family. He might never see them again. His new uncle treated him well, which he says was lucky, given that he was not the boy's natural son.

None of this is to suggest that parents never sign relinquishment documents that they do not understand. And it is true that the arrangements described above tend to be more informal than adoptions to another country by west-erners, since westerners, and the Hague Convention, insist on formal Western-type legal transfers of parental rights. So, when international adoption occurs, unintentionally or intentionally, the birth parents may not fully understand the nature of formal Western-style adoption. But usually they would understand that they are unlikely to see their child again until the child is grown or almost so. The key question, as we see in Isata's story, is what happens then?

Now we have acknowledged what everyone already knows: that in the last couple of decades, intercountry adoption has been plagued with the kinds of problems—fraud, deception, even outright kidnapping—that would make rea-sonable people want to shut it down. But we've also acknowledged that we want to keep it going and even expand it. One reason we still support international adoption is that, as we saw above in the case of Guatemala, these abuses occur much less frequently than media hype would have us believe—after televised police raids on adoption nurseries, birth parents would quietly return the chil-dren to the nurseries so that they could be adopted. Moreover, the most serious abuses, like child theft by strangers, represent a small fraction of the total number of international adoptions. This is not to suggest that we should tolerate them. But what harm these "trafficking problems" do is relatively minor compared to the enormous good that adoption conveys on the lives of thousands of children, including actually saving the lives of hundreds of those kids. As Bartholet puts it, "Opponents of international adoption *never weigh the evils on each side.* Instead they focus solely on the evils represented by adoption abuses, and then argue for restrictive regulation to address those evils. They don't consider the evils repre-sented by failing to place children in international adoptive homes, and the good that comes from placing them" (emphasis original).[77] Bartholet is weighing the benefits of IA against its costs, even in broad terms—something that is conspicu-ously missing from most of this literature.

Even if you weigh the costs of the abuses to be greater than the benefits of IA, we have a second reason to support adoption anyway, one that is specific to economic reasoning. Economists would argue that some of the rules governing the international adoption system virtually guarantee abuses of this kind. And a relatively simple restructuring of the system could largely eliminate them. But whereas adoption critics, at least those who don't want to outright ban the practice, propose reform requiring tighter regulation of international adoption, we suggest just the opposite. The system needs less regulation, not more, or at least a different kind of regulation: regulation that acknowledges the economic incentives facing usually very poor birth families. We turn to this argument after the next installment of Isata's story.

Why Won't You Tell Us Where Isata Is?

The M. family willingly signed papers allowing Isata to be placed with an American family to be raised and educated. But, as in some of the cases described in this chapter, in interviews with us, they claim they never understood that the placement would be a permanent legal adoption. In this section of Isata's story, we describe the M. family's struggle to have TCH meet the conditions they say were placed on the adoption from the beginning. We also hear from other birth parents about their experience with TCH.

According to the M. family, before Isata left for America in 2002 to be raised by the Sibleys, they were assured by TCH that Isata was to visit them regularly, that in ten years (i.e. 2012) she would return to Sierra Leone (to stay if she wanted to), and that they would have regular communication and progress reports from her new family. Within a couple of years of her departure, however, it was clear that these conditions were not being met. (In fact, if all these conditions were agreed on by TCH, the Sibley family was not informed of them, although the M. family did have the Sibleys' name.) As the years went by, the M. family put continued pressure on TCH to, at a minimum, provide information about Isata. Shaun described this struggle in a January 1, 2015, e-mail to us. His story involves the country director of TCH, whom we will refer to as David, though that is not his name.

> There was a time [in August 2012] that the whole family became desperate about getting information as to Isata's whereabouts and an update on her situation. In August 2012 our mom met with David and carried him [*sic*] to the Police Station. I and [younger brother] Abdul almost fought him at the police station because his words were not true; he was saying that their office [hadn't reported about Isata] because they had issues in dealing with printing and their internet connections were down. We were then promised by David that he would help us get the information and even give us numbers to be in contact with Isata's [American] family. These

promises were to be fulfilled in three weeks. The police men asked us to show proof that Isata is my parent's child. This was confirmed by my mom showing a photo of the whole family taken at the time of Isata's departure.

After the three weeks were up the whole family went to the police station to see the information David presented and also to get the contact information for the American foster parents; we didn't understand that Isata was adopted. I left work early that day to be at the Police station. To our surprise the promise of getting us the information and the contact details was not fulfilled. David only brought information to try to prove that my mom and dad were aunt and uncle to Isata, not her parents, and that they were not able to take care of Isata any longer, which was the reason why they had to send Isata to an orphanage. During this time, my mom and dad tried explaining all that transpired between them and David but the police men wouldn't listen. They wanted proof that Isata was really my parent's daughter. We almost wanted to fight David, but the police men were in his favor; as we tried going near him they said that if we move any step closer to him, we will be locked up. So that was how we ended up losing hope in fighting David of TCH.

According to Shaun, the police were initially concerned enough to take David's passport, but a few days later they had altogether lost interest in the case. The M. family suspected they had been paid to lose interest. This explanation is not implausible, as police corruption is endemic in Sierra Leone, as in much of the developing world. For example, our daughter once had to pay Leonean police to forget about a heinous crime she'd committed while visiting Freetown: she photo-graphed a mural on a wall "without a permit."[1]

In January 2013, while in Freetown, we heard similar stories about other birth parents who placed children with TCH. We visited the modest, well-kept home of the M. family while we were in Freetown. Shaun or Abdul had to translate for their mother, who spoke no English. After we talked for a while, everyone suddenly got up and left—again, we assumed we were supposed to follow. After a bit of a walk, we entered some unpaved alleys in a crowded neighborhood that in America would be considered a slum. The homes were very small, made of red clay, as were the roadways under our feet. This probably would not be considered a slum in Freetown—these were houses and were neatly made and relatively organized, not the ramshackle huts made out of anything stuck together that we had seen standing or leaning everywhere in what used to be the white person's hotel peninsula. At least some of these houses had electricity. These weren't shanties or tents. But public services were obviously limited; periodically we came across huge mounds of trash piled in a larger area of the road. At one of the homes, we entered a small, dark, and densely still living room through the front door—a cloth hanging from the jamb. The room was dominated by a TV set and held a large fan that the occupants turned off so that we could hear each other.

We came unannounced, annoying the owner slightly, as it was almost his prayer time. Nevertheless, he got out a folder of papers and gave us a long and detailed account of how David had misled other parents, some of whom arrived and gathered in the cramped space with us. This man had worked for TCH but had left their employ (at their instigation, in unclear circumstances that he related in a long story in which David played the villain). He had kept these papers and pictures when he left, and the papers typically gave the adoptive parents' full names. All the parents said that TCH had promised them that their child would return in ten years. The ten years was up. Isata, of course, was eighteen years old ten years later, but some of the children were younger.

One woman, in particular, sitting across from us, pleaded with us to help find her son, Peter. She wore pants and a shirt, was strong and thin, and had a square, angular face. She was quite striking. She showed us adoption records with pictures of him as he had looked ten years before, when he was four. She reached across the coffee table and took Tinker's hand and looked at her intently. She had asked about Peter at TCH, she said in her imperfect English, but David had refused to tell her anything. One of the M.'s translated for her.

When we left and started walking back to the M. house, this woman, Martha, walked with us for a while. Finally, she clutched Tinker's hand. "You will find Peter?" she pleaded. Martha waited for Tinker's response. This created an ethical dilemma. Peter was an American teenager, there was little doubt he'd be on Facebook, which meant we could find him in about ten minutes. We pointed out that probably anybody could find Peter on the Internet, including the man she knew who had worked for TCH, or Shaun M. This did not satisfy her. She asked Tinker again, "You will find Peter?" We explained, "If we find him, the most we can do is contact his American parents and tell them you want to know about him; we cannot send you Peter's address without their permission. She considered that reasonable. "You will find Peter?" she pleaded again, directly to Tinker, clasping her hand. Tinker said yes.

Back at the hotel, we found Peter's American address in less than five minutes. When we got home to the United States, we called Peter's adoptive parents and told them about meeting the birth mother. Happily, they had not been told that his birth mother had died; they knew she was alive. We told them that Martha very much wanted contact and that she could be contacted through Shaun M. We don't know if they ever communicated with her.

This story has a postscript, one which is quite common among stories of mishandled adoptions: none of the parents we spoke to in Sierra Leone, though they felt sorely misused, wanted their children to give up their American lives and move back to Sierra Leone. They just wanted to hear from them.

There is also a post-postscript. We were understandably angry at the apparent deception perpetrated on these parents by this children's-home-cum-adoption-agency. In the decades since GB's adoption we had given them tens of thousands of dollars to support their orphanage (Sierra Leone had since placed a moratorium on adoptions), and now it seemed that they had been lying to people. We felt obligated to report this in this manuscript and therefore also obligated to warn TCH that we would do so. After we contacted them in Freetown, they sent a representative to meet us who told us he was David's brother, or cousin (who, in Sierra Leone, are often referred to as siblings, as we've been told). To our explanation of what the birth parents had said, he merely nodded politely. Sensing his lack of interest, we asked for his assurance that he would tell David what we had said. Yes, yes, he said. At the end of our lunch he showed us pictures of diamonds and gold on his iPad, eventually trying to interest us in investing in local minerals with David and him as partners. We demurred on his offer. We also suspended the monthly contributions we had been making to this organization for eleven years.

But not without second thoughts. Was it really the right thing to do, cut off payment to that organization? How could it not be, given how so much of their behavior reeks to heaven of deception and fraud? But nothing about adoption in Africa is ever that simple. This organization did run a home that supported needy children. We knew that because we had been there. Not only had we been there, but we had dropped by unannounced, having heard of more than one case (as in the instance of the Sibleys' experience) of Americans visiting fabricated "orphanages" assembled for a day or even longer using neighborhood children.[2] But the unannounced visit found a large home with forty or fifty children running around the yard, the older ones wearing secondhand school uniforms. A tour of the building showed children definitely lived there. It wasn't as clear that education was occurring, though there were basic classrooms. Some of the children wore school uniforms that, we were told, were for them to go to school off site. So, who used the classrooms? Maybe the younger kids. But why did the kids seemingly go to different schools, and why weren't they in school right then? We could think of answers for most of our questions, but there seemed a lot of questions we had to explain away. Even if we were not completely convinced that the operation we saw justified the expenses listed in their financial reports, this organization at a minimum obviously did house, clothe, and feed a bunch of kids and provide them with very basic health care. They needed money to do that. Yes, some of their behavior seemed unethical by Western standards, but they weren't operating in the Western world. They were struggling to support vulnerable children in an environment desperately short of resources. Is it wrong to bend the rules to increase your revenue when you have so many hungry children to feed? Is it wrong even to hoodwink a couple of naïve, rich Americans if that helps support the abandoned children that the police keep bringing to your door? Not an easy call, as we see it.

In any case, we'll give you Diane's response to our challenges after the next chapter. We've already shown that the truth of these situations can become very unclear.

This part of Isata's story reinforces the notion that deception happens because adoptive and birth families do not meet to work out the details of the adoption in advance, and so those details get lost, or misshapen, and eventually decay into conflicting versions of the story. The rules established by the M. family about Isata's adoption were not explained to the Sibleys. And certainly nothing like a contract was established that specified what must happen in the adoption. Once an adoption has been finalized, intermediaries like TCH have little incentive to enforce any restrictions. Moreover, even if they had such an incentive, they lack any leverage over the adoptive families. Such restrictions can only be enforced by contracts between adoptive and birth families. And those can only be enforced by courts in the receiving country or by joint actions of the receiving and placing countries.

CHAPTER 6

Is Adoption Too Commercial?

For decades, international adoption has been a Wild West, all but free of meaningful law, regulation, or oversight.

E. J. Graff[1]

In *Family Bonds*, her fascinating account of a long journey through infertility treatment and into international adoption, Elizabeth Bartholet describes one of many lengthy waits in the hallway of a Peruvian children's shelter. She is in the process of a second adoption, this time of a boy named Michael. The shelter is called Viru, and it houses children whose parents can't care for them. There is a courtyard at the shelter with "a few broken swings and a few working ones.... There are large mud holes in the swing area full of unpleasant-looking water."[2] A few young children play in the courtyard; no adults supervise. Bartholet sees "one of the bigger kids knock a little one flat, sit on him, and begin to punch him" until a third child pulls the first one off the sobbing toddler. Bartholet feels helpless to intervene, knowing that if she offends the local staff it could easily jeopardize her chances of bringing Michael to America. What toll, she wonders, must life in that institution take on a child's spirit? "I think of the many people I have met who would be ecstatic if they could take one of these children home." But most of the children are not free for adoption. "Many have birth parents who may never visit and have no apparent capacity to function as parents, but who have not taken the formal steps necessary to free their children for adoption."

Most economists react instinctively to that sad statement from Bartholet with a question: What if you went to the village and offered the institutionalized child's next-of-kin two or three thousand dollars to sign release papers? Might that not get her out of the courtyard with the mud, the bully, and the broken swing set? Forever? If we are squeamish about the idea of paying cash for a child, what about

139

some alternative form of support: providing the family with health care, paying for improvements to their home, a loan to start a small business? Can it be denied that such a transaction would leave all three parties, the child, the birth family, and the adoptive family, better off than they were before?

Readers horrified by the apparent cynicism of that question—and there will be more than a few—can take comfort in knowing that virtually no sane person associated with adoption would ever even ask it. Or at least, no one would ever ask it out loud. Almost everyone involved with international adoption flinches at the slightest hint that birth families might be compensated for releasing their children to adopters. In her essay "Price and Pretense in the Baby Market," law professor Kimberley Krawiec says, "Throughout the world, in fact, baby selling is formally prohibited. And throughout the world, babies are bought and sold each day."[3] As Krawiec puts it, "legal regimes and policy makers around the world pretend that the market does not exist," but this only means that "fees, donations and reimbursements take the place of purchase price."

Those people who do acknowledge that these "purchases" take place almost universally lament them. Most people would say that the sale of children is precisely what's *wrong* with international adoption in the first place. Isn't it a main reason the number of foreign children adopted in the United States has fallen by half in less than a decade? It seems logical, doesn't it, that all of the current problems in the system—deception, fraud, even kidnapping—would be made even worse if a relatively open "market" were permitted? Historical evidence suggests just the opposite, that it is the *forbidding* of market transactions that precipitates fraud and corruption.

The Most Famous Historical Example of Prohibiting a Market

The characterization of international adoption as a "Wild West" by E. J. Graff, quoted at the head of this chapter, seems apt given all the scandals described in the previous chapter. One person who knew a lot about the Wild West was Mabel Walker Willebrandt, who, in 1921, at age thirty-two, became assistant US attorney general, making her the highest ranking female in the federal government at that time. Her job was to prosecute violators of the Volstead Act, the 1919 law that banned the sale of alcoholic beverages as required by the Eighteenth Amendment to the Constitution. Presidential candidate Al Smith called her "The Prohibition Portia."[4]

Willebrandt was born in the Wild West. Around the time of her birth, Willebrandt's hometown of Woodsdale, Kansas, battled—that is no metaphor—the neighboring town of Houghton to determine which would become the seat of Stevens County, a semi-arid square of land near the southwest corner of the state.[5] The governor had to send in militia to quell the violence. But if Stevens County was the Wild West, the land just below Stevens County was even wilder. At that time, what we now call the Oklahoma Panhandle was not a part of the United States. No state had jurisdiction there. In her book *The Inside of Prohibition*, written in 1928, Willebrandt describes that place.

> That strip of territory *was* literally, then, and was called "No Man's Land."
> It had not been brought under the authority of state law, and no law was
> enforced. It was a harbor for criminals. Just a few months before my birth,
> my father was almost killed and my uncle, serving with a sheriff's posse,
> was slain by a lawless band that swept over from that law defying area.[6]

Willebrandt saw the lawless panhandle of her youth as analogous to America during Prohibition. The whole country, she said, had become a "psychological no man's land which is the refuge for the dregs of society: the bootleggers, the thugs and potential murderers, the bribers, the grafters and criminals of every description who live by preying on honest men and women."[7]

Willebrandt's book was a starkly honest account of trying, and failing, to enforce Prohibition. She sadly recounted the staggering levels of corruption. Six hundred and fifty prohibition officers had been fired for taking bribes or for actually selling liquor in the first six years.[8] She had personally investigated a US assistant district attorney who, on an annual salary of four thousand dollars, had purchased an expensive seashore home with cash. The law was even flouted at the highest levels. "Senators and Representatives have appeared on the floor of the House and Senate in a drunken condition," she wrote.[9] Some even used their congressional freedom-of-the-port privileges to smuggle liquor into the country.

But Willebrandt was not ready to give up. She thought that the law of the land could and should be upheld. She was confident that the Volstead Act *was* enforceable if only there was sufficient political will to enforce it. There wasn't. The Eighteenth Amendment was repealed in 1933, but Willebrandt had already left the Justice Department in 1929.

Prohibiting the Victimless Crime

Why did Prohibition make America the lawless "No Man's Land" that Willebrandt described? The seventeenth century Dutch philosopher Baruch Spinoza said, "All laws which can be violated without doing any one any injury are laughed at." Even worse, Spinoza warned, "He who tries to determine every-thing by law will foment crime rather than lessen it."[10] This was certainly true of Prohibition. The law was a disaster for American society, yet quite a boon to certain criminals. The money earned from the sale of bootleg alcohol was truly staggering, by some estimates almost as large as the entire federal budget at that time (about $3.6 billion in 1926).[11] We get some idea of the scale of illegal activity just from the amount of extra cash needed for sub rosa transactions: "In 1925 the Bureau of Printing and Engraving printed nearly $300 million more in large-denomination bills than it had in 1920."[12] New York Mayor Fiorello La Guardia commented, "What honest business man deals in $10,000 bills? Surely these bills were not used to pay the salaries of ministers."[13]

Economists, among others, are skeptical of government attempts, like Prohibition, to suppress transactions that benefit both buyer and seller without directly harming others. It is difficult to enforce laws that many people regard as a meaningless infringement on their personal freedom. And while Prohibition is long gone, many of its problems still echo in America's current War on Drugs.[14] Each year, for example, seven hundred thousand Americans are arrested, and fifteen thousand go to prison, for offenses related to marijuana, a product considered less harmful than cigarettes or alcohol.[15] Jeffrey A. Miron estimates that the annual cost of this enforcement is about $7.7 billion, *not* including several billions in forgone tax revenues that legal marijuana sales could generate.[16] Even today, much of our drug policy remains in the No Man's Land that Willebrandt described.

In "The Economic Case against Drug Prohibition," Miron and Jeffrey Zwiebel explain what economists expect to happen when voluntary exchanges are outlawed by governments.[17] Such action raises the price of the product because suppliers face the cost of avoiding prosecution by evading detection—it is expensive to operate outside the law. It also raises price by preventing competition, as only those willing to break the law will become suppliers. Cartels are more likely to form, as they famously have in the market for cocaine. Most importantly, it encourages violence because disputes between suppliers cannot be settled legitimately in court. Not only buyers experience the higher cost; society must pay the expense of enforcing the laws against buying and selling. And finally, outlawing these transactions encour-ages corruption, as officials are bribed to look the other way. All of these higher costs associated with prohibition of an activity mean that the benefits of banning it have to be huge.

To summarize, restrictions like those on drugs and alcohol 1) decrease total sales, but not by as much as *legal* sales fall, 2) increase price and costs,

3) encourage violence, and 4) increase corruption, especially among police and government officials charged with enforcement.

The Cult of Nonpayment for Adopted Children

At this point you may wonder whether the prohibition of alcohol or drugs has anything whatsoever to teach us about international adoption, since adoption is generally not an illegal activity. While adoption itself may not be illegal, what *is* illegal, virtually everywhere, is the "buying" and "selling" of children to be adopted. While it may be acceptable the world over to raise another woman's baby, it is almost nowhere acceptable for you to *pay* her for her parental rights. The legal framework of adoption at all levels—state, federal, and international—strictly proscribes the compensation of birth families for adoption of children. It is almost universally seen as morally repugnant, as equivalent to the sale of a child, as akin to how humans were once sold into slavery. Even in Guatemala, where the law was silent on the subject of buying children, when the US embassy discovered that a baby was bought, "a visa could not be granted," and therefore the child could not legally be brought to the United States.[18] This was also the case in Cambodia and Vietnam, whose governments frequently looked the other way. And the 1994 Hague Convention on intercountry adoption states that the decision to place a child for adoption must not be "induced by compensation or payment of any kind."

The *any kind* phrase explicitly rules out not just monetary compensation, but even the sort of in-kind payments that America and other countries make to their poorest citizens, like shelter (through public housing), food (via food stamps), health care (coverage under Medicaid), and education (provision of free public schools). By the Hague rules, the adoptive parents get a birth mother's child, but she gets nothing (occasionally excepting some prenatal medical expenses). And the rules are sometimes implemented with striking rigidity. At a workshop we attended, a child welfare worker told the attendees that she was not allowed to bring a bag of rice, a traditional gift, to an Ethiopian birth family she visited, because it could be seen as compensating them for allowing their child to be adopted.

Under the Hague system, American families spend tens of thousands of dollars per child to adopt. Where does this money go? It goes to lawyers, adoption agencies, social service providers, courts, immigration offices, and facilitators of various kinds (a lot of middlemen), not to mention airlines, hotels, restaurants, cab drivers, and even bell hops. But not a farthing (theoretically) must trickle into the hands of the people making the greatest sacrifice: the birth families. This aspect of international adoption is, on the face of it, profoundly inequitable.

Some adoption professionals feel the inherent contradiction. At a conference in New York, we met an American adoption facilitator who recoiled at the idea of compensating birth mothers, yet struggled with the guilt of earning her living assisting in the "removal" of other women's children. John Lowell, head of the consulate office at the US embassy in Guatemala during the height of the adoption boom (2006–2007) told us that "they knew that birth moms received small payments in kind or in cash payments, and that others probably got larger amounts, but that's not what the cases hung on."[19] From a moral standpoint, one might not object to "a mother getting $1000 who then might be able to care for her other children. But she was getting $700–800 and then the lawyers or middlemen were getting $20,000," Lowell told us.[20] This type of result is typical of prohibited markets.

Firewall-Hague

So strong is the Hague Convention's determination to forestall the slightest hint of payment that its guidelines try to erect a firewall between the birth and the adoptive families. The US State Department's webpages on the international adoption process, for example, caution prospective adopters that "the Hague Adoption Convention generally *forbids* prospective adoptive parents from having any contact with the child's birth parents, and/or the child's legal guardians before the country of birth determines the child is adoptable according to Convention principles and refers the child for adoption to a family" (emphasis added).[21] The matching of child and family is entirely removed from the hands of either the birth or adoptive families—it is undertaken by some official.[22] Pre-matching contact between families, presumably, might occasion a surreptitious form of payment.

Admittedly, the Hague guidelines do allow some contact between the families *after* the match has been made, but it must be very clear that no kind of compensation can be in any way discussed. We recently attended a conference in which the head of a major adoption organization reported having developed a script that could be used to supervise any post-matching conversation between a child's birth and adoptive families. A script to supervise the most emotional conversation either party was ever likely to have? Who wrote this script, we wondered. Kafka?

The effects of Firewall-Hague can border on the absurd. We interviewed an adoptive couple—an American citizen born in Jamaica, whom we shall call Miriam, and her husband, a Laotian citizen of Thai and Loation ancestry who lived in Thailand much of his life, whom we shall call Lek.[23] They wanted to adopt a baby or child from Thailand, the country he considered his childhood home. Lek's mother, in Thailand, came to know personally a young woman—a girl, really—who got pregnant under awful circumstances and planned to put her baby up for adoption. Her father would not let her remain in her family if she kept the infant. The birth mother was happy for Miriam and Lek to raise her child. The baby was born, and, upon Skyping back home to Thailand one morning, the couple saw Lek's mom holding up a beautiful and healthy boy named (let's say) Jonathan. Miriam and Lek seemed almost to be parents. A child had been located, the child had been relinquished specifically to be adopted by Lek and Miriam, and the child was already living within their extended family. So, it was merely a matter of finalizing the adoption and bringing Jonathan home.

But nothing in international adoption is "merely a matter of" anything. Miriam was not Thai. And though Lek was half-Thai, which was close enough for local authorities, and though he'd lived in Thailand most of his life, he was born in Laos and had a Laotian passport. Jonathan could not be handed over to Lek as easily as he'd been handed over to Lek's Thai mom. There would need to be an official international adoption of this Thai child by a "foreign" couple. In the meantime, Lek's sister would be Jonathan's legal guardian, while Miriam and Lek would work with a licensed agency to formalize the adoption.

But no agency could work with them. The agency they approached, and other agencies they contacted, pointed out that the fact that he was already living in their extended family, far from making Jonathan a fish-in-the-boat, as it were, actually had the opposite effect. Thailand is a "Hague country," meaning it is fully compliant and is recognized as such by the US and other Western countries. By Hague guidelines, they could not adopt Jonathan. In fact, by Hague guidelines, Jonathan was the *one* child in the whole adoption universe whom they could specifically *not* adopt. Why? Because until a child had been officially assigned to the adoptive family, the convention proscribes contact between that family and the child's guardians, which is a bit hard to avoid if the child's guardian is, you know, your *sister*. The agency insisted they could not help Lek and Miriam adopt the baby that they were already connected to physically and emotionally. Under Hague rules, the birth and adoptive parents cannot find each other; someone *outside* the two families has to make the connection. The reason for this rule, adoption professionals will tell you, is to ensure that no child exchange gives off the slightest whiff of a market transaction and to avoid the appearance that IA is about "adoptive parents finding children" rather than "children finding parents."

As of May 2017 (several years after his birth), Jonathan's status remains in limbo. He lives with Lek's mom, Lek's sister is his legal guardian, and he's been told that Miriam and Lek are his mommy and daddy, with whom he Skypes regularly and who he sees at least once a year. But there seems to be no way that Lek and Miriam, as an American couple, can legally make this boy their son. He is now the one child they cannot legally have.

Inevitable Problems with the Cult of Nonpayment

These laws against payment, however well intentioned, cannot alter a harsh reality of adoption life: American families will pay tens of thousands of dollars for a child whose birth family earns hundreds of dollars per year, or less. So, someone who can get, say, a Guatemalan baby into the hands of a New York couple can earn a massive reward, at least by the standards of poor countries. But how does that someone induce a mother to give up her child? One can pay her surreptitiously, as in *Between Light and Shadow*, or kidnap the child, as in *Finding Fernanda*, or send away the children entrusted to your orphanage, as in (perhaps) the HANCI case in Sierra Leone. Most economists would argue that the theft, deception, and coercion suffered by birth families in poor countries occur not *in spite* of the bureaucratic rules against baby buying, but *because* of them.

Therefore, economic theory would predict that the Hague Convention would have effects similar to the historical interdiction of the supplies of drugs and alcohol. As countries sign and become compliant with the Hague, the number of legal adoptions would decrease and adoption fraud—to the extent possible—would increase.[24] Of course the State Department can stop *all* adoptions from a country by refusing to issue any visas, as is the case currently with the United States and Guatemala, Vietnam, and Cambodia. In this case, we would expect to see more illegal crossing of children (or pregnant women to give birth) over national boundaries for adoption. Sometimes doctors could fill out false birth certificates for the adoptive parents, as the doctor in Peru offered to do for Bartholet. We would predict that the Hague Convention would cause some combination of higher adoption cost, lower quality adoptions with less information, more dishonesty, and an increase in the level of official corruption. Tighter regulation should create stronger incentives to engage in that worst-of-all-problem in international adoption: kidnapping.

But How Could *Less* Regulation Mean *Fewer* Problems?

The argument made above is counterintuitive to most observers, particularly the critics of international adoption. Logic would seem to dictate that allowing parents to accept payment for a child would precipitate even *more* trickery, *more* coercion, *more* kidnapping and theft. But just the opposite should occur. The famous legal scholar and jurist Richard Posner (US Court of Appeals for the Seventh Circuit) has put it this way: "Seemingly exorbitant profits, low quality, poor information, involvement of criminal elements—these widely asserted characteristics of the [domestic] black market in babies are no more indicative of the behavior of a lawful market than the tactics of the bootleggers and rum-runners during Prohibition were indicative of the behavior of the liquor industry after Prohibition was repealed."[25] Because it is risky and expensive to operate outside the law, illegal vendors tend to be undercut by legitimate vendors of the same product in an open market. It's just as possible today, for example, to manufacture bootleg whiskey as it was in the 1920s, but does anyone still drink or produce moonshine? Today it's so convenient and inexpensive for people to get whiskey legally at the local liquor store that the bootlegging industry simply can't compete. Yes, it still exists in a few places, but as only the merest wisp of its Prohibition-era self, and its function is to evade excise taxes.[26] When markets work well (which they sometimes don't) competitive pressure from legitimate sellers can be expected to drive the illegitimate, dishonest sellers out of business.

Economic theory suggests that if the Guatemalan system had been more like the American, where couples can openly advertise their desire to adopt and birth mothers can negotiate the conditions of placement, and if receiving countries would issue visas, cases like *Finding Fernanda* would never have occurred. Would there have been what some would call "baby selling"? Definitely. Would there have been kidnapping, coercion, and fraud against birth mothers and regular misinformation to adoptive parents? Very little.

The system of private, independent adoptions, primarily for infants, as it functions in the United States is an instructive example. First of all, there is no firewall between birth and adoptive parents. Adoptive and birth parents are (basically) free to seek each other out, entirely so in open adoptions. To illustrate—again using an appallingly casual empirical method—if you type "a loving home" and "your baby" into Google, you get some 549,000 hits representing prospective adoptive parents seeking a child. Even the *Pennysaver* in our little Iowa town regularly contains ads from couples seeking a child to adopt. A pregnant woman wishing to relinquish her child has many, many adoptive parents to choose from, and though the potential adopters must be vetted and approved by state agencies, a regulatory process that should continue, the choice among the potential adopters is neither made by, nor approved by, some official or bureaucrat. The birth mother chooses *herself* who will raise her baby.[27]

What we just called the independent private adoption "system" in America is actually fifty different systems, because supervision of adoption is in the hands of state governments. To be sure, no state allows direct payment to a birth mother in exchange for relinquishing a child. But what all states *do* allow is the reimbursement of "customary and reasonable" birth parent expenses, such as medical and hospital costs related to pregnancy, some living expenses incurred during pregnancy, and attorney and court fees associated with the adoption. The stringency and enforcement of permissible payment rules, however, varies considerably among states. The restrictions are, in general, pretty weak. As of 2013, only seven of the fifty states prohibit certain types of expenses, ten states require no accounting, and three states impose no dollar limit on payments.[28] Naturally, these differences influence behavior. There is evidence to suggest, for example, that "when [pregnant women] live in states that do not allow prospective adoptive parents to pay birth-mother housing benefits, they flock to states more friendly in allowing these payments to give birth and place their children."[29] While the word "flock" is no doubt an exaggeration, there seems to be some movement toward less restrictive states.

Adam Pertman, an adoption expert, addresses the issue of surreptitious payment in his book *Adoption Nation*. "While few practitioners explicitly offer economic inducements, some use their websites to highlight the fact that everyone who signs up with them will be particularly well taken care of—the implication being that they'll receive far more than just good medical care."[30] He quotes long-time New York adoption lawyer, Benjamin Rosen, who, without judging its rightness or wrongness, says, "It's just a fact that more and more birth mothers want to know all the rules and want to be matched with couples in places where the legal climate's most permissive or least attentive... the *empowerment of birth mothers* is making it more of a seller's market" (emphasis added).[31] Moreover, given the level of contact that can occur in open adoptions in America, the opportunities for under-the-table payments in cash exist. It must surely happen in many cases, even if surreptitiously and illegally, as has been confirmed to us informally by adoption professionals.[32]

The American system is by no means an open market in children. It does not, for example, reach a "market-clearing price," which would be the price at which anyone wanting a child of a certain type (age, gender, etc.) can adopt that child in short order by paying the market-clearing price, while anyone placing a child for adoption at that rate will quickly find adoptive parents. We know the reimbursement level of birth mothers in the private system is below the market-clearing reimbursement level because obviously there are "shortages" of some types of children, mostly healthy white infants and toddlers, as evidenced by very long average wait times for prospective adopters.[33] The market price or reimbursement level is probably too low because full compensation is illegal and must be somewhat under the table. Also, not all states are generous with their compensation rules, and some birth mothers are unwilling to travel to a more generous state to have the infant. Conversely, some other types of children, often older ones, African Americans, and children with special needs, languish in foster care. For these latter children, the "market-clearing price" is negative—their adoptions need to be subsidized. The government does subsidize the adoption of children out of foster care, but the subsidy is definitely not high enough to get all of the children adopted. Nevertheless, the American system is much closer to a freely operating market than is international adoption.

And what is the result of this private "quasi-market" for adoption? In the United States, "trafficking" for adoption purposes is virtually unheard of, while defrauding birth mothers of their children is highly unusual and certainly not done on the scale observed in international adoption. The American system gives the birth mother many options, and because she can collect expenses from the prospective adopters, she has even more incentive to choose carefully whom she wants to adopt her baby. Private adoption in America puts the bargaining power into the hands of the birth mother. Excess payment—that is, payment above expenses—is not the norm in private adoption, but it does happen. When it occurs, it does not cause problems; it more likely eliminates or reduces some problems.

The Hague-compatible international adoption system puts the power, and the money, into the hands of intermediaries or government bureaucrats. As Krawiec puts it,

> Ironically, this institutional framework [restricting direct sale of babies] and the anticompetitive behavior that it enables are frequently defended as a means of preventing the commodification and commercialization of human beings, women's labor, or motherhood. As demonstrated, however, the costs of these rules are borne primarily by Baby Market Suppliers, who are disproportionately female and frequently from the lower end of the economic spectrum. The benefits, meanwhile, are disproportionately enjoyed by Baby Market Intermediaries.[34]

Thus, relaxing the regulations against compensating birth mothers is not likely to create more of the deception, fraud, and outright theft we so often observe in international adoption today—it will likely do the reverse. When birth mothers get to negotiate directly with a large number of prospective adoptees, it hugely increases their bargaining power. Contrary to claims often made by bureaucrats and other observers of international adoption, the rules against compensating birth families, and especially disallowing contact with potential adopters, do not protect birth families; they do just the opposite. The rules make the birth families *more* vulnerable to abuse, not less. As Claudia Fonseca, an expert on adoption in Brazil, has put it,

> Of course, many officials contend that the "no-contact" principle stems precisely from a desire to protect birth mothers in sending countries against undue pressures from gift-laden strangers seeking to adopt their babies. However, it might be relevant to remember that in the United States those who most vehemently opposed the no-contact principle— mounting campaigns for open adoption and the disclosure of sealed documents—were birth mothers as well as grown adoptees backed by strong minority politics.[35]

The logic here is straightforward: *you do not empower someone by taking away their power.* By denying a birth mother the right to meet, and freely negotiate with, prospective adoptive parents, you hobble her ability to control what happens to her child and what happens to herself in the wake of the placement. If anyone has a right to control such things, surely it is her. Yet the cult of nonpayment makes this incredibly difficult. The Leonean parents we spoke with, and those of the HANCI children, for example, did not want their children to return to live in Sierra Leone. They mainly wanted to have had enough control over the process to know where their birth kids were and how they were doing.

Some evidence about how much birth parents can be aware of adoption procedures comes from a 2013 report by the Donaldson Foundation that surveyed adoption professionals from both Hague-compliant and non-Hague-certified countries. All of the adoption facilitators from non-Hague countries said birth parents were consulted about adoption placements; only 41 percent of facilitators from Hague-compliant countries said they consulted with birth parents.[36]

What are we saying here? Are we saying that, in light of the above arguments, the American system of private, independent adoption is so efficient, so equitable, and so free of fraud and abuse that it should be meticulously emulated everywhere else in the world? Well, no, there is a problem with the American private system.

America Has the Opposite Problem

Because expenses are incurred prior to the actual placement, an American birth mother may get significant resources from the presumed adopters, especially housing costs, only to change her mind about releasing the child after the birth. Law professor Andrea B. Caroll says, "This scheme under which substantial living expenses are paid to a prospective birth mother who makes the ultimate choice to parent her child the vast majority of the time is fraught with problems.... Birth mothers often actually profit from the payment of their living expenses, necessarily raising the same concerns which have been used to justify a ban on baby selling."[37] In other words, compared to international adoption, the American model puts the shoe on the other foot; it's the birth mother who is in a position to defraud or exploit. Professor Carroll is a lawyer and her proposed solution to this problem, not surprisingly, is tighter regulation: banning the payment of birth mother's living expenses. This, in our opinion, will not eliminate the fraud, but primarily encourage more maternal compensation to take the form of under-the-table payment. Again, we would propose *less* regulation, not more.

Economists would argue that both the American and the international systems of adoption suffer from the same malady: they try to suppress mutually beneficial private transactions. The two systems suffer in different ways, but the problem is the same. Because direct monetary payments are prohibited, it's impossible to make *legally enforceable contracts* governing the exchange. The "child catcher" who pays a birth family in a typical African country a pittance for an adoptable child is, by definition, a criminal. He cannot be sued, because the transaction itself was against the law. In America, prospective adopters cannot offer a payment that is contingent upon the birth mother's relinquishment of the child. That payment would be illegal.

The inability to make legally enforceable contracts is precisely why Prohibition was so violent; when disputes cannot be settled peacefully in court, backed by the legitimate power of the state, parties will resort to other means. Hollywood frequently reminds us that the modern drug-related, drive-by shooting was pioneered by the tommy-gun-toting gangsters of the Roaring Twenties, as in the 1939 movie of that name with Humphrey Bogart and Jimmy Cagney. The drug violence happens for the same reason as the Prohibition-era violence: to claim exclusive territory in which to sell illegal substances.[38]

We believe that almost all of the fraud, theft, and chicanery associated with international adoption could be eliminated by this simple restructuring of the rules: *let birth families and adoptive families meet face-to-face and make whatever arrangements they want with respect to the adoption.* Keep the bureaucrats out of the meeting. The rich government's primary role should not be to prevent those direct negotiations from occurring, but rather to legally enforce whatever contracts result from them.

One might ask whether such contracts would in fact be enforceable. Can a poor birth mother in Ethiopia really sue an American couple for failing to, say, send annual reports on her child's well-being? We admit that this might be difficult, but it certainly is not outside the realm of possibility. For example, several NGOs brought suit against Madonna's two adoptions of children from Malawi.[39] They could as easily bring suits on behalf of birth parents whose pre-adoption contracts were violated. Also, many American lawyers will sue for contingency fees, that is, without the need for upfront payment by the plaintiff. A poor Ethiopian woman probably couldn't contact such a lawyer, but an Ethiopian attorney might well develop a relationship with an American counterpart. If there were enough cases of birth families suing adoptive families, it would be profitable for attorneys in the two countries to form these partnerships and enter this area of law. As we say in Iowa, "If you build it, they will come." What is necessary is a commitment by receiving country governments that their courts would enforce these agreements. In any case, the birth mother surely has a better chance of a satisfactory arrangement for her child via direct negotiation with adoptive parents than she does handing the child over to an intermediary. This is a fact that surely accounts, in part, for the support for open adoption among birth moms in the United States.[40]

A handful of adoptive couples in the US told us that one reason they decided to adopt internationally was the lack of contact with birth families and at least the perception of a greater severing of ties with birth families. They specifically cited their desire to avoid cases in the United States in which birth parents have tried to reclaim birth children from adoptive parents. Some adoptive parents surveyed for the Donaldson report also said they didn't want contact with birth parents. But, many of the latter parents changed their minds about birth parent contact after the adoption when they saw that it would be good for their child. In any event, our top priority is not potential adoptive parents, but the well-being of adoptive children and birth families, who would benefit from pre-adoption contact, and probably post-adoption contact as well.[41]

Babies and Bureaucracy in Brazil

An informative tale about the effect of regulatory intervention on adoption, both domestic and international, can be gleaned from the Brazilian experience of the early 1990s. Until the late 1970s, adoptions in Brazil, whether in-country or to foreigners, were regulated by the 1916 Civil Code. Under this system, says Fonseca, "there was no need to involve public authorities in the transfer of children from one set of parents to another. A private act registered with the notary public was all that was required in a process obviously designed to provide the pleasures of parenthood to childless couples."[42] This system applied to all couples, whether Brazilian or foreigners, though adopters had to be under fifty and could have no genetic children. Adoption was considered an "add on status, coexisting with, instead of replacing ties with the biological family." The arrangement could be revoked by either parent or child, and the "adopted person could resume his consanguineal identity with little ado."[43] This private, relatively informal, and highly decentralized adoption system endured for decades.

By 1982, however, rules for foreign adopters began to tighten: they were excluded from private adoptions, had access only to abandoned children, and their placements were subject to review by special state judiciary commissions.[44] Within a few years, the bureaucratic squeeze spread to the domestic system as well. Why did it occur? In the 1980s, Brazil managed to throw off twenty years of military dictatorship, adopting a new constitution in 1988 that transformed the political landscape. At this time, says Fonseca, "A rising tide of university-educated professionals, including social workers and community health workers, as well as a technologically more efficient state bureaucracy created a demand for greater intervention in people's domestic affairs."[45] One result was the 1990 Children's Code. In addition to putting extra restrictions on overseas placement, this new law radically revised the overall nature of official adoption, requiring that all placements be permanent and irrevocable; all trace of the adoptee's biological origin had to be "struck from his birth certificate, permanently severing ties to his [birth family]."[46] Access to birth records required judicial approval.

The Children's Code moved Brazilian adoption away from the decentralized, informal model that had functioned for decades, toward the tightly regulated, formal, and professionalized format that Western countries used for most of the postwar period. The impact on international adoption was immediate and profound. "The outcome of this more or less systematic repression was to inspire fear in many 'respectable' citizens who served as intermediaries in the adoption process."[47] Domingos Abrue reports how the Children's Code affected the *cegonhas* (storks), who were "women belonging to the middle and upper classes who spend part of their time trying to find children who are available for adoption as well as people who want to adopt children."[48] In practice, before the reforms, the arrangements were unregulated to say the least. "These activities all took place completely outside Brazilian law." While the women usually got compensated for these services, money appeared not to have been the primary motivation. Many, of course, were highly religious and wished to provide an alternative to abortion. Some called their work a ministry. "The major sort of value circulating between the stork and her clientele is prestige. The mediators of these [adoptions] discover a rich symbolic vein that can be exploited beyond any market calculation."[49]

Storks often helped birth mothers, both before and after adoption, with gifts of food and payment of medical expenses, as well as money, usually in small amounts. The legality of these payments was "ambiguous" but, as Abrue says, "On the practical level, it is very difficult to separate the purchase of a child from the financial aid furnished a poverty stricken birth mother."[50] Adoptive parents, especially wealthy ones, often found it impossible to resist providing some assistance to poor birth mothers. This largely unregulated system of informal arrangements was not populated by crooks or greedy mercenaries. In fact, storks who placed children with international couples were often highly reluctant to accept money to pass on to birth mothers because "everyone would think the child was being bought."[51]

Sometimes adoption mediators had their own private orphanages. "For many years these orphanages were tolerated by government agencies. Some had even formed partnerships with the state receiving help from the Children's Bureau at the district or state level." The owners of these "nurseries," far from being seen as evil traffickers, "enjoyed considerable popularity in the neighborhoods in which they were located."[52] They were especially useful in placing with international families the children that Brazilian adopters shunned, especially those of African descent. Many mediators adopted children themselves, greatly enhancing their reputations as people doing good work. The overall picture is one of an informal adoption system that was well serving the needs of children and both birth and adoptive parents.

But, in the 1990s, "with the advent of widespread criticism of intercountry adoption, international storks began to disappear."[53] The Children's Code placed adoption mediators under intense government scrutiny, sometimes including police surveillance. The tide of public opinion had turned, with surprising hostility, against the storks. Concerns about "the trafficking of children" eliminated the "rewards of prestige, honor, and recognition" that the storks had theretofore enjoyed from their work. Many abandoned it.

And if public opinion was not enough to drive out the facilitators, public policy took up the slack. The state of Ceará, for example, created a judiciary committee for international adoption whose "tacit mission was to eliminate not only the need for, but the very possibility of paid intermediaries operating in the field of adoption."[54] From one year to the next, 1993 to 1994, international adoption from that state fell from 223 to 54—more than a fourfold decline.[55]

The lesson we extract from the Brazilian story is that increased regulation and government control of the adoption process had a chilling effect on the informal placement of children within Brazil and internationally. It drove from the system not just the proverbial greedy lawyers and sleazy brokers, but intermediaries who were generally respected by the families they served and by local authorities who saw value in their work, even though some of it was technically illegal. And what precipitated this change of climate? It was not popular pressure to clean up a cesspool of fraud and corruption, though there was some of each; the system had been socially acceptable for decades. Rather, the Brazilian government, responding to media horror stories, mainly about events in other countries, succumbed to the irrepressible urge to regulate and control transactions that voluntarily occurred between consenting parties and moved the system toward a flawed Western/industrialized world model of adoption.

We realize, of course, that some reformers of international adoption are unlikely to lament the outcome of the changes in Brazilian adoption laws. The system was cleaned up! If the cleaning required a significant disruption of international adoption, so much the better, some would say. But who bore the cost of this "improvement" to the process? International adoption had a special role in Brazilian adoption because "the placement of certain children—especially those who were of visibly African descent or had special needs—was a serious problem among Brazilian adopters."[56] Because foreigners were more likely to accept kids who were hard to place domestically, the repression of international adoption fell disproportionately on those who were most vulnerable.[57] Was this really a victory for regulatory reform?

Romania Revisited: The Horror of a Free Market in Adoption?

Anyone who argues that an unregulated "market" in babies will eliminate deception, fraud, and abuse of birth parents has to confront the experience of Romania in the 1990s. That was the closest thing to a free-for-all in transnational adoption we are ever likely to see.[58] Remember Dr. Alexandra Zugravescu, head of the Romanian Adoption Committee, who called the time between August 1990 and July 1991 "the black period of Romanian adoptions"? TV coverage of the virtual warehousing of "Ceaușescu's children" under horrid conditions brought prospective adopters streaming into Bucharest by the thousands. They adopted nearly ten thousand children. In that frenzied year, as many as half of the children adopted came directly from their birth families, not from institutions. Facilitating this process were people like "M.," the baby broker in the Italian suit whom we met earlier strolling the lobby of the President Hotel assuring an American visitor that he could "find her a baby the following day."[59]

Nor, apparently, was this an idle boast. Kathleen Hunt, who wrote the story for the *New York Times* in March 1991 reported that on one evening, "M. triumphantly lounges on his usual couch in the corner of the lobby, surrounded by half a dozen radiant clients. One childless 40-year-old woman from Toronto lovingly holds the newborn G. [M.'s partner and half-brother] found for her in a peasant family for only $300, while another potential mother announces to M., 'If you can get me out of here in a few days, I'll give you all the cash I have left as a bonus!'"[60] G. reveals to reporter Hunt, with much pride, the secret of their success. "Many gypsy [Roma] people say they want 100,000 lei [about $2,900]. Then I come back and say, the American or Canadian will give you 30,000 lei—you want? If they say no, we leave and go in the car. Then the gypsy comes over and says it's O.K."[61] If G. has conflicting loyalties between his Western clients and his impoverished countrymen, they do not appear to trouble him much. "That's a big difference from 100,000 down to 30,000, right?"

None of this should surprise us—disgust us, perhaps, but not surprise us. In the chaos of a collapsed totalitarian state, a suddenly profitable business attracted profit seekers, as is always the case. Initially there was no law to control who entered this "industry." But even "profiteers" who escape the discipline of the law—where no law exists, or through bribery or political connections—are not immune to the discipline of the market. Eventually, as Hunt reports, M.'s sleazy business practices began to impinge on his success.

> One of the couples had been invited by M. to see a particular child, and instead were taken to an apartment to meet [another woman] Vania and her newborn. The couple was uncomfortable with what seemed to be the coercion of Vania. When they expressed their disgust, M. threatened them. Then Mihai appeared, introduced as M.'s driver. When the Canadians saw that Mihai "packed a piece" under his left arm, as they told it, they got out of there as soon as they could.

Then another one of M.'s clients discovered that the baby he had repeatedly assured her was healthy tested positive for hepatitis B. And "the same week M. lost two Irish clients when a second purportedly healthy baby tested positive for hepatitis B." His refusal to accept the old adage *the customer is not always stupid* continued to erode M.'s market share. "A third client, from Quebec, dropped him in horror when the 6-year-old girl he had located for adoption threatened to commit suicide if she was forced to leave her biological mother."

It is tempting to believe, as many people do, that only strict regulation can control the antics of market miscreants like M. and his cronies. We tend to assume that only the government can pull the bad apples from the barrel. But this ignores the widespread self-policing that competition typically effects in markets. Of course, we admit that markets don't always self-police, especially when a few giants dominate an industry—as the 2008 financial crisis showed—or when governments protect large companies from failure. But this hardly characterizes international adoption; it is a highly competitive industry, with many small players. Economists would argue that a mildly regulated system that tolerates baby brokering as a legitimate business is more likely to have the storks of Brazil and the adoptive parent advertisers in the local *Pennysaver* than the hoodlums of Romania, especially over time, as competition asserts its power. And this expectation is pretty consistent with historical evidence.

How Have the Hague Regulations Affected IA?

Recall from the above discussion that economic theory suggests that repressing mutually beneficial transactions tends to encourage black markets with their attendant higher cost, corruption, and, sometimes, violence, of which kidnapping is certainly one form. What effect has the tightening of regulations against compensation and the proscription of preplacement contact between birth and adoptive parents had on the international adoption system?

First, given that international adoptions have fallen by more than half in the last ten years, it would be hard to argue that the Hague Convention has helped to promote children finding families abroad. Indeed, looking at State Department adoption figures, we see that among countries sending more than a handful of children to America, nowhere in which the Hague Convention has entered into force (EIF) is the number of placements higher in 2015 than it was in 1999. The Hague did not revive adoptions from sending countries that had recently shut it down in the wake of scandals. In Cambodia and Vietnam, for example, the Hague entered into force in 2007 and 2012, respectively, but neither country has sent any children to the United States since achieving EIF. This is mainly because the US State Department has not been satisfied that their systems were sufficiently reformed.[62] Guatemala had achieved Hague EIF in 2003, before the 2009 shutdown, but has not yet resumed adoptions to the US. Some Hague supporters have claimed that the convention "saved" adoptions from places like the Philippines and Colombia, which had flawed systems before the reform. It is true that in those countries adoptions temporarily increased after EIF, but they are now down as well.

Of the top five sending countries to the United States in the last few years—China, Russia, Ethiopia, South Korea, and Ukraine—only China has implemented the Hague. Adoptions to the United States from China declined precipitously after the Hague came into force in 2006, though we do not claim that's necessarily only a result of the Hague implementation—these declines are happening even in non-Hague countries as a result of scandals in general. But, again, if the Hague convention has "improved" the process of international adoption, it does not appear to have improved the chances of a child in a poor country finding a permanent home in another country. Indeed, as we stated in the Preface, we were moved to write this book partly as a result of our puzzlement that so few African countries were placing children for adoption despite a massive orphan crisis. A statistical analysis by Marijike Bruening and John Ishiyama found that African signatories of the Hague convention tend to be the most restrictive in terms of placing children abroad.[63] This seems particularly sad to us.

Anecdotal evidence about the effects of the Hague, as described by professionals in the Donaldson report, are generally consistent with basic economic intuition. First, unsurprisingly, the time and money required to carry out adoption have both increased in proportion to the expansion of paperwork and the need to verify that paperwork. One respondent said, "There is a burden of bureaucracy that many times delays children from going to their families."[64] Another complained of "redundant protocols." The report itself says that "professionals have indicated that valid paperwork is checked and rechecked, creating bureaucracy redundancy and inefficiency that has a direct impact on the time a child spends living in institutional care."[65] Sometimes an inability to verify documents to Hague specifications leads to children becoming unavailable for either international or domestic adoption. As one respondent put it, "they stay in an orphanage until they age out or are put out."[66]

Moreover, the increased cost of agency accreditation may have affected competition within the industry. "It is such a burden that only large, big volume agencies can [survive]," said a respondent in the report.[67] Anecdotal evidence also suggests that the Hague Convention has reduced international adoptions in compliant countries. In the legislation implementing the Hague, some countries have set limits on the ratio of domestic to international adoption. India, for example, established an 80/20 rule: 80 percent of adoptions must be domestic, the remaining 20 percent can be international. How can this ratio be preserved when domestic adoptions fail to keep pace? Simple: leave some children in the orphanages who would otherwise be available to foreign families.

Has the Hague Convention reduced corruption? There is little reason to think so. One respondent in the 2013 Donaldson report said that "now the corruption is so high up that those involved are untouchable."[68] Nor, of course, has the Hague eliminated kidnapping or baby selling.[69] Both practices continue in India, for example, more than a dozen years after that country became Hague compliant, though some of those cases are for domestic adoption. A 2012 article in the *Daily Mail*, for example, reported the case of a couple who relinquished their newborn for forty thousand rupees (about $752) to finance treatment for their paralyzed two-year-old son.[70] As another example, a 2013 article in *The Atlantic* discussed several examples of kidnapping and selling of children for both domestic and international adoption in China. Some of those cases occurred before the Hague Convention went into effect in China in 2009, but some occurred afterward.[71]

Are We Imposing a Western Model of Adoption?

It has been suggested to us that by proposing that international adoption run more like the American private system we are trying to impose a Western model of adoption on the mostly poorer, mostly non-Western sending countries. We would suggest that we are doing just the opposite. While it was developed with the best of intentions for protecting poor birth families, the Hague Convention essentially enforces the pre-open-adoption Western system that prevailed in the United States and other western countries for decades. The Hague Convention, UNICEF, some large NGOs, and various officials in Western countries have pressured low-income countries into the time-consuming and costly process of becoming compliant with the formal, legal, Western-style system. The level of enthusiasm has varied markedly, from very cooperative (Rwanda and China) to noticeably sluggish (Vietnam and Guatemala). But even the reluctant sending countries must try to get on board or risk having adoption from their country to the West halted altogether or miss out on new aid-funded projects. Clearly, the Hague system represents the imposition of Western values on other countries. What we propose, on the other hand, is that two sets of parents, birth and adoptive, be given the freedom to create whatever adoption system best fits their mutual needs for the disposition of the child, presumably an arrangement more consistent with the cultural norms of the birth family. The only imposition of Western systems would be the enforcement of legal adoption agreements by primarily Western courts. The legal agreements would replace the informality that was the norm in most sending countries before the Hague.

We have made the rather radical argument that the problem is not that international adoption has become too commercial, but that, in some sense, it is not commercial enough. If we abandoned the cult-of-nonpayment and Firewall Hague so that IA could behave more like an actual market, as the American private adoption model approximates, we would get a more equitable and less corrupt system. If we could allow birth and adoptive parents to make their own private adoption arrangements, the hallmark of a market model, we would reduce the kidnapping, fraud, and deception that have existed in international adoption. We would reduce the power and compensation of the intermediaries and see more resources transferred to those who are making the greatest sacrifice: the birth families. Those families would find it easier to keep track of the progress of their children. Less regulation, more freedom for the two families; that is what we would suggest to reform IA. We understand, of course, that this proposal is counterintuitive. In the next chapter, we anticipate objections to this idea and try to address them. But first, we will give you a brief recap of Isata's story and then provide you with the response of the director of TCH to the charges that her adoption agency mishandled Isata's adoption.

TCH Responds to the Charges of Deception

As we have seen, the story of Isata's adoption is murky, as some stories of international adoption tend to be. Inconsistencies abound. For example, Pa M. first told us that his wife had signed Isata's adoption papers with an X, without understanding what she was signing (owing to her illiteracy). Later, Shaun laid out the details of an agreement the family had signed for Isata's placement in the United States. In this version of the story, they clearly understood what they were agreeing to. The Sibleys were told by Diane, the director of TCH, that Isata's parents were dead and that she'd been placed for adoption by an aunt and uncle. But the M. family was clearly a party to this deception, because (according to Isata) before placing her at TCH, Isata's birth mom told her that she would be going to America and would have a different last name: "Koroma" (let's say) instead of "M." She was made to practice saying her new name. Being known as Isata Koroma was one of the many things that she didn't like while she was living at the orphanage.

Why did the M. family do this? Surely it was to improve the chances of Isata being adopted. Although the Sierra Leone adoption law at that time doesn't seem to say that a child has to be a "true" orphan (two deceased parents) to be placed for adoption, nor does the US State Department, the State Department does require that a child officially have "orphan status." "Orphan status" can be achieved through signed relinquishment by birth parents among other means.[1] But it would be easy to believe that "true" orphans are more adoptable. Interestingly, Isata was not given simply an entirely false identity, but, in effect, a laundered one. That is, the M. family had actually taken in a true war orphan whose last name really was "Koroma" and raised her more or less as a daughter after Isata left, while placing Isata in the orphanage with that last name. During the 2013 reunion with her birth family in Freetown, Isata and Beckie were shocked to actually meet this person.

Was TCH aware that Isata was placed under a false name? Remember that each placement with a Western family was a source of substantial revenue for TCH, so they would have some incentive to cooperate in a less-than-forthright adoption process. Then again, they might have much to lose from being exposed as participating in illegal adoptions. Also, they would know that Isata didn't have to be a true orphan to be adopted. In any case, we told Diane of TCH that we would be writing about the behavior of TCH as reported to us by the Sibleys, the M. family, and the other families we spoke with in Freetown. We asked to speak to her by phone about this and the other accusations about lack of information going to the birth families. Requests and dates for an interview were postponed repeatedly due to illness. Eventually, our requests for an interview were simply ignored, but first we did get a very detailed e-mail response from Diane, which follows.

> I lived in Sierra for many years, took the statements of the biological or extended family members, worked with the government of Sierra Leone and the courts there, and with the US Embassy to try and make sure that all paperwork and information was correct and legal. I have heard, years later, that some of the biological families say they were not adequately informed or that the paperwork was not accurate—but any inaccuracies came from THEM and I can assure you from personal experience that the adoption process was explained to them in English, Krio and in their tribal language for many appointments and hours of interviewing them. The extended family members had to swear to documents for the High Court of Sierra Leone, had to appear in court to affirm their statements, the judge had to agree with the paperwork, and the US Embassy then had to verify all the documentation before a child could travel.
>
> I understand that extended family members may have had reasons for lying. Some of them thought the child could not be adopted unless they lied. But, I did not knowingly give out misinformation. Actually, I was the victim of this very thing myself. After adopting my daughter from SL, I found out that her birth mother was actually alive and was not her aunt, as the court papers attested. My daughter did a good job of crying about her dead

mother that she saw shot in front of her eyes, but it was a made up story because my daughter and her birth mother wanted her to go to the US. When I found out, my daughter was already adopted. I confronted the birth mother and offered to give my daughter back. She refused and said she didn't want her. But, now in adulthood, she has a relationship with my daughter (which is fine with me).

In my experience as an adoptive parent with 10 adoptions total, I did two US adoptions back in the 1980's. In both of those cases, the US birth parents lied as well. But no one knew it until years later. My son's birth mother said she was in perfect health, when actually she was an alcoholic and my daughter's birth mother lied about the birth father. I'm pretty sure that this isn't unusual, but it never occurred to me to blame the adoption agency. It always seemed pretty clear to me who would have a reason to lie, and I understood it from a human perspective. I'm also just really glad that I was able to have my kids! All of this to say that there is definitely more than one side to the story.

I also think using the "excuse" that the family members in SL did not understand the adoption process makes sense if you are trying to establish a relationship with the child, and make sure that they can still "benefit" from the child now that the child is older. If the bio family says they understood full well about the permanency of adoption, how can they explain their behavior now?[2]

In the same e-mail, Diane explains that she has been ill and won't be able to talk to us until she is better. "I have had many complications from my recent surgery and have been in a fight for my life for the past 2 weeks." She also says that she and David know nothing about David's "brother" (quotation marks hers) or anything about meeting to invest in diamonds.[3] Finally, she says, "we [David and I] would really like to know who is impersonating or misrepresenting him."

As we said, after this e-mail, requests for a phone interview were ignored. Certainly some of her statements are true. The birth family members did have to legally swear and attest to various things on various documents. Sometimes they "signed" with their thumbprints, as Isata's mother did, and as did our son GB's mother (who is also Isata's adopted sister Sia's mother). These documents had to pass the

High Court of Sierra Leone and satisfy the US embassy. The birth family (or mother) had to appear before the High Court. It is unlikely, as Diane says, that the High Court would have conducted its proceedings only in English.

What we glean from this communication from Diane, and from the previous installment of Isata's story, is that there is a great deal of incentive on the part of both birth families and adoption facilitators to withhold information. Presumably, TCH at least could have contacted the Sibleys to let them know that the M. family was clamoring for information that Isata was OK. Why didn't they? It may have partly been to protect the Sibleys from the requests for money they knew might come from the M. family. When our daughter Mary visited TCH in Sierra Leone during her college years and asked to locate GB's aunt, David told her that they wouldn't do that because not only would we get asked for money, but TCH would have all of the birth families coming to TCH asking for money. Mary didn't think this answer was adequate, but TCH was hosting her, and she felt it was polite to accept that answer. But TCH's reticence to have Mary contact GB's "aunt" might also have been to avoid exposing the fact that she was actually his mother and not his aunt, as we had been told.

Again, to some, these types of deceptions would be reason enough to shut international adoption down. But are they absolutely endemic to the process? As we have argued, we rarely observe anymore such deceptions in American adoption, largely because we have moved to an open adoption system where birth and adoptive families can make their own private arrangements.

What if a family like the Sibleys could have met with the M. family before the adoption? If the Sibleys had been aware that Isata had an immediate birth family, they might have elected not to have adopted her and instead to have adopted a "true" orphan. That is not necessarily a worse outcome than what occurred, and some would call it better overall. It might also have been the case that the adoption would have proceeded as it did, with all parties having a better understanding of what was expected. We cannot identify the counterfactual. But it is worth remembering that ultimately a very vulnerable child got a chance at a safer life in America, which is something that *both* the adoptive *and* birth family very much wanted.

CHAPTER 7

Objections
Won't Less Regulation Make Things Worse?

We understand that the suggestion that adoption be less tightly regulated rather than more is at best counterintuitive and at worst repulsive. So, we anticipate important objections readers will have to this suggestion and address them.

Won't Birth Mothers Be Pressured to Give Up Their Children?

Even if the brokers aren't shady characters like M. and G. from Romania, you may ask, won't market forces put pressure on birth mothers to give up children against their will? Even if competition protects the adoptive parents, who or what will protect the birth mothers? In the *New York Times* story by Kathleen Hunt where we met M. and G., we saw the mother Vania being coerced by M. to give up a baby she clearly did not want to part with, which made the prospective adopters flee. Vania's story continues.

> Mihai [M.'s piece-packing driver] and Aurelia [his wife] took [another Canadian] adoptive family to the same mother, Vania. To their horror, they found her "hysterically screaming 'I am not a whore.'" As they turned to leave, they recalled, "Vania's husband, a little guy with a thin mustache, came running after us, offering their other baby, Valentin, for adoption."

Some would say that Vania's anguish illustrates precisely why adoption should *not* be opened up to market forces. To put it, perhaps, more mildly than it

ought to be put: Vania did not regard the sale of her baby as a "mutually beneficial" commercial transaction; therefore, such an exchange should never have
been allowed to occur. But notice: it didn't occur. In these two cases, at least,
the transaction broke down when the buyers withdrew. With a bit of deconstruction, the awful scenes in Vania's apartment can be seen as examples of the
market working. In general, would-be adopters recoil at the prospect of stealing
someone's baby. Likely, they will refuse to participate in that sort of abuse, as
they clearly did in Vania's case. But their refusal is contingent upon actually
seeing the abuse. That is, adoptive parents can better prevent abuse if there is
no firewall between them and the birth mothers and if the transaction is visible
to the world because it isn't illegal. In the 2013 Donaldson report, adoptive
parents said that the benefits of pre-adoption contact included "confirm[ing]
the intent to relinquish," "feel[ing] that no abuses had transpired," and making
sure that "birth parents… fully understand that adoption is meant to be permanent."[1] Openness and transparency are necessary conditions for eliminating
fraud and deception. The obviously improper relinquishment of Vania's baby
was prevented not by the intervention of Dr. Zugravescu and her Romanian
Adoption Committee once it was formed, but by the simple expedient of
having sellers and buyers meet face-to-face.

Moreover, it is worth remembering that, at one time, American adoption
reeked with coercion: Teen mothers in grim birthing facilities were harangued
into handing over their newborn babies. Or worse, were told their babies had
been born dead. What ended this abuse? Not increased government regulation. It was eliminated in part by the open adoption movement, wherein birth
mothers meet prospective adopters and decide who should adopt their baby.[2]
The Donaldson report asserts that "over the last 15 years in the U.S., contact
between first parents and adoptive parents… has evolved as research has found
it benefits all parties."[3]

Fear for the reputedly powerless Third World birth mother is widespread
among both opponents and supporters of international adoption, including some
parents who are seeking children. Journalist Lee Aitken, writing for *Money* magazine in 1992, described her negotiations with a Romanian broker named Tudor
Frangu.[4] Tudor was a "sullen, bearish" former taxi driver whose cynicism made
M. and G.'s look pale in comparison. Aitken, then a childless, unmarried editor
at *People*, had come to Romania during "the black period" seeking a healthy baby
girl. Tudor was referred to her by someone Aitken described as a Canadian "adoption mogul." "Tudor arrived at my room one evening carrying [a baby named]
Adriana and explained that he had taken her out of an orphanage 600 kilometers
away but then had been unable to get her mother's permission for adoption by an

Irish couple. Tudor said he was driving Adriana back the next day, but offered to leave her with me overnight. Foolishly, I agreed."

Aitken, who was a reporter after all, immediately found Tudor highly suspicious. But, she writes, "by the time I discovered he was devious and cruel too, I had fallen in love with the baby—as he knew I would." When Tudor came to reclaim Adriana the next morning, he said he had changed his mind about returning the child to the orphanage and disappeared with her for two days. "I was frantic," Aitken says. When he resurfaced, Tudor tried to persuade Aitken that the child's mother was a sex addict, living with a Gypsy lover whose family was advising her to demand a huge sum for the baby. Tudor, however, said he was going to use a sidekick of his to woo the mother away from the Gypsy, charming her with flowers, an in-town apartment and restaurant meals—all of which would be paid for by Aitken, of course. As a bonus, he would forge the mother's ID card so that court proceedings could happen in Bucharest instead of the remote town of the mother's birth. These services, he informed her, could all be had for a mere $5,500.

"Tudor's story was so implausible, his behavior so erratic and manipulative that common sense told me I should walk away," Aitken said. Her Romanian friends were appalled by Tudor. But Aitken knew that Adriana "would have a good life if I could just endure Tudor long enough to get her away from him." She offered him three thousand dollars for the whole package but demanded to meet the birth mother. It turned out, of course, that the birth mother, Roxana, "obviously wasn't a sex maniac or an indifferent parent" but a "shy peasant woman who kissed my hand upon introduction and treated her baby with affection." Though they couldn't directly communicate, Aitken and Roxana connected well and everything seemed set for the adoption to proceed.

But first Aitken had to go back to America to finalize arrangements for the adoption. When she returned to Bucharest, having accomplished in three weeks what might normally take six months, Aitken found that Adriana, as she had feared, had been promised to another American couple. "I wept for days," Aitken said. Efforts to contact Roxana to try to change her mind came to naught. The young woman had turned cold. To compound Aitken's suffering, one evening she saw Roxana and the baby eating in the restaurant at her hotel, and on another occasion Aitken watched mournfully while Adriana played on the lobby floor.

From Aitken's perspective, the villain in this drama was clearly Tudor Frangu, the deceitful and "bullying" baby broker. For his part, Tudor had few illusions about their relationship. "I know you hate me," he told her. But, Aitken says, "What I hated was the power he had over me and Adriana and Roxana."

We found Aitken's story to be poignant—and believe she was lied to and manipulated by Tudor. But we interpret her experience rather differently than she does, at least in its economic aspects. To us, the account suggests that it was Roxana, not Tudor, who had the power. At her first meeting with Roxana, for example, Tudor advises Aitken to "act like I didn't care for the baby and wanted a boy," which Aitken refused to do. Why did he suggest that? Tudor was hoping to lower the price that Roxana would accept for the baby, presumably to increase his own share of the exchange. Apparently, he could not dictate a price to Roxana because she could always take the baby back to her village or to another baby broker. She controlled something, like it or not, she knew to be a valuable asset, Adriana, and that gave her power in the exchange. It gave her much greater control over her own fate and that of her baby daughter. Ultimately, Roxana chose the other couple over Aitken for her own reasons, probably partially financial, something Aitken didn't want to accept.

Other accounts suggest that Romanian birth mothers were aware of, and exploited, the intense competition for healthy babies. In *The Adventure: The Quest for My Romanian Babies*, George Klein describes his trip in 1990 to a remote village to find the birth parents of a four-month-old "olive-skinned" girl named Consuela he had located in an orphanage in Arad. Klein and some Romanians who were assisting him, Alexandru, Floriana, and Gheorghe, traveled a two-lane "main highway," before turning into a gravel road that eventually became dirt. The parents' house, when they found it, had been abandoned because they could not afford the rent. Playing in the yard of the new residence were three of Consuela's four older siblings. They were dirty and their clothes were ragged.[5]

The children said the mother was working on the nearby collective farm. Once there, the visitors parked by an old barn; the mother came out to meet them, and negotiations began. As Klein writes, "Alexandru [the translator] got out of the car and began to talk to [the mother] in Romanian. Floriana, Gheorghe, and I got out and leaned on the side of the car. Gheorghe whispered, 'You wore a white shirt and tie. That's a nice touch.'" Four times during the next twenty minutes, Alexandru gestured toward Klein and said to the mother, "Pro-fes-sor Un-i-ver-si-tate, A-mer-i-ca!" "At the end of the conversation," Klein recalls, "she [the mother] said to [Alexandru], in Romanian, 'The French, the Germans and the Italians all wanted my baby. I always said, no. But, to you, I say, maybe. I'll see you at your office on Monday.'"[6] Klein doubted the woman would in fact come on Monday, but she did, and the adoption of Consuela was successfully arranged.

Was the birth mother paid for the baby? Klein neither says that she was, nor that she wasn't, and we have no right to presume it happened. But the important point is whether the birth mother was exploited in this arrangement. We might ask whether this woman had really turned down French, Germans, and Italians who wanted her baby or whether that claim was a negotiating tactic. We don't know, but it hardly matters. The key thing is that the birth mother was clearly aware of her power to determine who got her baby, that the decision was hers and not that of some government official. In the adoption "free-for-all," she had the freedom to exercise her power to negotiate.

The Hague guideline against contact between birth and adoptive families is also considered problematic by some officials in sending countries. The assistant to the minister of Family Affairs of Sierra Leone expressed doubts about this provision, as did Charles Margai, the plaintiff's attorney in the case wherein the Leonean Supreme Court reopened international adoption after a moratorium on the practice in that country.[7] Sierra Leone has a tradition of pre-adoption contact. For example, in one of the orphanages we visited, American couples came and developed relationships with children over a week or month at a time, maintaining Skype contact thereafter while they waited for the adoption to be finalized, or later, waiting for the moratorium on adoption to end. People in the minister's office expressed optimism about getting Hague officials to agree to such contact as they worked toward Hague ratification. Given the difficulty Vietnam and other countries have had getting Hague approval, we were less sanguine.

We interviewed Charles Margai in his Freetown office in January 2013. He is the nephew of the first president of Sierra Leone after independence, son of the second president, and a former presidential candidate. The High Court case that ended the moratorium was that of a boy who was about to become sixteen, the age limit for being adopted, but who had a prospective adoptive family that had known him and been waiting to adopt for several years. In its decision, the High Court basically said that it, the judicial branch, should decide whether adoptions were allowed on a case-by-case basis, not the welfare department of the executive branch that had declared the moratorium.

At the end of the day, we wonder for whom was this "black period" of Romanian adoption, as Dr. Zugravescu of the Romanian Adoption Committee on Adoption deemed it, really so black? Possibly for her and other government officials: "It pains me that this could happen," she said.[8] But Dr. Zugravescu was not one of the people handing over a child—it was often the birth mothers themselves who did that, and the lack of bureaucratic oversight gave these women much more control over what happened to their children. And who better than the birth mother to decide a) whether the child would be better off adopted by Americans and Western Europeans and b) who the child's new parents should be?

Needless to say, of course, we do not advocate that the birth mother can hand her child over to absolutely anyone. But the rigorous vetting process that Western countries require of adoptive parents before issuing a visa makes it highly unlikely she could relinquish the child to abusers or exploiters. We emphasize that these regulations vetting adoptive parents are ones we do *not* propose relaxing.

But Doesn't a Market Exploit the Poor?

To claim that introducing a market, any market, makes participants better off presumes them to be capable of making "rational" economic choices. Many think this problematic. Oreskovic and Maskew warn against excessive reimbursement of birth mothers because "such payments can... have substantial coercive effects."[9] Extremely poor birth families, presumably, may not be able to resist offers of compensation. Hence offers of payment can actually harm them.

Moreover, critics of IA might ask if it is really a *choice* to place your children for adoption. Harvard philosopher Michael J. Sandel has argued that a choice made in the face of desperation is not really a choice at all. In his popular book, *What Money Can't Buy*, Sandel illustrates this issue by analogy. "A peasant may agree to sell his kidney or cornea to feed his starving family, but his agreement might not really be voluntary. He may be unfairly coerced by the necessities of his situation."[10] The same reasoning might apply to adoption: a family facing a crisis may see relinquishing a child for payment as the only option in their desperate plight, so they have not really "chosen" to place the child for adoption. Economists would argue, however, that the choice to sell a kidney, or analogously place a child, did not create the peasant's desperate situation, rather it offers him a way to ameliorate it. He at least gets to pick the rock over the hard place, or vice versa. In other words, saying "You shouldn't have to choose between your kidney and your family, so we'll foreclose the kidney sale (or the adoption), though unfortunately that still leaves your family hungry," does not improve the peasant's situation. Moreover, in the adoption case, unlike the kidney sale, relinquishment could quite significantly improve the well-being of the child.

From the economist's perspective, seeing payments for adoption as coercive assumes that the birth parent, the "seller," will eventually regret the transaction. In other words, giving up a child for money is never a rational choice, so we must outlaw payment to protect the unwitting from making what *we* know, but they don't, is a really big mistake. Perhaps this is true in many cases. "Seller's remorse" is not uncommon in housing markets, and losing a child is surely more wrenching than leaving a house. But we cannot assume, as many people seem to, that a decision to place a child for adoption in exchange for payment is an irrational decision. Or necessarily a *bad* decision. As we have seen, many poor parents are quite willing to send children to be raised in America believing they will have a better life. One can easily imagine a birth mother with several children who was not planning to send one abroad *until* she discovered that the baby she was carrying could be released to an American couple, to live in an American home, and she would receive (let's say) three thousand dollars in compensation. She will release the child if and only if she can get the three thousand. Is this a bad choice? What if that money would allow her to fix her house or pay school fees for her other children while simultaneously providing the baby with much greater opportunities for education and employment, among other things? Placing the baby might enhance the well-being of the entire family; it might be a terrific "deal." Especially if she can negotiate an adoption agreement in which the child will not completely lose touch with the birth family.

It is both arrogant and unjust for Western policy makers to assume that a poor birth mother is incapable of making a rational decision in the face of possible compensation for her child. Why mandate that she must never, ever be offered payment? It is doubtful that she requires, or is desirous of, our "protection." Why do *we* know what is best for *her*?[11] Doesn't she have the right to make this choice?

Does International Adoption Cause Child Abandonment?

In July 2013, the UNICEF website contained a story about the return of a fourteen-month-old girl named Meseret to the Ethiopian village of her birth—a birth that had ended her mother's life.[12] Meseret's father had placed her in an orphanage at six days old. "I gave her away so that she could grow up and get a better education than is available here," he is quoted as saying in the piece. An officer at the regional Bureau of Women Children and Youth Affairs (BWCYA) explained that parents like Meseret's father were being promised that if their child went abroad they would get "all types of rewards, you will get more money." The article stated that "the recent rapid increase in inter-country adoptions has spawned a proliferation of child care institutions." The regional child protection officer said that some of these institutions were not meeting minimum standards and "were not seeking the best interest of the child, but their own private benefit." Accordingly, UNICEF was working with the local BWCYA offices to reunite the children with their families.

A similar situation has evolved in Uganda, which is not a Hague Convention signatory. Mark Riley headed a task force, supported by UNICEF and the Uganda Ministry of Gender, Labour and Social Development (MoGLSD), that is developing an alternative care framework to cope with rising numbers of institutionalized children. According to Riley, "There is a mushrooming number of baby and children's homes, current estimates are 500+, which are removing children out of families and communities and placing them into institutional setting[s]."[13] Many of these homes are "exploiting children for economic reasons through child sponsorship schemes and international adoption," both of which generate income for the homes.[14] Some homes are actually boarding schools that get funds from donors under the guise of being orphanages. In fact, we visited one such "orphanage" in Kampala in 2013. Few of these children's homes actually look for "Ugandan solutions" for children in their care. And, the report said, "International adoption [is] often favoured over any domestic solution."[15] In other words, these homes *reversed* the order of the Subsidiarity Principle and put international adoption as the *first* choice alternative. Riley argues, probably correctly, that this preference reflects the much greater revenue potential of international adoption compared to solutions within Uganda.[16] The report calls for immediate action. In fact, the document says, "Unless the situation is brought under control, Uganda will have the most child care institutions per capita in Africa."[17] UNICEF's central argument here is that not only does intercountry adoption take orphans away from their extended birth families, it encourages living parents to abandon their own children. As Karen Dubinsky puts it, "Individual social workers as well as such major social welfare organizations as International Social Service and Save the Children have argued at least since the 1970's that transnational adoption hinders the development of a domestic social welfare system and encourages child abandonment in favor of an imagined 'better life' elsewhere."[18]

Romania offers an empirical example. In a 2003 paper arguing that the Romanian moratorium should not be ended, Andrew Bainham of Cambridge University writes, "Since the moratorium has been in place, the official statistics for abandonment have dropped dramatically. In other words, children are abandoned precisely because of the availability of international adoption. If this is banned, there will no longer be any attraction in abandoning children or, to put it more accurately, giving them up to the care of others-for money."[19] In *Romania for Export Only*, ardent intercountry adoption opponent Roelie Post quotes the 1997 UNICEF report *Intercountry Adoption and Children's Rights in the CEE Region* as saying that "in early 1995, the [Romanian Adoption Committee (RAC)] was receiving hundreds of phone calls a month from parents announcing their plans to abandon their child and wished the latter be placed on the RAC list for potential adoption internationally—this being the legal way to respond to continued demand."[20]

On the face of it, this seems to be a significant problem with international adoption: causing parents to abandon their children. Even if IA brings some children out of orphanages, it may bring others in, at least temporarily. But here again, we economists would argue that this problem is not inevitable; it's a consequence of how the system is regulated. Parents abandon children in large numbers when it's the only legal way to make the adoption happen. If face-to-face meetings with adopters are illegal, and children can only be taken from orphanages, then that is where the children must go if parents want to arrange an adoption, as many parents obviously do. So, in the Romanian example, because Dr. Zugravescu of the RAC was determined to eliminate the "dirty business" of private adoption, many parents resorted to preplanned abandonment. Similarly, during a time in Rwanda when only Mother Teresa's orphanage was permitted to place children internationally, and that institution was filled to capacity, babies were routinely abandoned by the side of the road near Kigali or on the steps of an orphanage. In general, even where it is illegal to formally abandon a child, as in Ethiopia and some other African countries, we see this sort of behavior.[21] Surely, empowering private arrangements would reduce that. It would make birth parents more likely to choose international adoption over abandoning their children to an institution, especially if compensation were allowed. Parents would be less likely to turn a child over to an orphanage if the orphanage was capturing adoption fees that might otherwise go to them.

But Shouldn't We *Preserve* Families Rather Than *Break Them Up*?

A lawyer in Uganda asked us to imagine that instead of thirty thousand dollars being spent to take away a child, the money were given to the child's local village. Did we realize how much good that money could do? Probably an awfully lot of good, we supposed. But who was going to put up that money? Apparently not the Ugandan government, or the World Bank, or UNICEF, or any one of dozens of NGOs operating in Uganda, as evidenced by the fact that the village remains incredibly poor. We agree that families should not be so poor that they feel the need to put children up for adoption. But they are. Suspending international adoption will not raise the income of any village or family. And we can't ask children to remain institutionalized until we get around to eliminating world poverty—that may not be soon enough for them.

Moreover, it is rarely mentioned that international adoption could be a way to bring resources to a poor community from an entirely new source: the adoptive family. IA could represent a transfer of wealth from comparatively "rich" households in the United States and Europe to extremely poor ones in Africa and Latin America. But it doesn't. Unfortunately, the Hague Convention is designed to ensure that it won't. Currently, international adoption represents a transfer of wealth from American and European families to lawyers, adoption facilitators, and various governmental agencies, not the poor families themselves. And sometimes that involves a lot of money, tens of thousands of dollars. According to AdoptiveFamilies.com, an Ethiopian adoption in 2014 or 2015 could cost as much thirty-five thousand dollars, only about half of which went to travel and documentation fees; the rest went to various intermediaries and service providers, typically in the capital city.[22] If some of that money—or indeed *any* of the money—went to the poor themselves, it might be a great deal of help. It might help preserve the remainder of that family. It might also help preserve other families, given what people in our line of work call the multiplier effect of spending. When an outsider injects money into a community, it stimulates other kinds of spending as well; it raises peoples' incomes, it creates jobs. Thus, the payment of a few thousand dollars, or even a few hundred dollars, into one family in a poor village helps more than just that family—it helps the whole community. This makes it easier for *other* families in the village to support their children and stay together. No doubt IA already does this to some extent, especially in cities. But it could do so more effectively if more of the adoption money went directly into the hands of poor families in poor communities rather than to intermediaries.

Moreover, it is likely that international adoption could help keep some families together by stimulating other kinds of giving. In the years since GB joined our family we've given to African child-care institutions several multiples of the thousands we spent on his adoption. It is difficult to imagine our having done that without first adopting GB. The little boy who wanted "de beeg chicken" made it hard to ignore the plight of similar boys and girls left behind in Sierra Leone. And having located his birth family, we are now able to help them as well. Or consider Madonna, who was much criticized for circumventing the eighteen-month residence requirement for bringing her son David and daughter Mercy home from Malawi. She is known to have given millions of dollars to support Malawian children. Isn't it more likely that this wealthy donor will continue to support Malawian children now that two of them sit at her dinner table? She perhaps would anyway, but those two faces certainly won't hurt.

Still, it is hard not to see the UNICEF approach to helping families with vulnerable children to be the right one. That is to say that, even if a well-designed IA system could avoid breaking up families, it must surely take a back seat to family unification programs, mustn't it? Let's go back to the Ethiopian village where UNICEF and the Bureau of Women, Children, and Youth Affairs are reuniting fourteen-month-old Meseret with her father, who had placed her in an orphanage when his wife died in childbirth. This reunification (apparently) was not requested by the father. A BWCYA official is quoted as saying that "after *convincing the families* we don't just give the children back. We prepare a package that we believe a returning child will need, and that will reduce the burden on the family" (emphasis added).[23] Meseret's package included clothing, household items, and a "cash grant." The reunification program also helped families set up "projects that generate income." The website does not specify what these projects were, which is unfortunate because the World Bank has been trying to set up "projects that generate income" for African families for eighty years with surprisingly little success. UNICEF may help millions of poor families in other ways, but we're saying that reuniting the child and the family doesn't solve the problem that got her sent to the orphanage in the first place. UNICEF partners with NGOs in many developing countries to reunite families in this way with reunification packages.

A reunification package will help, but how long will it last? Consider the reunification program in Sierra Leone as of 2013, described to us by the director of an orphanage in that country. A UNICEF worker attempts to find a living member of the immediate or extended family for each child in a given orphanage and in a low percentage of cases succeeds. This is a good thing to do. Then UNICEF attempts to convince that relative to "reunite" with the child, even though they may not have ever lived with the child or even had much to do with her. This *might* be a very good thing, as well. How do they do it? In 2013, UNICEF gave the family one hundred dollars as part of a reunification package. In Sierra Leone, a hundred dollars was still a lot of money, one-fifth of per capita income in 2013, so extended families usually agreed to reabsorb the child into their household. But then what? One orphanage director described to us how, on UNICEF instructions, he delivered a preadolescent girl to a birth uncle who ran an auto body shop.[24] The uncle's home and his business were entirely populated with young men—this girl would be the only female. The girl did not want to stay with the uncle, so the director simply refused to leave her there. The in-country director of an orphanage in Sierra Leone once asked a UNICEF representative point-blank: "Does this program work?" "No," he replied "It doesn't work. It might work if we could do the planned follow up," that is, to check the continued well-being of the child, even to make sure the children remain in the family, "but there is not enough funding [for that]." An orphanage director in Ethiopia agreed. This director said that UNICEF has reunification programs that are done "in a harsh way, they are not concerned with the sustainability of the program, they don't follow what happens to the children."[25]

The director of a children's home in Rwanda described a meeting with many orphanage directors and a nonprofit organization, Hope and Homes for Children, that was working with USAID, the Sierra Leone government, and UNICEF to "close all 33 orphanages" in the country through reunification with birth families. The director asked the organization's representative, "What if the family member you find isn't a good or well-functioning parent?" The answer: "We will teach them to love."[26] Again, families send children to orphanages for some reason, sometimes even as a result of abuse, and a reunification package does not fix that reason, or, as the children's home director said to us, "They can't teach them how to love." It certainly might tempt them to take the child in—at least for a while. Then the child, as the head of the home suggested to us, could be used for farm labor, or a girl, as a Ugandan school principal said to us, could be sold for a bride price.

An anonymous reviewer of this book made the same point about reunification programs in the Former Soviet Union (FSU), an area in which she had personal experience. Alcoholism is a huge factor in getting kids sent to orphanages in this region, and unless that problem is resolved many families will remain dysfunctional. Also, many who relinquish children in the FSU are themselves alumni of these institutions and sometimes have little notion of how to parent a child. These situations make it difficult for reunification programs to work well.

Some professionals on the ground are skeptical of reunification schemes that place children with extended family. Dan Lauer of Holt International told us that as the result of a poor economy, the Ethiopian families he knew had already taken in all of the kids they could handle. Jana Jenkins, an adoption facilitator in Rwanda, asks, "Does Rwanda really have what it takes to follow up on all those cases? A lot of times kids come running back to the orphanage. They're kind of a stranger to their families."[27] Moreover, reunification has a sketchy record of success. We spoke to the woman who ran the family reunification program and other children's programs for Holt International in Uganda—including during years before Holt began adoptions from the country—about how and when family reunification succeeds. She said that it works for a small percentage of children in orphanages but that the key is long and careful follow-up over years after the child is returned to the family. So, we can expect UNICEF's efforts to work if they have the will and the budget to follow up at this level.

An orphanage director in Ethiopia told us that, for UNICEF, the reunification program is specifically linked to its opposition to international adoption. The question UNICEF is asked is, "If international adoption is a last resort, and therefore should rarely occur, what is going to happen to all the children in orphanages?" Their response is threefold: 1) family reunification to greatly decrease the number of kids in orphanages, or, in the case of Rwanda, to close all orphanages; 2) increased domestic adoption, which, as we discuss below, does not occur in large enough numbers to solve the problem; and 3) more funding for UNICEF-specific programs to help poor families, programs that we argue won't solve the major underlying problem of massive poverty. For example, the reduction in international adoptions from Ethiopia to 5 percent of what it had been before was accompanied by an announcement of added funding for UNICEF programs in Ethiopia to help vulnerable children.

To us, these reunification schemes have a slightly ironic flavor. Organizations that would likely protest if money motivated a family to *give a child away* seem untroubled when money motivates them to *take her back*. But perhaps we're being too cynical. Regardless, reuniting kids with their birth families may sometimes be better, for a low percentage of children, than having them in institutions, but it is not *always* better than international adoption.

We do, however, offer a caveat. Though almost everyone in the international adoption community with whom we have discussed this says, often with some bitterness, that UNICEF opposes IA, the organization has not openly disavowed it. The US State Department avers that UNICEF is not opposed to adoption.[28] Opposition can be inferred more from what UNICEF doesn't say publicly than what it does. For example, on December 26, 2012, UNICEF posted to its website a statement by Executive Director Anthony Lake on the proposed Russian adoption ban that would forbid Americans from adopting Russian children.[29] In this brief statement, Lake says, "We encourage the government [of Russia] to establish a robust national protection plan to strengthen Russian families." He also reminds Russia that "alternatives to institutionalization are essential, including permanent foster care, domestic adoption and international adoption." That is the only mention made of international adoption. The statement makes a few other points, but it does not recommend that the ban be lifted, nor does it criticize the ban or otherwise even mention international adoption in a statement that is *about* a ban on international adoption. In fairness to Lake, however, it is surely a political risk for an agency like UNICEF to chide a powerful UN member. But elsewhere UNICEF's silence blares out just as loudly. A UNICEF webpage entitled "The Child Without Family Care" discusses the need for general poverty reduction and for social welfare policies to support families and even recognizes *institutional care* "as a last resort and as a temporary measure" for children without homes (emphasis added). There is no mention of international adoption.[30]

To further decipher UNICEF's attitude, recall the task force run jointly with the Uganda Ministry of Gender, Labour and Social Development (MoGLSD) that is developing what it calls an alternative care framework for Uganda. The task force praises a recent MoGLSD campaign to promote domestic adoption over international adoption. The initiative is described as "hugely successful," having resulted in "30 Ugandan families adopting non-blood relatives."[31] Hugely successful? These thirty adoptions represent less than one-sixth of the two hundred adoptions from Uganda to the United States that the report says occurred in 2011, a number of international placements it describes as "relatively low compared to other countries." On the basis of UNICEF's own figures, we infer that putting children in the homes of local nonrelatives may be well worth promoting, but it is not a substitute for international adoption.[32]

Finally, the Subsidiarity Principle places domestic nonrelative adoption ahead of international adoption as an alternative for children in need of homes. But domestic adoption faces some significant difficulties. Mr. Nzaramba, the former assistant to the Rwandan minister of Gender and Family Promotion, while telling us that Rwanda was making progress on domestic adoption, told us these efforts ran into the problem of how the new child fit into the family.[33] Prospective domestic adopters (and legislators) balked at the idea that the adoptee would have the same rights of inheritance as their birth children. Professor Marijke Bruening has said the same thing about Ethiopia. Birth children will object to sharing an inheritance with an adopted child.[34] Jana Jenkins, the just-quoted Rwandan adoption facilitator, makes the point that "Africans are very good at taking care of extended family, but it kind of goes against the grain to take care of a child that's not blood-related."[35]

A Market Might Work for Babies, but . . .

In Rwanda, an American woman who was teaching middle school told us that our proposal would never work as intended. Allowing adoptive parents to negotiate with birth families would trap even more children in institutions, she said. "No one will adopt older children, everyone will buy babies, so if you think your plan will get kids out of orphanages, then you're just wrong!" Her attitude offended us. "Excuse us," we said to her. "That is no way to talk to your parents!"

Nevertheless, we have to admit that our daughter made a good point. As we said at the outset, our primary concern is to find permanent homes for children who are currently institutionalized. We want to get kids out of awful orphanages—or even good orphanages—and into families.[36] But will opening up international adoption really accomplish this? If prospective adopters can advertise their intentions to openly negotiate with birth parents, as they can in America, won't many (most?) choose healthy newborns over older children stuck in orphanages? If our proposal traps even more kids in institutions, it will have certainly backfired. We don't want babies relinquished by living parents to reduce or eliminate adoptions of older children or orphans. Because there is no way to know in advance whether that would happen, the question is entirely empirical.[37] This aspect of our proposal could be worrisome.

But with respect to this issue of babies driving out adoptions of institutionalized children—who are typically older or have special needs—we are comforted by a number of things.[38] First, in some cases, Guatemala being one, the preferences for getting young children directly from families is partly an artifact of the regulation regime. A US embassy cable to the State Department explains this: "One of the paradoxes of adoption in Guatemala is that for these literally abandoned, parentless, or institutionalized children, desperately in need of families, the adoption process takes two or three years."[39] A private adoption through parental relinquishment might take only a few months. The discrepancy occurs because an institutionalized child has to be officially declared abandoned or orphaned. "The judges are excessively cautious and only allow the child to be adopted after years have gone by and the meager official efforts to find the parents or extended family have failed."[40] Thus, any preference for getting babies directly from their families is exacerbated by the way adoptions of institutionalized children are handled. This difference in timing is true in some other countries: signing relinquishment papers is quick, whereas declaration of abandonment in an orphanage takes more time. Changing the regulations allowing for the adoption of children in orphanages by, for example, changing who is legally responsible for (and therefore who can be compensated for) children in orphanages, could change the timing incentives.

A second reason to be optimistic is that many parents who wish to adopt internationally are explicit about wanting an orphan or older child as opposed to one with an existing immediate family. This is reflected in the fact that much of the scandal in the last few years surrounded the adoption of children thought to be orphans who later proved to have living parents. But if birth families and adoptive families are encouraged to meet and negotiate arrangements, surely this sort of surprise will be much less common. Certainly, if the adoptive family demands such a meeting, it will be much harder for agencies to pretend that children they are placing in fact have no family. The prospective adopters can at least require some contact with an extended family, along with a DNA test, which probably should be required with all international adoptions, to verify the child's status.[41]

Another point of comfort is that the set of children in institutions is not a fixed population; each year some children enter the system and some children leave. So, for example, we can be sure that five years from now most orphanages around the world will house many five-year-old children and that today those kids are all still infants. It follows that any babies who are adopted now will presumably not join the future five-year-olds in those institutions. Furthermore, the families whose children are most likely to end up in those institutions are the same ones most likely to place babies for adoption: the very poor and vulnerable. If a birth mother who anticipates her inability to raise a newborn is induced to place the infant for adoption, in part because she'll be compensated, thereby allowing her to feed her other children, placement in an orphanage might be avoided both for the adopted child and the birth mother's other children. Hence, *some* children destined for orphanages will not get there. They will go to America or Europe instead.[42]

Moreover, as institutionalization tends to impede child development, there is value in getting children into permanent homes *before* some family crisis drives them into institutions. In reviewing the scientific literature, Schoenmaker, et al. state that "at the highest level, early adoption without prolonged institutionalization shows the most positive outcomes for children without permanent parents."[43] So if compensation induces some parents to place children for adoption earlier than they might otherwise, this will likely improve a child's welfare. We hypothesize (in the absence of data) that a country with a more open and tolerant adoption system should eventually have fewer kids in institutions.

Using the Dreaded P-Word

Another reassurance about our fear that the adoption of infants from families might replace the adoption of older children and institutionalized babies has to do with the dreaded p-word: price. People wince when the words *child* and *price* are spoken in the same breath. But if you think the word price is upsetting when associated with children, try using the term "price differential." Utter that phrase in a meeting of adoption professionals, and you may well hear someone gasp. We've done both. "Are you implying," you may be asked indignantly, "that some children are more valuable than others?" It seems horrible, though undeniably true, that children of different ages, or different health statuses, or different races or ethnicities, command different prices in the market for adoptable children. What does this say about our society? If parents are willing to pay more for a white baby than a black baby, doesn't this imply that our society sees black people as less valuable? The question may sound stupid to anyone who knows anything about American history, but it is slightly more complicated than it seems at first blush. Ask a university dean, for example, the relative value of hiring a black female professor versus a white male with the same credentials and you may conclude that America likes black women much more than it likes white men, which we greatly doubt. Market price is not determined by demand alone; it is determined by demand in relation to supply.

How American society actually "values" white people versus black people we are unqualified to say, but we're confident that the market price of babies tells us little about it. In general, the relationship between market price and value is widely misunderstood by much of the public, as well as many of those charged with making public policy. A bucket of water, for example, has less than a millionth of the market value of the same bucket filled with diamonds, but no one regards diamonds as ultimately more valuable than water. Oxygen costs nothing, but is the most vital commodity that we consume. Price tells us much about the value of the last unit exchanged, but very little about the value of all units of a particular good. As economists say, market price is determined "at the margin."[44] The cost of adopting a healthy white infant is much higher today than fifty years ago, mostly because of a drop in supply beginning in the 1970s with the advent of the Pill, legalized abortion, and changes in social norms.[45] Contrast this with the 1880s, when adoptable white babies were so abundant that the market price actually fell below zero. In those days, birth parents would pay ten dollars to so-called baby farmers who promised to place them for adoption, though having no market value, they were sometimes disposed of in much nastier ways.[46] But the negative price for white babies in the 1880s does not allow us to conclude that American society derived less total value per capita from its children in 1880 than in 1990. What that market price tells us is that with so many children available, the *marginal* child was indeed less valued.[47]

To belabor this argument slightly, an illustration of what price cannot tell us is the supposed disappearance of wealth during the 2008 financial crisis. Journalists asked what happened to the trillions of dollars in asset value that seemed to vanish into thin air overnight. The answer is that such wealth never existed. The market value of a share of stock tells us what the next person would get paid who sold approximately one share of that stock. It does not tell us much more than that. It certainly doesn't tell us what would happen if half or two-thirds of those shares were sold all at once. So, multiplying the market price of a share of stock by all of the existing shares does not tell us what all of those shares are worth in the market. It is not the amount of money that could be obtained by liquidating all of that stock. So, to go back to our previous example, a negative market price for babies in the 1880s did not mean that American society derived negative value from its children (except, possibly, at bedtime).

Having said all of that, a price differential does tell us something about relative preferences for different types of children *at the margin*. The fact that a newborn white baby is much more expensive to adopt than a biracial nine-year-old in the foster care system tells us that if the adoption of both children cost the same amount of money there would be many more people willing to take the white infant than the biracial nine-year-old. This is simply undeniable.[48] We have heard it argued that because such price differentials show implicit disrespect for one type of child over another, they should be prohibited; the price of adopting should be the same for all types of children. But that is like shooting the messenger. The price differential is less itself a problem than a *symptom* of a problem. But the price differential also offers a potential solution to part of the problem. Lower prices for certain categories of children are likely to increase the adoptability of those children, however uncomfortable that makes us feel. To mandate that the cost of adoption be the same for both types of children is to condemn some of them to remain unadoptable or to wait a long time in foster care.

The American child welfare system recognizes this of course. To get children from the welfare system to permanent homes requires a negative price; foster parents are usually paid rather than charged to care for the child. And states provide various levels of subsidies to help foster kids become adoptees.[49] We may lament the large price differential between the white infant and the biracial eight-year-old, but if we refuse to tolerate this price differential, what would happen to the older, biracial child?[50] The fact that older, black, and male children often face long wait times before adoption indicates that the subsidies are generally not large enough.

To bring this back to international adoption, we would expect a price differential to emerge between infants still in families and older children in institutions. The latter should cost less to adopt. This would certainly help mitigate the problem of new babies driving older and institutionalized children out of the adoption market. It would also make adoption more accessible to middle-class families.

How Do We Avoid Creating Baby Factories?

Recall Antonia from *Between Light and Shadow* who had sold multiple babies and claimed that it was common for women to have babies just to sell them to the gringos. Do we really want to encourage this behavior? Moreover, there are far more grim tales of "baby factories" in Guatemala than the story of Antonia. In 2006, before the adoption moratorium, an American physician named J. White, who volunteered on a medical mission, gave a personal account of an encounter with a Guatemalan birth mother.

> Last week a thirteen-year-old girl named Marta came into my office. Her father works on a coffee plantation. She grew up on the verge of starvation in a cardboard house, with eleven siblings, six of whom are still alive. A man came in a car a year ago and offered her family three hundred dollars—a year's wages for her father—for each baby she can make and give to him. She now lives and works in his house, tends his garden, washes his clothes, was impregnated by men unknown to her.... The babies are delivered by the owners of the house. No hospitals. No doctors.... There are six other girls in the house in the same situation.[51]

We expect that most adoptive parents would likely balk at getting a child from a mother who is a baby factory, who is just doing it for the money. Hopefully no one wants to get a child from ruthlessly exploited captive young girls. How do we avoid this? Once again this speaks to the value of having the birth and adoptive families directly communicate. Exploitation thrives in the murky world in which babies appear in orphanages or in the hands of intermediaries without adoptive families knowing where they came from. Greater transparency would reduce this. Fortunately, DNA tests, which were routinely used in Guatemala, can reliably establish maternity. If we decide this is a regulation we'd like to have, embassies can keep records of the number of visas issued to the children of a given mother. This should make it possible to limit the number of visas issued to her children, or at least to inform the adoptive families of the number of children a given mother has placed for adoption. Most importantly, encouraging adoptive families to connect with the birth families would make it much harder to profit from the kind of nightmarish situation that Marta was in.

We summarize our discussion of potential objections to our proposal that adoption and birth parents be permitted to meet and negotiate their own adoption arrangements. Far from believing that birth mothers will be harmed by this model, we think it will empower them. That has clearly been the effect of the open adoption movement in America. That some mothers will be pressured to sell their children can be addressed by contact with adoptive parents; the latter are unlikely to agree to be party to such exploitation. Similarly, DNA tests and records of previous adoptions are likely to make it hard for "baby factories" to form. The argument that international adoption should be replaced with family reunification ignores the fact that reunification is not always and everywhere the better option for the child, or even always best for the birth family. Reunification rarely addresses the family problem that caused the child to be institutionalized in the first place. A more troublesome possibility is that adoptive families may choose babies over older and/or institutionalized children. This could be addressed, at least in part, by streamlining the process by which institutionalized children are adopted; a long and complicated search for extended family, as in Guatemala and Romania, makes it hard to place these children. If extended family could be quickly contacted, or the search truncated at a reasonable point, it would facilitate the adoption of institutionalized children. And, as we discuss in the next chapter, if the extended family can be compensated, they will have an incentive to come forward. Moreover, many adoptive parents, like the authors of this book, actively seek to adopt kids who are older and/or in orphanages.

But Is Selling Children a Victimless Crime?

Even if these private negotiations are as mutually beneficial to the birth and adoptive families as we market-favoring types claim—and many would dispute that—a question remains unanswered. Are the laws against baby selling the type that can, as Spinoza put it, "be violated without doing anyone any injury"? Even *if* all the parents are satisfied with the arrangement, perhaps the child is harmed by having her parental rights be sold. We take up this question in Chapter 8.

After the Reunion

We left the M. family and Isata at the reunion with everything going well, after some difficulties were ironed out. But the good vibrations were not to last. The following summer, after Isata got a job, the M. family began asking about her earnings. Shaun mentioned to Beckie that were Isata in Africa, she would be expected to give a portion of her earnings directly to her parents. In an e-mail to us, on the other hand, Shaun denied that any money is expected from Isata.

Isata says, "I found out that my dad wanted to be a chief in his village and wanted to marry a second wife. And he wanted money from my parents [the Sibleys] to help him do that. I try to understand that culture, but I just don't like that idea [of having two wives].... He expects me to understand his culture, but he doesn't have to understand mine. When I told him I had gotten my first job, my summer job, my dad immediately asked when I could start sending money regularly.... And it's all just too much. They write me [e-mail, or on Facebook] all the time, several times a week. I just can't do that.... I am trying to get a balance, I want to be involved but not too involved in their business."

Shaun wrote, "At the airport [as they were leaving] Isata promised to call or write to the family once every week or twice a month and also another visit was expected in 2013 which didn't happen.... There has not been good thoughts about the reunion any more, due to how the Sibley family are behaving to the M. family.... [The Sibleys] keep from even communicating as though the M. family were expecting financial support from them. All that the M. family ever needed from them was the concern to show that they care, that's all."

In any case, disappointment in the reestablished relationship is quite palpable on both sides. As of this writing, the two families have essentially stopped communicating. The disagreement is effectively based on cultural differences and expectations. (Race, on the other hand, has not been an important issue in Isata's adoption.)

After reading this long story, the reader is entitled to wonder what lesson we draw from it regarding whether it is wrong to deprive a child of her birth culture via international adoption.

It is reminiscent of other stories we have heard and that others have written about. One example is the story of Heidi in the film *Daughter from Danang*. Heidi was adopted as a child in the famous (or infamous) Operation Babylift at the end of the Vietnam War to Tennessee, where she still lives as an adult. In the film, she travels to a reunion with her birth mother and family in Vietnam. At first the visit goes well, but when the birth family starts asking for financial support, the woman begins to feel that they wanted to see her again for the money and not because they love her. (We do not believe Isata feels this way about her birth family). Again, there is a cultural misunderstanding. At a two-year follow-up at the end of the film, Heidi is refusing communication with her birth family.

And what of our son GB? Because we know that it would be the cultural norm for GB or his family to help his (birth) parents financially, and because we know they are much poorer than we are, we have sent them money, especially during the Ebola outbreak in Sierra Leone. We paid the school fees for the girl who GB, when he joined our family, called his "small, small sister." We have educated GB about this African cultural norm of children helping their families and told him of the decision he will need to make when he is established in a job and earning a living. In the not too distant future, we hope to return to Sierra Leone and meet with his birth mom. We hope he will be willing to come with us this time.

One final word on these stories: Issues of cultural differences between birth and adoptive countries have been a problem area, at least for birth parents; racial differences between adoptive children and adoptive families in these stories have not been a problem (though we would never claim it couldn't be). There were misrepresentations in these adoptions, to varying degrees; in Isata's case enough to perhaps be categorized as "child trafficking" through adoption, at least according to some critiques. The adoptive children themselves are, as adults, happy with the outcomes, and even the birth parents would not undo the adoptions, even if they might want current relationships changed. Most importantly from our perspective, were the families in Isata's case to have met and negotiated the terms of the adoption, including perhaps communication throughout the child's lifetime, the kinds of misunderstandings, disappointments, deceptions, and even fraud that occurred could surely have been avoided.

CHAPTER 8

Repugnant Ideas That Became Mainstream

Economists are pretty much immune to repugnance.

Steve Levitt[1]

We have argued that tolerating the "sale" of children—more accurately, the sale of parental rights—would help revive international adoption by reducing the fraud and deception that have occurred in the system and hastened its implosion. In this chapter, we look at other economic ideas and policies that once horrified the public but are now either widely accepted, or on their way to becoming so. What was once viewed as repugnant can become, not just acceptable, but viewed as helpful to society.

In the 1890s some large American companies began a practice the "mere suggestion" of which showed "the frightful depths to which human nature, perverted by avarice bred of ignorance and rasping poverty, can descend."[2] The capitalists had found a way to ruthlessly extract huge profits from the children of the poor. In her lively and fascinating book, *Pricing the Priceless Child*, Viviana Zelizer describes the nationwide struggle to outlaw this nefarious activity. The American Humane Society for the Prevention of Cruelty to Children fought to have it declared a criminal offense. In hearings before the Massachusetts legislature in 1895, "clergymen, physicians, judges and politicians took the stand to denounce this 'diabolical practice.'"[3] What was this new monstrosity of child exploitation? Slavery? No, that was already at long last illegal. Making children work long hours in dangerous and dirty factories? No, that had already been going on for decades. This new outrage was *selling life insurance for children.*

Life insurance companies had been around since the 1600s, but they generally sold policies for husbands and fathers, the primary source of family support. In 1875, however, the John F. Dryden Company began insuring children under the age of ten. "Perhaps because premiums were as low as 5 or 10 cents per week, the business grew beyond all expectations. By 1895 . . . the Prudential alone had received over $33 million in premiums" and employed 10,000 agents.[4] The number of insured children had reached three million by 1902.

Then, as now, big companies making huge profits aroused the ire of social reformers, sometimes with good reason, but sometimes not. In 1885, the governor of Massachusetts asked the legislature to make child life insurance illegal, as did the governor of Pennsylvania in 1889.[5] In as many as eighteen states, bills were introduced every few years to make the insurance of young children illegal, though only in Colorado, in 1893, did these efforts succeed.

Why were so many people opposed to life insurance for children? Because, as the *New York Times* said in 1895, it presented a "temptation to inhuman crimes."[6] Insurance might induce poor people—not the middle or upper classes, mind you, just poor people—to murder their own children! The *Times* acknowledged that for the "respectable poor," children's life insurance was a good thing, a form of savings and protection against funeral expenses. "But there is a drunken profligate class to whom a little money is worth any sin to get it, and by these the life of a child is not held for much."

Just look at what had happened in England! Reverend Benjamin Waugh told readers of the *Contemporary Review* in 1890 that "the terrible estimate given two years ago that [in England] a thousand children a year were murdered for insurance money has at length received an official confirmation." The reverend thought this revelation would surely "doom the system" of insuring young children.[7] Of course these "murders" were not generally in as obvious a form as strangulation or bludgeoning, which were easily detectable, but in a more subtle, and more cruel, form: neglect. Waugh described the "crafty practices whereby child killing is accomplished and yet inquests are escaped."[8] We may wonder how, if they were so hard to detect, Reverend Waugh knew that a thousand cases of neglect-unto-death were occurring every year. Presumably from the coroners examining poor children who had succumbed to disease—supposedly a suspiciously large number of those children were insured.

Even absent murder and deliberate abuse, said Charles C. Read, among the most voluble critics of the practice, insuring young children was an unscrupulous exploitation of the "poor and ignorant people." "Money that should buy bread to sustain life goes to the insurance agent," often with the result that children were hungry and poorly clothed. Greedy companies employed many "sharp, shrewd and enterprising men" who comb the tenements "floor by floor and room to room... to secure insurance upon the lives of everyone they meet."[9] In Read's opinion, the poor were being pressured into buying a product that wiser heads like his own knew not to be in their best interest.

By the early 1900s, however, opposition to children's life insurance had mostly faded away. The horrors predicted by the critics simply failed to materialize. There were no thousand English children murdered by their parents each year for the sake of insurance payments.[10] Would people do such a thing just because they're poor? Very rarely, it turns out. Indeed, some commentators found it a "contemptible slander" to say that "the poor love their children less than the millionaires."[11] And while it was certainly true that companies made millions selling insurance to poor families, they hardly sanctioned children's deaths—insurers make money when their clients *stay alive*. Companies profited precisely because lots of people wanted to insure their children against the shame and horror of a pauper's burial. Today, virtually no one calls child life insurance a moral outrage.[12]

Ghosts of Repugnance Past

Children's life insurance once was (to some) what Harvard economist and Nobel Prize winner Alvin Roth calls a "repugnant good."[13] As the term implies, these are goods or transactions that arouse moral revulsion when they are subject to market exchange. There are lots of examples: sex, forced (or indentured) servitude, transplantable organs from live donors, narcotics, votes, scalped tickets, and, of course, adoptable babies and children. Roth points out that a number of goods and services have, like children's life insurance, overcome social repugnance to achieve market respectability. Perhaps society in general does not care if some of these remain repugnant—dwarf-tossing, a game that Roth describes that is popular in some areas, but extremely repugnant in most, may not worry us by staying repugnant. But society could gain, has gained in the past, from acceptance of other repugnant goods.

One obvious case is usury: charging interest when lending money. In 1179, the Third Lantern Council, convened in Rome, declared usury to be an excommunicable sin for all Christians. This posed a serious impediment to progress. As historian Niall Ferguson says, "Without the foundation of borrowing and lending, the economic history of our world would scarcely have got off the ground."[14] And indeed, the world didn't see growth in per capita incomes until the period 1000–1500 AD.[15] To grow, economies must invest *current* resources toward the production of *future* resources. And the lender of current resources requires something in exchange for abstaining from consuming them. Moreover, he may never get his investment back. Ferguson reminds us of what Shakespeare's Shylock said regarding a loan to the Merchant Antonio: "Ships are but boards, sailors but men: there be land rats and water rats, water thieves and land thieves; I mean pirates; and then there is the peril of water, winds, and rocks."[16] The lender must be compensated for these risks. Without lending, there would be few resources for growth, and without interest, there would be little lending.

Fortunately for European civilization, Jewish law allowed lending on interest to gentiles, though not to fellow Jews. Because Jews were often prohibited from joining guilds and professions, the Medieval Church essentially thrust the commercial credit industry upon the Jewish community. As banking was, and still is, a critical industry, some Jewish bankers accrued enormous wealth, along with enormous anti-Semitic resentment. Western society has long since reconciled itself to the necessity of charging interest on loans. Some Islamic societies still have not (though most get around this religious stipulation).

Another repugnant good was the human cadaver. More accurately, the repugnance was in giving the human cadaver over to be dissected. At the beginning of the nineteenth century, Edinburgh University was one the world's foremost centers for the study of human anatomy. The study of anatomy required human corpses. But by the Murder Act of 1751, the only bodies available for scientific dissection were those of murderers who had hanged.[17] This imposed a severe constraint on scientific advancement, as there were simply not enough convicted murderers, usually not viewed as a social problem. A black market in cadavers arose. So-called resurrectionists would dig up dead bodies shortly after burial and sell them to instructors of anatomy. To protect the newly departed, some graveyards from that period had watchtowers or, for the wealthier dead, individual graves might be enclosed in cages or locked in vaults.

The cadaver crisis in Edinburgh reached a crescendo in 1828 when two innovators named Burke and Hare streamlined production by eliminating one long and tedious step: waiting for people to die on their own. Burke and Hare murdered seventeen people and sold their fresh cadavers. When these acts were discovered, there were public protests and some famous anatomists were burned in effigy in Edinburgh's Surgeons' Square.[18] The public prosecutor convinced Hare to turn state's evidence against Burke, who was convicted, hanged, and, yes, subsequently dissected. To stem the tide of grave robbing, Parliament passed the Anatomy Act of 1832. The act licensed anatomists and allowed them to accept unclaimed cadavers from prisons and workhouses. More importantly, it also allowed next of kin to donate bodies for dissection in exchange for payment of the eventual burial costs. Thus was formed a regulated, quasi-market in human corpses wherein payment was made "in-kind" in the form of funeral expenses. This reform essentially eliminated the resurrection industry. It also helped promote the extraordinary transformation of medicine from a primitive collection of folk remedies to an actual modern scientific enterprise.[19]

A contemporary example of a good gradually wending its way from repugnance to acceptability is the marketable emissions permit. These permits are essentially licenses to pollute. Economists see pollution as a market failure caused by a poor incentive structure. Because "emitters" of pollution don't have to pay the costs that their effluvium imposes on "receptors" of pollution, unregulated markets produce an "inefficiently large amount" of pollution. We don't tend to label some people as bad guys and other people as good guys. Morality isn't much discussed.

In 1920, British economist Arthur Pigou suggested that the problem could be resolved by using taxes or fees to create disincentives to pollute. If, say, a smelter belched noxious smoke, its owner must pay a fee per unit of smoke emitted.[20] The idea was that the fee would induce the firm to pollute less, by either cutting output or adopting a less noxious production process. Polluting the air would not be illegal, but it would no longer be free. In 1968, John Dales suggested a more sophisticated version of the "polluter pays" concept: issue a fixed number of permits to pollute based on the amount of pollution deemed allowable, and let the permits be bought and sold, like stocks and bonds.[21] Competition within the permit market would drive down the cost of abating the pollution.

The "pay to pollute" principle was morally offensive to many people. Philosopher Robert Goodin said, "The problem with green taxes or pollutions charges or permits... is that they seem to say, 'It is OK to pollute, provided you pay,' when the proper message is instead, 'It is wrong to pollute even if you can afford to pay.'"[22] He likened pollution permits to medieval religious indulgences, with which, for a fee, the Church would wipe away past sins in the eyes of God. Michael Sandel says that a system of pollution permits "says in effect that emitting pollution is not like littering, but simply a cost of doing business. But is that right? Or should some moral stigma attach to companies that spew excessive pollution into the air?"[23]

Despite some moral opposition, the 1990 amendments to the Clean Air Act mandated that states issue tradable permits for sulfur dioxide emissions from power plants. The first markets for pollution were formed. The press calls the system "Cap and Trade." The scheme worked so well that even environmental organizations are now embracing the permit approach as a way to reduce greenhouse gasses. Johan Eyckmens and Snoore Kverndokk report, for example, that in Norway "environmental organizations are now trading carbon offsets on the internet (to offset carbon emissions from airplane flights) even if they argued against pollution trade just a few years ago."[24] The Environmental Defense Fund says that "Cap and Trade is the most environmentally and economically sensible approach to controlling greenhouse gas emissions."[25] Judging by their websites, the Audubon Society and the Wilderness Society seem equally convinced. The Sierra Club, even if still harboring some reservations, sees the concept as a workable approach. The repugnance to pollution markets has waned sharply.

A Victimless Crime?

In the last chapter, we addressed the practical issues associated with allowing parents to accept compensation for exchanging parental rights. Even if the two sets of parents are satisfied with the negotiations, the children are generally not consulted. So, here we consider the more philosophical or psychological sticking points, namely is harm done intrinsically if a person, or child, or baby is sold for adoption purposes? Many people in the adoption triad currently would emphatically say yes. We consider some of their objections.

Let's begin by acknowledging that some objections to baby selling are considerably less sensible than others. Judge Posner, quoted above, took quite a bit of heat for an article he and Elaine Landes published in 1978 suggesting that a regulated market in adoptable babies was not beyond the pale of consideration.[26] The idea did not resonate—some think that article contributed to Posner being passed over for a seat on the Supreme Court.[27] In a 1987 speech at Boston University, Posner reported, "An official of a national adoption organization wrote me recently (and more importantly, the *Wall Street Journal*) that, as he understood the article, I advocate allowing the wealthy parents of a child who needs a liver transplant to buy a child and 'harvest' its liver for their own child."[28] Said official, of course, did *not* understand the article. In private correspondence, he even admitted to Posner that he hadn't actually read the Landes-Posner piece, but had based his letter to the *Wall Street Journal* on newspaper accounts about the article. It shouldn't need to be pointed out that in a market model like that of Landes and Posner, adoptive children face no greater danger than they would with their birth parents. "Laws forbidding child abuse and neglect would continue to be fully applicable to adoptive parents even if baby sales were permitted."[29] Nobody in America is allowed to abuse their child, no matter how that child came to be theirs.

Indeed, we would expect that, as Landes and Posner pointed out, adoption increases a child's safety. Before they can adopt, an American couple must submit to at least one home study, frequently more, not to mention providing legal background checks, soliciting letters of recommendation, and doing lots of other expensive and tedious things designed to establish their suitability to raise the child. We consider these to be very, very good regulations. Yet, birth mothers (to say nothing of birth fathers) do none of these things. In fact, to deliver and raise a baby one need supply fewer official credentials than are required to buy a six-pack of Miller Lite.

If there is one assumption we can reasonably make with respect to adoption it's that the two parties who most care about the child in question are the birth family and the prospective adopters. We expect the genetic family to value the child because that's how evolution works, and we expect adoptive parents to value any child for whom they're willing to pay tens of thousands of dollars. Neither valuation holds unfailingly in every single case, but *in general, in most cases*, we can surely expect the two sets of parents to care more for a child than adoption agents, facilitators, or government officials. Why then, would anyone propose leaving them out of the matching process merely because some money might change hands?

But It's Fundamentally Immoral to Sell Human Beings

We realize, of course, that most people regard any scheme permitting the "sale" of human beings as an absolute nonstarter and that they hold this view without the slightest ambivalence. We've quoted Ethan B. Kapstein, who states, "A free market for babies is out of the question: while infants can fetch a high price, they are not, and should never be treated as, commodities."[30] Moreover, some argue that even *if* the sale of a child benefits all members of the adoption triad, it still harms society as a whole. In a well-known article in the *Harvard Law Review*, Janet Rabin argues that selling children attacks the very nature of "personhood" and threatens society's view of "human flourishing." Rabin says that "conceiving of children in market rhetoric would foster an inferior conception of human flourishing, one that commodifies every personal attribute that might be valued by people in other people."[31] When used in conjunction with exchanges involving humans, the term "commodification" conjures up some ugly associations. Sandel goes so far as to suggest that this is the defining feature of human slavery. "Slavery was appalling because it treated human beings as commodities, to be bought and sold at auction."[32] Sandel's statement shows the extreme negative connotation of any connection between humans and commodities.

Economists, or the authors at least, are less likely to shrink in horror at the idea of some aspect of a human's life, for example, the right to parent her until age eighteen, as an object of sale. We think that in one form or another it happens routinely. Back in 1920, for instance, some folks in Boston famously sold a babe (of sorts) to some New Yorkers for what was then an enormous sum of money. On January 6 of that year, a headline in New York's *The World* proclaimed, "Yankees Buy Babe Ruth and Home Run Bat for over $100,000." It was the highest price ever paid for a ballplayer, and Ruth, who got none of the money, had little choice but to accept the sale. This exchange truly appalled many people, especially Red Sox fans, but not because Ruth was treated as a commodity. He was, after all, compensated handsomely and was always free to walk away, although only at enormous cost to himself. Ballplayers still get sold to this day. On a moment's notice and without consultation, they can be sent to work for another team in another city and their only alternative is to risk destroying highly lucrative careers. Surely this is treating someone as a commodity.[33] We cannot, of course, equate an adult's choice to accept commodification with the circumstance of a child who has no choice, but being treated as a commodity is not always and everywhere absolutely unacceptable in Western society.

Slavery, as Sandel says, certainly does commodify people, but its real horror lies in the fact that it's grand theft, perhaps the grandest theft of all: the stealing of someone's entire being. Abolition, after all, did not radically alter the daily lifestyle of the former slaves. The people picking cotton in Alabama in 1868 were more or less the same people who picked it in 1863, but with the difference that in 1868 they had to be paid, even if very poorly, and they were mostly free to leave. But their labor could no longer be openly stolen. Slavery and international adoption do have one important feature in common: neither the birth mother nor the slave is compensated for their loss.

But really, no child is owned. Some adult always has parenting rights over a child until she reaches the age of majority, at which point she becomes a free agent. Parents cannot, for example, sell the child for purposes of exploitation, and such rights as parents have are subject to termination by the state in cases of neglect or abuse. Selling parental rights is not like selling a child, and certainly not like selling a child into slavery.

But Doesn't Commodification Harm the Child?

Recall the child who was stuck in the Peruvian shelter, knocked off her swing, and pummeled by one of the older inmates. Bartholet said that "many have birth parents who may never visit and have no apparent capacity to function as parents, but who have not taken the formal steps necessary to free their children for adoption."[34]

It could be argued that were a child in the orphanage Bartholet describes relinquished by her birth family in exchange for money, that act would effectively "commodify" her. So what? Imagine how the child sobbing on the playground would react if someone said, "Look, Sweetie, I can get you out of this crummy orphanage and into a nice home in California, *but*—and I'm not gonna sugarcoat this, kid—you will have to accept being *treated as a commodity*." Seriously, is that the main thing she would be worried about? One could also argue, however, that while this young child might not mind commodification *now*, she will one day have to confront the notion that her birth family valued money more than they valued her. That idea could indeed be painful. But will it be worse than staying in the institution? Will it be worse than the realization, which some kids face, that they were adopted only because long and expensive fertility treatments had failed to produce a genetically related child? Will it be worse than knowing that you weren't supposed to exist at all? We, and probably lots of readers, know birth children who cheerfully report that they were complete "accidents," that their mother's pregnancy was entirely unexpected and initially unwelcome. But, as usual, their parents quickly fell in love with them, and that made the untimeliness of their arrival emotionally irrelevant. Comical even. Parental love doesn't always conquer all, but it conquers a lot, and we suspect that "commodification" is something it could generally handle. Therefore we, for two, require some serious empirical persuasion if we're to believe that staying in an orphanage, or in a family that can't feed you, is better than knowing you were "treated as a commodity" in the adoption process.

We can cite two specific examples of adoptee attitudes toward commodification that we happen to be familiar with. One is a young Burundian woman we'll call Denise who was a student at a liberal arts college in the United States. International adoptions from Burundi are rare, but Denise was adopted by a Burundian man living in America, which made it acceptable to the local authorities. At age six, Denise was in a displaced persons camp, having narrowly escaped the Hutu genocide of Tutsis in Burundi in 1994. Her parents did not escape the murderers. As a way of helping his shattered homeland, the adoptive father and his wife—who already had birth children—visited the camp to find a child to adopt. The American couple met with Denise's birth siblings about the adoption. The siblings were very much in favor of it. We don't know if money changed hands in these initial discussions. But we do know that Denise's American/French parents regularly sent money to her birth siblings throughout the years she was growing up. They arranged to send the support to an aunt who then disbursed it to the family based on need. When Denise was old enough to get a job, she proudly began to help with these payments. She eventually planned to fully take them over. Did she feel commodified that money changed hands between the two families? No, she felt proud of her dad for his willingness to help. While in college, she visited Burundi and had a joyful reunion with her birth siblings.

A second example is that of our sons. Compensating their birth families had never been an issue until we located GB's birth mother. But while writing this book, we had a discussion with our sons about the issue of payments. Both boys knew that we paid thousands of dollars for their adoptions. Neither was at all bothered by the commodification question. Not even our older son, who is not persuaded by our proposal to allow compensation of birth parents. Our younger son is indifferent—what matters to him is that he made it here. Perhaps the children of economists make a poor test case, but our point is that kids are not fated to feel "commodified" by payment. It depends on how their families, and their societies, frame the issue for them: as an act of love or as crass materialism.

We admit, of course, that anecdotes such as the above prove nothing. No doubt there are examples of adoptees who *do* feel commodified by the adoption process, or would feel that way if they had knowledge of being "purchased." The point we are making, however, is that given the profound advantages that adoption can give a vulnerable child, and given that private negotiations, including potential payment, can improve the process, the burden of proof is upon those who say that commodification is a reason to prevent such payments.

In-Kind Payment as an Alternative to Cash

Professor Alvin Roth has written that repugnant markets, such as those for human organs, are so viscerally distasteful to most people that economists are unrealistic to try to convince policy makers to allow them. He is famed for, among other things, his path-breaking work on the system of voluntary kidney donation. Professor Roth did not try to institute an open kidney market, which economists have long favored, because kidney sales are strongly opposed by both sentiment and law in the United States. Only Iran allows open kidney sales, and apparently only Iran has eliminated the waiting list for kidney donations.[35] Instead, Roth helped create a matching algorithm that greatly improved the process of matching donors with recipients, thereby saving many people's lives.

Professor Roth's insight on repugnant markets could easily be applied to our proposals about adoption. Perhaps instead of cash payments, birth families could be compensated in-kind. For example, adoptive parents could agree to pay school fees, for some fixed period of time, for other children in the family. Or they could create a health care fund from which the family could draw. Perhaps they could help build the family a new house; there are many, many such possibilities. This type of arrangement also could protect the birth mother from a husband or boyfriend getting use of the money for purposes that she opposes, something that research indicates can happen. This modification would complicate the process of open adoption, but it might go a long way to making it more palatable.

A Market Even We Don't Like

If, as Steve Levitt says in the quote at the beginning of this chapter, economists are immune to repugnance, then we are not good economists, because there is a market that even we find repugnant. And yet, we believe that this repulsive market is critically important and that attempts to suppress it do more harm than good. Thus, we think it particularly helpful to consider it here.

Africa's elephants, like its orphans, are a highly vulnerable population, only more so, in the sense that at least people don't shoot orphans for sport. In March of 2011, Bob Parsons, the CEO of the internet-hosting company GoDaddy, posted a video of himself shooting an elephant in Zimbabwe.[36] Repugnance immediately reared its digital head. People for the Ethical Treatment of Animals (PETA) called for an immediate boycott of GoDaddy. Iain Douglas-Hamilton, founder of Save the Elephants, said, "It's a very sad, tragic thing when elephants have to be shot. I find the glorification totally out of place."[37] As if to illustrate what is either really *good* about capitalism, or really *bad* about capitalism, a GoDaddy competitor, Namecheap, raised twenty thousand dollars for elephant conservation by donating one dollar for each new subscriber to its internet service. Parsons, however, was unapologetic. Indeed, he claimed that by destroying a "problem animal" he was helping local villagers, some of whom are seen on the video wearing caps with the GoDaddy logo while stripping the hide and meat from the bloody carcass.

African countries vary considerably in how they try to protect their elephants. In the 1970s, Kenya responded to a catastrophic decline in herd size by banning all forms of elephant hunting. People like Bob Parsons were not allowed to kill elephants for fun. It was also illegal to sell raw ivory in Kenya and authorities made emphatic bonfires out of enormous stacks of captured tusks. But the hunting ban and the burning of ivory made these animals even more valuable to poachers. The law was profoundly ineffective: from 1977 to 1989 Kenya's elephant population fell from more than 160,000 to less than 20,000 animals. One can find on the Internet (though we don't recommend it) pictures of elephant carcasses after the tusks had been chainsawed from their faces. A 1990 international ban on sales of African ivory (CITES) helped the herds increase, but only to forty thousand by 2012.[38] Now, almost all of Kenya's elephants are confined to national parks to protect them from poachers; outside the parks, they are virtually gone.

Botswana, Zimbabwe, and Zambia, on the other hand, did not ban elephant hunting. In fact, they promoted it. Under a program called CAMPFIRE, sponsored by USAID, anyone wanting to shoot an elephant could purchase a permit to do so.[39] Permit revenue was shared with the local villages, so every time an elephant was shot, the local community benefitted. A dead elephant brought in money; live elephants were a dangerous nuisance. Intuitively, this sounds like a sure-fire method for wiping out the herds. But market outcomes can be counterintuitive. Between 1989 and 1995, the combined elephant population in the three countries using CAMPFIRE *rose* by about 15 percent even as the rest of Africa *lost* almost 25 percent of these animals.[40] By 2005, the number of elephants in Zimbabwe had more than doubled.

Why did promoting elephant hunting do a better job of protecting elephants than *banning* it? Banning hunting doesn't eliminate the incentive to procure ivory; it increases the incentive by raising the price of the product. And a ban requires government enforcement. Louisa Lombard, a conservation researcher, wrote in the *New York Times* that "since the 1980's, under the mantle of conservation efforts with funding from [Western countries] African Park Guards have fought a rarely discussed low-level war against poachers."[41] It's essentially a guerilla war in which poachers fight park rangers, foreign soldiers, and local militias led by international mercenaries. Guerilla wars tend to be endless and bloody. Lombard says, for example, that "some anti-poaching guards claim to have killed hundreds of poachers."

The CAMPFIRE program, in contrast, doesn't rely on government officials to protect the elephants. The system is highly decentralized. The revenue from hunting permits, which can cost as much as twenty thousand dollars, accrues primarily to the local village council, along with the value of any ivory, meat, or hide from the carcass.[42] Consequently, local residents have powerful incentive to protect "their" herds from poachers. As Jon Hutton of the African Resources Trust said, "When rural communities are allowed to benefit from harvesting the wild, they try to protect the wild, not destroy it."[43] The elephants became assets, and people want their assets to grow, not disappear, so CAMPFIRE increased the population significantly.[44]

On the other hand, many people find elephant hunting to be morally repugnant.[45] In a *Wall Street Journal* editorial, the Humane Society's vice president, Wayne Pacelle, said, "If we could shut down sport hunting in a moment we would."[46] We are highly sympathetic to this point of view. The CAMPFIRE program "protects" elephants by sacrificing some of these intelligent and highly social creatures to the amusement of people who are primarily rich, white, and male, like Bob Parsons. To us, it makes a great deal more *moral* sense to completely ban the hunting of elephants.[47] Why do we have to kill these lovely animals? Let rich white men find other ways to amuse themselves. Ivory is not oil or bauxite; our economy can run quite smoothly without it. Little would be lost, and much gained, if elephant hunting stopped entirely.

But hunting bans don't seem to work. Why would rural poor people stand up to armed poachers unless the elephants could somehow help them support their families (instead of trampling their crops and being a nuisance)? Under CAMPFIRE, the village values elephants for the revenue it receives from controlled hunting, and consequently villagers have incentive to protect the herds. Bob Parsons is paying for elephant conservation. We may not like his *motives*, but that is beside the point. A policy that succumbs to instinctual moral revulsion, rather than facing the harsh reality of human behavior, could well lead to elephant extinction. That is an even more repugnant outcome.

A similar dilemma arises with respect to adoption. To save more vulnerable children, and to simultaneously help birth families financially, we may need to swallow a bitter pill of moral repugnance: birth parents "selling" their kids, or parental rights, to adoptive parents. But because policy must work in the world we *actually* live in, not the world we *wished* we lived in, this pill may turn out to be well worth swallowing. Our review of the evidence suggests that it is.

We have illustrated that, historically, certain types of market exchanges that were viewed with revulsion have made the transition to respectable, often highly useful transactions. As we saw, predictions of horrific behavior resulting from these exchanges, such as the wholesale murder of insured children, simply do not materialize. We also saw that market outcomes can be counterintuitive: banning the hunting of elephants did not eliminate poaching nearly as effectively as establishing a regulated sale of hunting permits. And we saw in the previous chapter that the private quasi-market in infants occasioned by the open adoption movement in the United States has not lead to great abuse of poor birth mothers; if anything, it helps empower them.

CHAPTER 9

Adoption
Joy and Sadness

Why any kid would wanna be an orphan is beyond me.

Miss Hannigan, *Annie* (the movie)

A few years after GB joined our family, Tinker was invited to speak in a class called Reproduction and Technology taught by two colleagues of ours, a sociologist and a biologist. She spoke to the students about the process of deciding, in Kurt's case, whether we would adopt domestically or internationally and, in GB's case, which specific child we would choose from a group of available children. At the end of the talk, one student raised her hand. "Didn't you feel like you were... ah... *shopping* for a child... like, uh, picking one off of a shelf?" she asked. Well, yes, we did feel like we were shopping for a child because that, if we're honest, was pretty much what we were doing. And no, though it felt like the responsible thing to do, it didn't feel very good, and it still doesn't feel great these many years later.

The description of our first adoption in the Introduction went something like this:

> When we decided to add a second child to our family in 1991 through adoption we wanted to find one in need of a home, and having been told that black and biracial infants can be hard to place, we opted to go in that direction.

But the process wasn't as smooth as that. The path to adopting Kurt was emotionally quite difficult, fraught with anxiety and guilt, some of which lingers to this day.[1]

The more complicated story is that the first kids we considered adopting were on a list called "Iowa's Waiting Children" published by Iowa's Department of Human Services. We can't remember how many kids there were, maybe twenty or so, a number in sibling groups. What we do remember is that these children had been removed from profoundly dysfunctional homes for some terrible combination of abuse and neglect, and the stories in their dossiers were heartbreaking to read. For example, one pair of sisters had only one requirement for an adoptive family: "someone who won't hurt us." Reading their histories made us feel that unless we abandoned our careers and bought a big farmhouse to fill with these children we could not consider ourselves decent human beings, never mind candidates for sainthood. And we soon discovered just how unsaintly we were. It feels bad to report that we did not fill a big farmhouse with Iowa's Waiting Children; we did not adopt even one of them. Why not? Because they seemed to us to be so disturbed, so damaged, so full of pain and sorrow, that we were afraid. Perhaps we were wrong about these kids and about whether we could manage to be good parents to them. Very good friends of ours adopted a son from foster care with non-speaking autism, very wrongly diagnosed as a child as being "mentally retarded." He is graduating Phi Beta Kappa from Oberlin College this year, carrying an A average. Of course, it has been a lot of hard work for all three of them, but obviously adoption from foster care can work out very well. Still, we thought these kids from the Iowa care system would require not just devoted and excellent parenting, but conceivably a change in our entire lifestyle and might even require that one of us sacrifice his or her career. And, honestly, we were just not willing to sacrifice enough to change our lifestyle that much or lose one of our careers. It all seemed too risky. So, we passed on Iowa's Waiting Children, after swallowing, not for the last time, a bitter pill of self-censure.

Having decided against adopting out of foster care, international adoption seemed the next logical step. We talked to the Holt Agency, who suggested we consider a little boy in Costa Rica by the name of John Albert, a sweet-faced seven-year-old with thick dark hair. Looking at his video, we fell in love with him immediately. He had, the agency said, a cleft lip and palate and fetal alcohol effects, a milder version of Fetal Alcohol Syndrome (FAS), which is caused by drinking during pregnancy and can produce a wide array of cognitive problems. We didn't know a lot about fetal alcohol effects, but we figured we could handle it; John Albert didn't even have full-blown FAS.

We knew that, once started, the adoption process would take some months to complete, but emotionally we and our oldest child, six-year-old Mary, began integrating John Albert into our family. We tried to learn some Spanish by putting notecard labels on items around the house, like doors (*la puerta*), the sink (*el lavabo*), the refrigerator (*el refrigerador*). We compiled a book of snapshots, including ourselves, our house, lots of extended family, and of course the dog, that we planned to send him as soon as we had confirmed the adoption. We were ready.

Then, the fog of delusion began to dissipate. We were excitedly discussing our plans at a party one night when a glum-faced colleague very gingerly made a modest suggestion. "Before you do this," she told us, "you might want to read Michael Dorris's book, *The Broken Cord*."[2] So we read it. And it scared the hell out of us. Dorris's 1990 book recounts his experience of adopting (as a single male, virtually unheard of in 1971) a three-year-old Lakota boy, "Adam," who would eventually be diagnosed with Fetal Alcohol Syndrome. We hadn't understood how bad it could be. So, we started doing research on FAS. We read reams of literature and consulted top experts on the disorder at the University of Iowa Hospitals in Iowa City. WebMD, for example, although not available in 1990, says that facial abnormalities; growth, learning, and behavior problems; and birth defects are all symptoms of FAS.[3] In America, it is one of the leading causes of preventable learning disabilities. One day, in the office of an FAS specialist in Des Moines, Mark asked her point-blank, "Is it possible that this child will have to be cared for by us until we die, and after that, cared for by our daughter?"

"Yes," she said, "that is possible."

From a distance of twenty-five years, we feel a sense of shame in writing these next words: we decided not to adopt John Albert. No one blamed us for changing our minds. Indeed, most people assured us that it was sensible, it was prudent, it was morally responsible not to adopt John Albert—we had Mary's welfare to consider, after all. We went so far as to get help from a psychologist about making the decision. And adoption experts warn against entering into a situation you'll be unable to handle—a failed adoption is a disaster for all concerned, but most of all for the adopted child. So maybe turning away from John Albert was a reasonable decision. But after all of this time, it still feels like a failure of our courage.

As everyone knows, it is much "safer" to adopt a healthy infant than an older child, which is why healthy infants are in short supply. But, as we have explained, while the demand for white babies might exceed supply, the demand for black and biracial infants, especially boys, does not. Such infants, we were told, were still hard to place. The Holt Agency suggested that we consider an African American or biracial child, and we agreed, after Tinker read the research on transracial adoption and we consulted a couple of African American friends. We had a referral almost immediately.

Ten years later, when we began the process to adopt again, this time a boy from Africa, and contacted The Children's Home (TCH) in Sierra Leone, we again had choices to make. And again, these choices were painful. The first child recommended to us was a five-year-old named Daniel. We read the description of Daniel e-mailed to us, and something about the way he was described suggested to us that he had Attention Deficit Disorder. We asked Diane, the director, so she checked with the orphanage and reported to us that it might well be the case. Having some experience with ADD, we did not feel ready to raise a boy with that problem and still give Kurt and Mary the attention they deserved and needed.

The next child referred to us was a seven-year-old named Squire. Diane was quite frank and open with us about Squire's background. He was born in a rural village where his mother ran a small grocery store. Somehow, she had run afoul of some others in the village who were bent on revenge and used the war as an excuse to exact it. When they became soldiers, they came back to the village and murdered her. They then decapitated her and drove around town with her severed head mounted on the front of their jeep. Squire witnessed this. His father's fate was arguably worse: the rebels chopped off all four of his limbs. For a time, Squire was the only one available to care for him. We wanted to take Squire because here was a boy who truly needed a loving family. But could we handle him? How would the trauma that Squire had suffered affect his mental health and behavior? Could we handle a child with PTSD? We didn't know that much about it and were afraid that we couldn't, that if the syndrome emerged it would disrupt our family more than we could manage or than we wanted to impose on Mary and Kurt, so we weren't willing to risk adopting Squire. Put bluntly, again, it would require more bravery than we could muster.

There was a third child who, given the story we were told of how he became orphaned, had likely also suffered trauma. This was GB. His parents, so the court documents said, had been murdered by the rebels as they fled from Makeni on their way to the capital. But he had been very young at the time, not much older than two. And we knew something else important about him: he had been with his mother during those critical first two years of life. This, we knew, was essential to forming healthy attachments. Of course, GB might suffer emotional problems, but there seemed a good chance that we, and he, could cope with them. So, we began the adoption process for the boy who became our son Gibrila.

But still there were choices. The Children's Home suggested that we take another child, a girl named Sia, who was, they said, a child who had lived in the same house as GB. Later they told us that Sia was GB's younger cousin. We didn't learn until much later that she was actually GB's half-sibling, nor did we realize that the two considered themselves brother and sister until after the adoption took place. Even so, we were willing to consider the idea. Was there some kind of discount on fees, we asked, when you adopted a second child? There wasn't. We didn't think we could afford to spend another fifteen to twenty thousand dollars at that time, though if we had understood how close the children were, we would have scraped together the money. In the end, Sia was adopted by the Sibleys in Oregon, a very loving family indeed, and she and GB have now resumed their relationship.

Some critiques of adoption say that parents who adopt internationally seem to have a savior complex and that instead of feeling like saviors, these parents ought to feel guilty about having made this choice. We do feel guilt. But our bad feelings are not about the children we did adopt; they're about the ones we did not adopt. So, even if the adoption critics are right in accusing us of indulging a "savior complex," the process did not leave us feeling saintly.

Something Is Always Less-Than-Perfect

Though adoption may produce a happy outcome, it is inherently born of some less-than-perfect family situation. Never mind kidnapping; even an entirely fully-informed voluntary placement—even a placement with substantial compensation—involves the pain of a mother parting with her child. For older children, there is the added trauma of parting with their mothers (sometimes through death). Even the hypothetical person some see as the worst-case-possibility of a birth mother, the woman who becomes a "baby factory," is almost always motivated by desperate poverty. So even the most highly successful adoption, with a child happily ensconced in a loving family, seems to exploit someone else's misery.[4] We saw this clearly in Isata's story. The M. family was very determined to get their child out of Sierra Leone and into what they decided was a better life. But they suffered the agony of not knowing what happened to her, wondering whether they would ever see her again, or whether she was even still alive. No wonder some people are hostile to international adoption.

What, however, is the best alternative? In 2013, at a conference entitled "International Adoption: Orphan Rescue or Child Trafficking?" a well-known critic of IA explained how the whole system was irreparably corrupt. Mark raised his hand to ask a question. "If one hundred infants are adopted from

Uganda, we can expect that all of them will reach the age of five; but if they stay with their birth families we expect that only ninety-two will survive that long. How does the death of those eight children enter into the ethical calculus of opposition to adoption?" "You're comparing adoption," he said, "to what we have now. It ought to be that those children shouldn't die." He was right, of course—it shouldn't be that way. But what chance do we individuals have to alter that fact? In an ideal world, we would eradicate world poverty. Economist William Easterly has pointed out that in the past half century the West has poured a trillion dollars into African development with astonishingly little to show for that effort. Debates over how, and even whether, rich countries should intervene to help poor countries still rage. Meanwhile, a number of sub-Saharan countries are poorer today than they were at the time of independence.[5]

Yet if it is beyond the power of one family to help all of Africa, it is well within their power to help one African child. Or two or three. If they are permitted to do so, they can also help the families that gave birth to that child. There is always, as we have admitted, some sadness surrounding this exchange, but the sadness came first, not the adoption.

The Bottom Line

Do we really expect to influence adoption policy? The short answer is that directly influencing policy was not really the goal of our writing. Our target is the widespread mentality about international adoption that has helped bring about its near collapse.

Adoption, as we have argued, has been turned over to the bureaucrats. The logic of tight regulation is that children are virtually helpless and, to ensure their protection, government officials must vigorously supervise their transfer from one family to another. In general, we think this kind of caution is well warranted. After all, our laws don't allow parents, birth or otherwise, to physically abuse their children or to deny them food, shelter, or education, for example. In adoption policy, this protectionism seems to reach its zenith. Western parents wanting to adopt internationally must be visited by social workers both before and after the adoption; must submit letters of recommendation; and must have their police records, their income, and their assets officially scrutinized. In adopting GB, we even had to verify the licenses of the notaries who authenticated our documents. Overall, we think this kind of regulation makes a good deal of sense. It is not without drawbacks, of course; it increases costs, costs which are already prohibitive for some middle- and lower-middle-class families. But strong safeguards need to be in place.[6]

In contrast, birth families, even extended birth families, who receive children through reunification programs do not undergo the same level of safety checks. On its website, UNICEF tells us that in Africa it "convinces the family" to reabsorb the institutionalized child and gives an aid package to assist them. This can be a good thing to do for a child in an orphanage. But is it always better than being adopted abroad? Western families adopting African children do not need convincing; they are willing to spend thousands of dollars and endure the frustration of slogging through a bureaucratic quagmire to bring the child into their family. Yet, the Subsidiarity Principle treats as axiomatic the proposition that any in-country family will do a better job of raising the child than any foreign family. Why? Why are foreigners, in effect, the family-of-last resort?

The Subsidiarity Principle reflects, in part, the sense of shame that governments feel in having foreigners raise their children. International adoption can make sending-country governments seem incapable of protecting their own young, or perhaps indifferent to their children's fate. Subsidiarity has also achieved widespread acceptance among Western officials and even among adoption professionals. We speculate that this stems from an unwillingness to assert the politically incorrect proposition that children in rich countries enjoy "better" lives than children in poor countries—that view seems to embody the very essence of Western arrogance. Better to support the Subsidiarity Principle than to model Western arrogance and exploitation. Recall, for example, the statement from Save the Children that "poverty and a lack of resources *should never* be a reason for the separation of a child from his or her family" (emphasis original).[7] However, when you have received a letter from an African mother begging you to take her twelve-year-old son, you begin to question the wisdom of that proposition. The kind of children who are adopted abroad, whether from orphanages or from their original families, tend to be not just poor, but the poorest of the poor. They usually are the most vulnerable to malnutrition and disease, have the lowest life expectancies, and the fewest opportunities for education. As we calculated above, in a seven-year period in the first decade of the 2000s, international adoption from just two countries to the US saved the lives of hundreds of children.

But the Subsidiarity Principle was not formulated by poor mothers whose children face this kind of vulnerability. It was promulgated by government officials and other professionals who are themselves probably not poor and who are perfectly capable of raising their genetic birth children. Perhaps that sounds harsh and unfair. But is it unreasonable to ask why the priorities for vulnerable children are set not by their families, but instead entirely by officials? As we have seen, many, many parents in poor countries are eager to give their children a better life abroad, so eager that they will sometimes place them in institutions, or so eager that they will sometimes engage in fraud to make these adoptions possible. Who has the right to decide that these adoptions must only be a last resort?

We are not advocating abandoning anything that is politically incorrect in some willy-nilly fashion, simply for the sake of fighting the prevailing dictates of political correctness. That type of policy making is as foolish as adhering to the politically correct simply for the sake of avoiding looking racist, or homophobic, or imperialistic. Typically, there are good reasons why politically correct actions became considered "politically correct." We simply suggest examining these policies carefully for their effects on real people; in the case of international adoption, we have examined the effect of reducing IA to a trickle on vulnerable children and their birth families around the world.

International adoption, it is claimed, leads to child abandonment. But abandonment is often the only option available to birth parents to get a child adopted. The rules prevent direct contact and open negotiation between birth and adoptive families on the grounds that such negotiation might lead to the "sale" of children. And such sales are utter anathema to the officials who control adoption and to observers and commentators in the media and the academy. Child selling, or, actually, the transfer of parental rights, is considered "trafficking" and lumped together with kidnapping and with the transport of women and children for slave labor or sexual exploitation. But it has very little in common with these crimes. Moreover, direct communication between birth mothers and adoptive families is exactly how we eliminate such abuses. Sixty years ago, when out-of-wedlock birth had to be hidden and girls were sent away to give birth in special homes, abuse was common. Mothers were intensely pressured to give up their babies, or worse, told their child had been stillborn. The open adoption movement helped end this.

Even if "baby selling" were as cynical as adoption critics fear, motivated solely by money rather than consideration of a child's future, is it necessarily, therefore, not in her best interest? Imagine yourself an infant; given a choice between a family who would *sell* you for two thousand dollars and a family who would *buy* you for twenty thousand, which would you prefer to join? In our view, the obsessive fear of baby selling that seems to pervade every discussion of adoption does far less good, and far more harm, than most people realize.

Moreover, the absolute refusal of international adoption policy to even contemplate compensation of birth families makes the practice profoundly inequitable. Thousands upon thousands of dollars are expended presumably without a penny going into the hands of those making the biggest sacrifice. This inequity plays directly into the hands of critics who regard IA as neo-imperialist exploitation of the poor. The proscription of preplacement contact as a means of forestalling any hint of payment seems somewhat hypocritical when advocated by Americans—our open adoption movement, and the quasi-market it has engendered, have enormously empowered the once-exploited birth mothers.

Having said all that, do we honestly suppose this book will convince many people to accept what is almost universally considered a nefarious practice: pre-adoption contact and decriminalization of birth family compensation? We hope so. But our real hope is to put a dent, however tiny, in the mentality that fosters the "cult of nonpayment," as we have called it, that builds a firewall between birth and adoptive parents. This abhorrence of payment needs to be challenged; the topic of compensation should not be as utterly taboo as it obviously now is.

Our adoption experiences have taught us a great deal, not merely as parents and as people, but also as social scientists. The courses we teach have covered such issues as the racial composition of poverty, the differential unemployment rates of blacks and whites, and the stubborn racial gap in educational achievement. Before we got our sons, these were statistics; we never had to think about them personally. Now we have a better conception of what it means to be black in America—something more white people need to understand more deeply. And researching this book has allowed us to observe firsthand what we had previously recognized only in the abstract: that the rules and practices of international adoption discourage transparency and promote deception. Among other things, we discovered, as we had suspected, that GB's birth mother was not killed by the rebels; she was very much alive, and, importantly, we could help her financially.

We continue to believe that international adoption is a blessing for children, a blessing born of sadness to be sure, but a blessing nonetheless. Even if adoption represents a second-best solution to the problems facing a vulnerable child, it offers a viable solution and one that can give great joy. We think it a terrible shame, therefore, that the system now seems to be in steep decline. We provide the perception of two economists of why this is happening and how the situation could be improved. If this book does nothing more than to encourage a single family to adopt a child internationally, or persuade one policy maker to think less rigidly about compensation for birth families, it will have been well worth the effort of writing it.

We close with a story we ran across on our last trip to Kigali while rereading a famous book about the Rwandan genocide, *Shake Hands with the Devil*, by

Lieutenant General Romeo Dallaire, the Canadian commander of the UN peacekeeping mission there at the time.

On a bright May morning in 1994, the general and two staff members were driving on a road along which "most of the people in the surrounding villages had been slaughtered," when he saw a child of about three on the roadside.[8] The boy was caked in dirt, his hair was white with dust, and he was "encrusted with flies, which were greedily attacking the open sores that covered him." Dallaire followed the boy into a hut where his dead family lay decomposing, and, on carrying him out in his arms, the general found, "I made up my mind, this boy would be the fourth in the Dallaire family. I couldn't save Rwanda, but I could save this boy."

This decision, however, was entirely at odds with the policy toward adoption that the general himself had firmly established. "Before I held this boy I had agreed with aid workers and representatives of both warring armies that I would not permit any exporting of Rwandan orphans to foreign places.... I would argue that the money to move a hundred kids by plane to France or Belgium could help build, staff and sustain Rwandan orphanages that could house three thousand children."[9]

But holding this child, the general admits, "eradicated all of my arguments."[10] After all, what would be better for this boy: living in an institution or living in a loving family?[11] His path seemed clear; he would take and adopt this boy. Would the money saved from flying this child and others abroad actually be spent on Rwandan orphans? Apparently, the general was succumbing to the infamous "savior complex" that adoption critics complain about. "I could see myself at the terminal in Montreal, like a latter-day St. Christopher with the boy cradled in my arms, my wife, Beth, there ready to embrace him." But the adoption was not to take place. An armed teenage soldier of the RPF, the army that drove out the genocidaires, told the general firmly that his comrades would care for the boy; the general could not take him to the hospital as planned. The general, unwilling to risk a confrontation that could put lives at risk, let the boy go. The soldier disappeared into the bush with the child. Neither we nor the general ever learned of the boy's fate.

For the general, not adopting this boy symbolizes failure, how "ineffective and irresponsible we [the UN and World Powers] were when we promised the Rwandans that we would... allow them to achieve a lasting peace."[12] To us, it also symbolizes something else: how adoption may be a strong motivation to help a child when no other motivation will work, and how weak the theoretical arguments against international adoption are when confronted with a real child in desperate need of a home and family.

NOTES

PREFACE

1. The details of the stories about Isata and Sia come from interviews and email exchanges with Jason, Beckie, and Isata Sibley over the period from October 2012 to July 2015. Information about Isata's birth family comes from interviews with her brother, whom we call Shaun M., and her father, whom we call Pa M., in Freetown, January 2013, and subsequent email exchanges with Shaun M. from July 2013 to July 2015.

2. These figures are for the twenty-three countries receiving the most adoptees. Peter Selman, *Key Tables for Intercountry Adoption: Receiving States 2003–2012; States of Origin 2003–2011*, March 26, 2014, *www.hcch.net/upload/selmanstats33.pdf*. Also available on request from pfselman@yahoo.co.uk.

3. Now Cuttington University.

4. This book discusses only sub-Saharan Africa. North Africa is mostly Muslim, and Islam does not approve of adoption in the Western sense of the term.

5. We only use true names, including that of this orphanage, when we have been given explicit permission or when the person referred to has a public role in the adoption world.

6. Ethan B. Kapstein, "The Baby Trade," *Foreign Affairs* 82, no. 6 (Nov–Dec 2003): 115.

7. See, for example, Barbara Katz Rothman, "Motherhood under Capitalism," in *Consuming Motherhood*, eds. Janelle Taylor and Linda Layne (New Brunswick, NJ: Rutgers University Press, 2014), 19–30; Madelyn Fruendlich, *The Market Forces in Adoption*, vol. 2, *Adoption and Ethics* (New York: Donaldson Adoption Institute, 2000); Jack Darcher, "Market Forces in Domestic Adoption: Advocating a Quantitative Limit on Private Agency Adoption Fees," *Journal for Social Justice* 8, no. 2 (Spring/Summer 2010): 729–772; Deborah Spar, *The Baby Business: How Money, Science, and Politics Drive the Commerce of Conception* (Cambridge, MA: Harvard Business School Press, 2006).

INTRODUCTION

1. Quoted in Chaitali B. Roy, "Child Trafficking New Form of Slavery," *Arab Times*, Kuwait English Daily, May 19, 2014.

2. Scott Straus, *The Order of Genocide: Race, Power, and War in Rwanda* (Ithaca, NY: Cornell University Press, 2008), Kindle edition.

3. Peterson reports that in March 1992, in a lead-up to the larger genocide, there was a massacre in Bugesera for which "an order went out to the local authorities, who told people that there was going to be a special collective work session 'to clear the bush'; everyone knew this meant to kill the Tutsi. The killing of women and children was called 'pulling out the bad weeds.'" Quoted in Scott Peterson, *Me Against My Brother: At War in Somalia, Sudan and Rwanda* (New York: Routledge, 2001), 270–271. For more on the Hutu/Tutsi genocide, see Jean Hatzfeld, *The Killers of Rwanda Speak*, trans. Linda Coverdale (New York: Farrar, Straus and Giroux, 2006) and Jean Hatzfeld, *Life Laid Bare: The Survivors of Rwanda Speak*, trans. Linda Coverdale (New York: Farrar, Straus and Giroux, 2006).

4. Peterson, *Me Against My Brother*, 270–271.

5. The minister, Aloisea Inyumba, died in December 2012. Mr. Nzaramba was later transferred to another department of the government.

6. For a thorough discussion of the harm done by institutionalization, see Rebecca J. Compton, *Adoption Beyond Borders: How International Adoption Benefits Children* (Oxford: Oxford University Press, 2016).

7. Quoted in Trish Maskew, "Child Trafficking and Intercountry Adoption: The Cambodian Experience," *Cumberland Law Review* 35, no. 3 (2004/2005): 621.

8. Kevin Voigt, "International Adoption: Saving Orphans or Child Trafficking?" CNN, September 18, 2013, *www.cnn.com/2013/09/16/world/international-adoption-saving-orphans-child-trafficking*. We have tried unsuccessfully to find the original source of this statistic, which is quite widely quoted. It should be viewed with proper caution.

9. Rachel Swarns, "A Family, for a Few Days a Year," *New York Times*, December 8, 2012.

10. Daniel Nasaw, "Vietnam Stops US Adoption Programme," *Guardian*, May 1, 2008.

11. Kathryn Joyce, *The Child Catchers: Rescue, Trafficking, and the New Gospel of Adoption* (New York: Public Affairs, 2013), 136.

12. Voigt, "International Adoption."

13. US State Department, Alerts & Notices, "International Adoption: Learn about a Country, Alerts and Notices—Ethiopia," April 5, 2011, *travel.state.gov/content/adoptionsabroad/en/country-information/alerts-and-notices*.

14. Zeryhun Kassa, "Ethiopia: Stakeholders, Public Has to End Foreign Adoption," Ethiopian Radio and Television Agency (Addis Ababa), December 26, 2013.

15. US State Department, Alerts & Notices, "International Adoption: Learn about a Country, Alerts and Notices—Ethiopia," May 2, 2017, *travel.state.gov/content/adoptionsabroad/en/country-information/alerts-and-notices*.

16. Joyce, *The Child Catchers*, 137.

17. Selman, *Key Tables*.

18. Most notably among the adoptive parents is David Smolin, a law professor at Samford University, who adopted two girls from India. We learned in a personal interview with him in June 2012 that he and his wife discovered that the two girls they adopted from India had in effect been stolen from their birth mother. It is inaccurate to call Smolin an opponent of international adoption, however. As he told CCN, "I'm not a proponent of shutting down intercountry adoption," but when a large amount of

cash comes to developing countries with weak governments, "it reproduces systematic problems over and over again." Quoted in Voigt "International Adoption."

19. UNICEF, *Africa's Orphaned Generations* (New York: UNICEF, November 2003), *www.unicef.org/sowc06/pdfs/africas_orphans.pdf*, 3.

20. Elizabeth Bartholet, "Intergenerational Justice for Children: Restructuring Adoption, Reproduction and Child Welfare Policy," *Law, Ethics and Human Rights* 8, no. 1 (2014): 121.

21. See, for example, Elizabeth Bartholet, "International Adoption: Thoughts on the Human Rights Issues," *Buffalo Human Rights Law Review* 13 (2007).

22. Jessica Elgot, "Madonna, Angelina Jolie Criticised for African Adoptions by Mozambique Supermodel Tasha da Vasconcelo," *Huffington Post UK*, February 7, 2013.

23. David Smolin, "Poor Children for Rich People," in "Celebrity Adoptions and the Real World," *New York Times*, May 10, 2009.

24. Smolin has made this clear in a number of public talks and in a private interview with the authors.

25. Growing up in the 1960s, we can recall people who opposed interracial marriage not because of prejudice (they said) but because it was "unfair to the children."

26. "UNICEF Data on Orphans by Region to 2010 [Chart]," Children and Youth in History, item no. 293, accessed August 27, 2014, *chnm.gmu.edu/cyh/primary-sources/293*.

27. Ofeibea Quist-Arcton, "For Ebola Orphans in Liberia, It's a Bittersweet New Beginning," Goats and Soda (Blog), NPR, December 4, 2014, *www.npr.org/blogs/goatsandsoda/2014/12/04/368408240/charities-help-ebola-orphans-start-over*.

28. See, for example, Joyce, *The Child Catchers* and Laura Briggs, *Somebody's Children: The Politics of Transracial and Transnational Adoption* (Durham, NC: Duke University Press, 2012).

29. E. J. Graff, "The Seamier Side of International Adoption," in "Celebrity Adoptions and the Real World," *New York Times*, May 10, 2009.

30. We had not chosen to sponsor this child. We were sending money to the orphanage for whatever use they wished, but because people are more likely to give to help a particular child, they automatically assigned a "sponsored child" to us.

31. Hillary Whitman, "African Adoption Should be Discouraged 'At All Costs,' Group Says," CNN, May 31, 2012, *www.cnn.com/2012/05/29/world/africa/africa-child-adoption*.

32. Heather Jacobson, *Culture Keeping: White Mothers, International Adoption, and the Negotiation of Family Difference* (Nashville, TN: Vanderbilt University Press, 2008).

33. This may partly be because Russian adoptees so often have more severe problems. In "Cold War Kids: The International Dispute Over Russia's Orphans" (*Harper's Magazine*, October 2013), Irina Aleksander quotes neuropsychologist Ronald Federici saying, "'That there are there are three things indigenous to Russian adoptees.' The first is the psychological damage caused by abandonment and neglect in state-run institutions. The second is the neurological damage caused by 'drinking and

drugging' and the third is the 'physical, sexual and emotional abuse that ran rampant in these institutions.'"

34. Lynn H. Nicholas, *Cruel World: The Children of Europe in the Nazi Web* (New York: Alfred A. Knopf, 2005).

35. David Fanshel, *Far from the Reservation* (Lanham, MD: Scarecrow Press Inc., 1972).

36. Sloan Philips, "The Indian Child Welfare Act in the Face of Extinction," *American Indian Law Review* 21, no. 2 (1997).

37. Judy Klemesrud, "Furor Over Whites Adopting Blacks," *New York Times*, April 12, 1972.

38. Among academics, the very use of the term "race" is contentious because there is no clear biological basis for separating people into distinct racial categories. And, historically, differentiation among races has often been based on arbitrary criteria, such as the "one drop rule" in the United States. We will continue to use the word race, however, to refer to physical differences typically termed "racial."

39. Jans Jeong Trenka, Julia Chinyere Oparah, and Sun Yung Sin, eds., *Outsiders Within: Writing on Transracial Adoption* (Cambridge, MA: South End Press, 2006), 4.

40. Rita J. Simon, Howard Altstein, and Marygold S. Melli, *The Case for Transracial Adoption* (Washington, DC: American University Press, 1994), 39.

41. A conference we attended at the Pepperdine University Law School in February 2013 was even titled "International Adoption: Orphan Rescue or Child Trafficking?"

42. David Smolin, "Intercountry Adoption as Child Trafficking," *Valparaiso Law Review* 39, no. 2 (2004/2005): 282.

43. E. J. Graff, "Call It Trafficking," *American Prospect*, January 3, 2013. *prospect.org/article/call-it-trafficking.*

44. Gina Kim, "International Adoption's Trafficking Problem," *Harvard Political Review*, June 20, 2012, *harvardpolitics.com/world/international-adoptions-trafficking-problem.*

45. Hague Conference on Private International Law, *Convention on Protection of Children and Co-operation in Respect of Intercountry Adoption, Concluded 29 May 1993* (The Hague: HCCH, 1993), *www.hcch.net/en/instruments/conventions/full-text/?cid=69.*

46. Nigel Cantwell, *The Best Interests of the Child in Intercountry Adoption*, Innocenti Insight (Florence: UNICEF Office of Research, 2014), 5. *www.unicef-irc.org/publications/712.*

47. George Fitzhugh, *Sociology of the South; or, The Failure of Free Society* (Richmond, VA: A. Morris Publisher, 1854), from University of North Carolina-Chapel Hill, Documenting the South: Library of Southern Literature, accessed May 29, 2013, *docsouth.unc.edu/southlit/fitzhughsoc/menu.html*, 7.

48. Ibid., 21.

49. Ibid., 84.

50. But the reader will wonder how any intelligent person could ignore the horrors of slave ships on the Middle Passage or the agonizing breaking up of families when slaves were sold. Those, Fitzhugh said, were not part of slavery, but of the slave *trade*. And who ran the slave trade? Yankees.

51. Johanna Oreskovic and Trish Maskew, "Red Thread or Slender Reed: Deconstructing Prof. Bartholet's Mythology of International Adoption," *Buffalo Human Rights Law Review* 147 (2008): 102.

52. Fitzhugh, *Sociology of the South*, 278.

53. Tobias Hubinette, "From Orphan Trains to Babylifts," in Trenka, Oparah, and Shin, *Outsiders Within*, 43.

54. It was our good fortune not to have had fertility problems, but we have seen friends and family struggle to conceive, as well as witnessed gay and lesbian families try to negotiate the adoption system. We do not mean to dismiss their difficulties, needs, and emotions.

55. Joyce, *The Child Catchers*, 250.

56. Quoted in ibid.

ISATA'S STORY, PART I

1. We changed the name for reasons that become clear later in the book.

CHAPTER 1

1. Peter Opa, "Child Poverty: Difference between Africa and America," OpEdNews.com, November 21, 2013, *www.opednews.com*.

2. *The World Factbook* (Washington, DC: Central Intelligence Agency, 2012–2013).

3. Erin Siegal, *Finding Fernanda: Two Mothers, One Child, and a Cross-Border Search for Truth* (Boston: Beacon Press Books, 2011), 96.

4. Calculated by computing expected death rates for infants and children one to five, respectively, in Guatemala and the US, using UN mortality statistics. Calculated as $[\text{deaths}/1000_{\text{Guatamala}} - \text{deaths}/1000_{\text{US}}] \times [\text{adoptions}/1000]$. Mortality statistics from Millennium Development Goals Indicators, *mdgs.un.org/unsd/mdg*; adoption statistics from "Intercountry Adoption, Statistics," US State Department, *travel.state.gov/content/adoptionsabroad/en/about-us/statistics.htm*.

5. World Health Organization, *World Malaria Report 2014* (Geneva: WHO Press, 2014) *www.who.int/malaria/publications/world_malaria_report_2014/en*.

6. Quoted in Roger Bate, "Without DDT, Malaria Bites Back," *Spiked*, April 24, 2001, *www.spiked-online.com/newsite/article/11697#.WYI3mIgrJPY*.

7. Jeffrey Sachs and Pia Malaney, "The Economic and Social Burden of Malaria," *Nature* 145 (February 7, 2002).

8. "Malaria: The Challenge," The Malaria Consortium, accessed August 9, 2014, *www.malariaconsortium.org/pages/malaria_challenges.htm*.

9. "Factsheet on Intestinal Worms," World Health Organization, last modified May 2015, *www.who.int/intestinal_worms/en*.

10. Edward Miguel and Michael Kremer, "Worms: Identifying Impacts on Education and Health in the Presence of Treatment Externalities," *Econometrica* 72, no. 1

(January 2004). WHO recommends the periodic administration of anthelminthic for soil transmitted helminths (STH) for children (from one to fifteen years of age) living in areas where the prevalence of STH is estimated to be over 20 percent. "Soil-Transmitted Helminth Infections," World Health Organization, last modified January 2007, *www.who.int/mediacentre/factsheets/fs366/en.*

11. "Prevalence of Undernourishment (% of Population)," World Bank, accessed September 7, 2014, *data.worldbank.org/indicator/SN.ITK.DEFC.ZS.*

12. Dana E. Johnson, "Thirty Years of International Adoption: Lessons Learned" (presentation to Putting Family First Conference, sponsored by the Joint Council on International Children's Services and the Adoption Council, Arlington, VA, June 22–24, 2015).

13. Compton, *Adoption Beyond Borders*, 26–36. Notably, one area in which internationally adopted children lag behind their new non-adopted peers (though still out perform their former peers) is in executive function as measured over time. Executive functions include higher-level problem solving, planning, and control of impulsive behavior and are controlled by the brain's prefrontal cortex. As Compton, who is a biological psychologist, says, "development of the prefrontal cortex is affected by early-life social deprivation" (32).

14. Authors' calculations based on figures from *The World Factbook* (Washington DC: Central Intelligence Agency, 2013).

15. The latter figure is included because in many poor countries secondary and postsecondary schooling represent a smaller fraction of the total spending.

16. We are aware of the limitations of using expenditure per student as a measure of educational quality. See, for example, Gary Burtless, ed., *Does Money Matter?* (Washington, DC: Brookings Institution Press, 1996) and Helena Holmlund, Sandra McNally, and Martina Viarengo, "Does Money Matter for Schools?" *Economics of Education Review* 29, no. 6 (December 2010): 1154–64. But the spending gaps identified in this table surely overwhelm such measurement errors as are discussed in this literature.

17. Jeffrey Chaudhary, et al., "Missing in Action: Teacher and Health Worker Absence in Developing Countries," *Journal of Economic Perspectives* 20, no. 1 (Winter 2006).

18. R. Inglehart and H-D. Klingemann, "Genes, Culture, Democracy and Happiness," in *Culture and Subjective Well-being*, eds. E. Diener and E. M. Suh (Cambridge, MA: MIT Press, 2000).

19. Richard Layard, "Has Social Science a Clue?: What is Happiness? Are We Getting Happier?" (Lionel Robbins Memorial Lecture Series, London, March 3–5, 2003).

20. Irene Jay Liu, "Smuggled Chinese Travel Circuitously to the U.S.," NPR, November 20, 2007, *www.npr.org/templates/story/story.php?storyId=16422719.*

21. Malcolm Gladwell and Rachel E. Stassen-Berger, "A Booming Business in Smuggling of Chinese—New York Tragedy is One of Many Cases of Profiting on Dreams," *Washington Post*, June 7, 1993.

22. Ryan Roberts et al., "An Analysis of Migrant Smuggling Costs along the Southwest Border" (working paper, Office of Immigration Statistics, Department of Homeland Security, Washington, DC, November 2010) *www.dhs.gov/xlibrary/assets/statistics/publications/ois-smuggling-wp.pdf.*

23. *The World Factbook*, 2013.

24. Marc Silver, "Bodies on the Border," *New York Times*, August 17, 2013.

25. Scott Glover, "Pair Arrested in Green Card Marriage that Resulted from Web Ads," *Los Angeles Times*, December 7, 2007.

26. "Any individual who knowingly enters into a marriage for the purpose of evading any provision of the immigration laws shall be imprisoned for not more than 5 years, or fined not more than $250,000, or both" (8 U.S.C. § 1325[c]). It must be admitted, however, that the actual penalty can be *considerably* smaller. See, for example, Edecio Martinez, "Mexican Actress Fernanda Romero Gets 30 Days in Sham Marriage Case," CBS News, April 27, 2011, *www.cbsnews.com/news/mexican-actress-fernand-romera-gets-30-days-in-sham-marriage-case*.

27. Erica Pearson, "Proving Love to the Feds: Inside the Unit that Makes Sure Green Card Marriages are Real," *New York Daily News*, May 20, 2012.

28. Sara Dillon, "Making Legal Regimes for Intercountry Adoption Reflect Human Rights Principles: Transforming the United Nations Convention on the Rights of the Child with the Hague Convention on Intercountry Adoption," *Boston University International Law Journal* 1 (Fall 2003): 179.

29. Christie Schoenmaker, et al., "Does Family Matter? The Well-Being of Children Growing Up in Institutions, Foster Care and Adoption," in *The Handbook of Child Well-Being: Theories, Methods and Policies in Global Perspective*, eds. Asher Ben-Arieh, et al. (New York: Springer Science and Business Media, 2014), 2218.

30. Kelly McCreery Bunkers, Victor Groza, and Daniel P. Lauer, "International Adoption and Child Protection in Guatemala: A Case of the Tail Wagging the Dog," *International Social Work* 52, no. 5 (2009): 650.

31. Elizabeth Bartholet, "International Adoption: The Human Rights Position," *Global Policy* 1, no. 1 (January 2010): 95.

32. Save the Children, Child Protection Initiative, *International Adoption*, policy brief, June 2012, *resourcecentre.savethechildren.net/node/6250/pdf/6250.pdf*, 1.

33. Ellen Pinderhughes, et al., *A Changing World: Shaping Practices through Understanding of the New Realities of Intercountry Adoption* (New York: Donaldson Adoption Institute, October 2013), *www.adoptioninstitute.org/wp-content/uploads/2013/12/2013_10_AChangingWorld.pdf*, 9.

ISATA'S STORY, PART II

1. Joseph Opala, "What the West Failed to See in Sierra Leone," *Washington Post*, May 14, 2000.

2. Douglas Farah, "Children Forced to Kill," *Washington Post*, April 8, 2000.

3. Norimitsu Onish, "A Brutal War's Machetes Maim Sierra Leone," *New York Times*, January 26, 1999.

4. In 2013, Charles Taylor was found guilty and sentenced to fifty years in prison by a UN-sponsored tribunal.

5. Communications are from a private correspondence in December 2015. They have been edited slightly for grammar and clarity.

6. "Sierra Leone Profile," News Africa, BBC, January 15, 2015, *www.bbc.co.uk/news/world-Africa-14094194*.

CHAPTER 2

1. *Abandoned in Guatemala: The Failure of International Adoption Policies*, produced by Paul Feine and Alex Manning, Reason TV, 20:00, October 6, 2011, *reason.com/blog/2011/10/06/reasontv-abandoned-in-guatemal*.
2. Corey Kilgannon, "Doctor Saves African Boy, and Vice Versa..." *New York Times*, May 31, 2003.
3. We must acknowledge, however, that while Gibrila may not pine for his birth *culture*, he sorely misses his birth *climate*. He constantly complains about the cold in Iowa. When he first arrived in April 2002, we were having a chilly spring, colder weather than he had likely ever experienced. A few months later, in midsummer, we started air conditioning our Victorian house. At that time, a large air conditioner set in the dining room wall was used to cool the whole first floor. Naturally, whenever Gibrila walked through the dining room on his way to the kitchen, he felt the cool blast from that machine. One day he pointed to the machine and said to Tinker, "Dees make de room *COLD!*" He was clearly mystified by this. Americans live in a cold climate, and when the weather finally gets a little bit warm, they use a machine to make the house cold again. He quite obviously thought this insane. He has made it clear that when we visit him as an adult we can expect to drive to Florida or Arizona.
4. Even for boys, who anecdotal evidence suggests may feel less connection to their missing past than girl adoptees.
5. Will Bennet, "My Zulu Boy was Legally Abducted," *Independent*, May 6, 1996.
6. Quoted in Michael Freeman, "Culture, Childhood and Rights," *Family in Law Review* 5, no. 15 (2011): 21.
7. Quoted in Latiefa Albertus and Julia Sloth-Nielsen, "Relocation Decisions: Do Culture, Language and Religion Matter in the Rainbow Nation?" *Journal of Family Law and Practice* 1, no. 2 (Autumn 2010): 86.
8. Ibid.
9. Whitman, "African Adoption Should be Discouraged."
10. J. L. Roby and Stacey A. Shaw, "The African Orphan Crisis and International Adoption," *Social Work* 51, no. 3 (July 2006): 203.
11. Veronica S. Root, "Angelina and Madonna: Why All the Fuss? An Exploration of the Rights of the Child and Intercountry Adoption within African Nations," *Chicago Journal of International Law* 8, no. 1 (Summer 2007): 324.
12. Ibid., 345–346.
13. Prior to the efforts of the Holts, there was also widespread adoption of orphaned refugee children after World War II.
14. "Bertha and Harry Holt," Adoption History Project, University of Oregon, last updated Feb. 24, 2012, *darkwing.uoregon.edu/~adoption/people/holt.htm*.

15. David R. Black and Shona Bezanso, "The Olympic Games, Human Rights, and Democritisation: Lessons from Seoul and Implications for Beijing," *Third World Quarterly* 25, no. 7 (2004).

16. Matthew Rothschild, "Babies for Sale: South Koreans Make Them, Americans Buy Them," *Progressive* 52, no. 1 (January 1988), 18.

17. Quoted in ibid., 20.

18. Ibid., 21.

19. Quoted in ibid., 21.

20. Tobias Hubinette, "The Adoption Issue in Korea: Diaspora in the Age of Globalization," *Stockholm Journal of East Asian Studies* 12 (2000).

21. *POV*, "First Person Plural," written and directed by Deann Borshay Liem, PBS, Dec. 18, 2000 (premiere broadcast). Transcript of the relevant section, "History of Adoptions from Korea," available at *www.pbs.org/pov/firstpersonplural/history*.

22. Tobias Hubinette, *Comforting an Orphaned Nation: Representations of International Adoption and Adopted Koreans in Korean Popular Culture* (Stockholm: Stockholm University, Department of Oriental Languages, 2005), 69.

23. Ibid., 74.

24. Ibid.

25. Elizabeth Bartholet, *Family Bonds: Adoption, Infertility, and the New World of Child Production* (Boston: Beacon Press, 1999), 91.

26. "Reason.tv: Abandoned in Guatemala—The Failure of International Adoption Policies," Hit & Run Blog, Reason.com, October 6, 2011, *reason.com/blog/2011/ 10/06/reasontv-abandoned-in-guatemal*.

27. *Abandoned in Guatemala*, Reason TV.

28. Will Stewart, "Fury as US Woman Adopts Russian Boy…," *Daily Mail*, April 9, 2010, online edition, *www.dailymail.co.uk/news/article-1264744/American-sends-adopted-Russian-boy-behavioural-problems.html*.

29. Ibid.

30. Clifford J. Levy, "Russia Seeks Ways to Keep its Children," *New York Times*, April 15, 2010.

31. As quoted in Aleksander, "Cold War Kids," 66.

32. Levy, "Russia Seeks Ways."

33. Aleksander, "Cold War Kids."

34. Levy, "Russia Seeks Ways."

35. Aleksander, "Cold War Kids," 65.

36. Ibid., 66.

37. US State Department, Office of the Spokesperson, "United States—Russia Bilateral Adoption Agreement," media note, October 18, 2012, *2009-2017.state.gov/p/eur/rls/ prsrl/c49244.htm*.

38. Adam Taylor, "The Man Behind the Magnitsky Act Explains Why Now is Time to go After the Russian Elite's Assets," *Washington Post*, March 3, 2014. *www.washingtonpost. com/news/worldviews/wp/2014/03/03/the-man-behind-the-magnitsky-act-explains-why-now-is-the-time-to-go-after-the-russian-elites-assets*.

39. Alissa De Carbonnel, "Russian Lawyer Likely Beaten to Death: Kremlin Council," Reuters, July 6, 2011, *www.reuters.com*.

40. "Russia Human Rights Legislation Passes Foreign Affairs Committee," statement by Ileana Ros-Lehtinen, Committee Charmain, Committee on Foreign Affairs, US House of Representatives, June 7, 2012, *archives.republicans.foreignaffairs.house.gov/ news/story/?2401*.

41. Will Englund, "Russia Chafes as House Passes Magnitsky Act," *Washington Post*, November 6, 2012, *www.washingtonpost.com*.

42. Quoted in Aleksander, "Cold War Kids," 72.

43. See Dana Naughton, "Exiting or Going Forth? An Overview of USA Outgoing Adoptions," in Gibbons and Rotabi, *Intercountry Adoption*.

44. Alan Elsner, "Trial and Execution: The Dramatic Deaths of Nicolae and Elena Ceausescu," *World Post*, July 22, 2010, *www.huffington post.com*.

45. Ronald D. Bachman, ed., *Romania: A Country Study* (Washington, DC: Federal Research Division, Library of Congress, 1989), *www.loc.gov/item/90006449*.

46. Ibid.

47. Karen Breslau, "Overplanned Parenthood: Ceausescu's Cruel Law," *Newsweek*, January 22, 1990.

48. Ibid., 36.

49. Bachman, *Romania: A Country Study*, 74.

50. Christina Nedclu and Victor Groza, "Child Welfare in Romania: Contexts and Processes," in Gibbons and Rotabi, *Intercountry Adoption: Policies, Practices and Outcomes*, 92.

51. Ibid, 92.

52. "Inhumane Conditions for Romania's Lost Generation," ABC News, June 8, 2000, *abcnews.go.com/2020/story?id=124078*.

53. Mary Battiata, "20/20 Inside Romanian Orphanages" *Washington Post*, October 5, 1990.

54. Carol Lawson, "Doctor Acts to Heal Romania's Wound of Baby Trafficking," *New York Times*, October 3, 1991.

55. Peter Selman, "Global Trends in Intercountry Adoption: 2001–2010," *Adoption Advocate* (a publication of the National Council for Adoption) no. 44 (February 1, 2012), *www.adoptioncouncil.org/images/stories/documents/NCFA_ADOPTION_ ADVOCATE_NO44.pdf*.

56. Thomas Schuler, "'Child Wanted, Cash Paid' The Shady World of Adoption," *Atlantic Times*, March 2010, *www.atlantic-times.com/archive_detail.php?recordID=2113*.

57. Kathleen Hunt, "The Romanian Baby Bazaar" *New York Times*, March 24, 1991.

58. Alexandra Zugravescu and Ana Iacovescu, "The Adoption of Children in Romania," in *Intercountry Adoptions: Laws and Perspectives of "Sending" Countries*, ed. Eliezer D. Jaffe (Leiden: Martinus Nijoff Publishers, 1995), 52.

59. Different organizations use different translations of this committee's name and therefore different initials to represent it: RAC, RCA, or CRA. Unless used in a specific quote, we will use the form used by USAID, RAC.

60. Lawson, "Doctor Acts to Heal Romania's Wound."

61. Zugravescu and Iacovescu, "The Adoption of Children in Romania," 50.

62. Independent Group for International Adoption Analysis, *Final Report: Re-Organizing the International Adoption System and Child Protection System* (Bucharest: IGIAA, March 2002), 18.

63. Although, it must be acknowledged that the Hunt article preceded the passage of new adoption law by a few months. We don't know whether the law drove M. out of business.

64. Michael W. Ambrose and Anna Mary Coburn, *Report on Intercountry Adoption in Romania*, prepared for USAID in Romania, January 22, 2001, *pdf.usaid.gov/pdf_docs/Pnacw989.pdf*, 5.

65. Ibid., 6.

66. Jane Perlez, "Romanian 'Orphans': Prisoners of Their Cribs," *New York Times*, March 25, 1996.

67. Quoted in ibid.

68. Or even millions. A 1993 study by the Bucharest-based Institute for Researching the Quality of Life found that "only 10.3 percent of the country's children lived in decent conditions." Camelia Manuela Lataianu, "Social Protection of Children in Public Care in Romania from the Perspective of EU Integration," *International Journal of Law Policy and the Family* 17, no. 1 (April 2003): 100.

69. Ibid., 22.

70. Quoted in Roelie Post, *Romania: For Export Only, The Untold Story of Romanian "Orphans"* (Hoekstra Drukkerij: Sint Annaparochie, Netherlands, 2007), Kindle edition, location 237.

71. Blog post by Sandra Hanks Benoiton, InternationalAdoptionBlogs.com, June 14, 2006, retrieved from ChineseAdoptionBookmarks.com. *chineseadoptionbookmarks.com/sites/090579/International-Adoption-Child-Adoption-Categories-Nastiness-and-shoddy-practices-Corruption-The-UN-index.html*.

72. Andy Beckett, "Profile: Emma Nicholson: Not Her Sort of Party," *Independent*, December 31, 1995.

73. Ibid.

74. Unfortunately, the relationship between Nicholson and Amar later deteriorated, though it is not clear how or why. A 2004 article in the *Telegraph* reported, "Now 23, unemployed and homeless, Amar claims he has been abandoned by Lady Nicholson... Lady Nicholson, now an MEP for a constituency in the South East, denied she had abandoned Amar and said he had left her." Richard Alleyne, "'Sometimes I Wish I Had Not Been Saved,'" *Telegraph*, March 5, 2004. The article also refers to Amar as a "quasi-adopted son." What is clear is that Amar had a number of difficulties growing up, including severe facial scarring, and that these affected his ability to cope with life and his relationship with Nicholson. After thirty years as parents we know better than to try to judge what happened or to assign blame in a difficult parent-child relationship.

75. Emma Nicholson, *The Secret Society: Inside and Outside the Conservative Party* (London: Indigo, 1996), 30.

76. Ibid., 215.

77. Beckett, "Profile: Emma Nicholson."

78. Post, *Romania: For Export Only*, location 1365.

79. Quoted in Roy, "Child Trafficking."

80. Ibid.

81. Virginia Hughes, "Detachment: Can Research on Romanian Orphans Be Ethical?" *Aeon Magazine*, May 12, 2014.

82. The troubling aspect of the MacArthur study, at least outside the scientific community, was the fact that the 136 children under study were randomly assigned to either remain in the orphanage or join a foster family. The logic of randomization, as always, was to ensure the two "treatment" groups would not differ systematically on some measure (e.g. appearance, intelligence, behavior) that was correlated with the outcome. See Hughes, "Detachment."

83. Roy, "Child Trafficking."

84. Tom Wilson, "Romania Rethinks Adoption Ban Despite Child-Trafficking Concerns," *Deutsche Welt*, April 26, 2014.

85. Yves Denechere and Beatrice Scutaru, "International Adoption of Romanian Children and Romania's Admission to the European Union," *Eastern Journal of European Studies* 1, no. 1 (June 2010): 144.

86. Post, *Romania: For Export Only*, location 1975.

87. Ibid., location 1975.

88. Denechere and Scutaru, "International Adoption."

89. Post, *Romania: For Export Only*, location 919.

90. Denechere and Scutaru, "International Adoption."

91. Post, *Romania: For Export Only*, location 4068.

92. Reported in *Le Monde*, October 5, 2002. Quoted in Denechere and Scaturu, "International Adoption," 146.

93. *Permanent Extension of Most-Favored Nation (MFN) Trade Status to Romania, Hearing Before the Subcommittee on International Trade and Finance on H.R. 3161 and W.S. 1644.* 104th Cong. (June 4, 1996), 38.

94. Post, *Romania: For Export Only*, location 2375.

95. Do we exaggerate? Technically, under Article 39 of Law 274/2004, a foreign couple could still adopt a Romanian child if they managed to meet one small condition: they were the child's *actual biological grandparents.*

96. Jeffrey Thomas, "Congressional Resolution Urges Romania to Amend Adoption Ban," *Washington File*, April 11, 2006, *news.findlaw.com/wash/s/20060411/200604111238591.html.*

97. Charities Concerned with Children in Romania, "Romania's Concealed Childcare Crisis" (advertisement), *Financial Times*, June 12, 2006, reproduced by Child Rights Information Network, *www.bettercarenetwork.org.*

98. Emma Nicholson, "Romania Banned International Adoptions as an 'Evil Trade in Children'" (letter to the editor), *Financial Times*, June 13, 2006, 14.

99. Megan Collins Sullivan, "For Romania's Orphans, Adoption is Still a Rarity," NPR, August 19, 2012, *www.npr.org/2012/08/19/158924764/for-romanias-orphans-adoption-is-still-a-rarity.*

100. Hughes, "Detachment," 14.

101. Sullivan, "For Romania's Orphans."

102. Quoted in ibid.

103. The term "genocide" was coined in 1944 by a Polish-Jewish lawyer named Raphael Lempkin to describe Hitler's intention to utterly eliminate Jews (and others) as a people. Lempkin envisioned a broader concept than deliberate mass murder. This concept, called "cultural genocide," was introduced at the 1948 United Nations' *Convention on the Prevention and Punishment of the Crime of Genocide*, but subsequently became controversial among UN member states. (See, "What is Genocide?" *Holocaust Encyclopedia*, Unites States Holocaust Memorial Museum, accessed February 22, 2014, *www.ushmm.org*). Importantly, however, the final document contained a clause that has been invoked numerous times by critics of interracial adoption practices. Article 2 states that "genocide means any of the following acts committed with intent to destroy, in whole or in part, a national, ethnical, racial or religious group:" Among those following acts is "(e) Forcibly transferring children of one group to another group." United Nations, *Convention on the Prevention and Punishment of the Crime of Genocide,* 1948 UN Treaty Collection, accessed May 3, 2017, *www.treaties.un.org/Pages/CTCTreatie.*

104. David Crossland, "Nazi Program to Breed Master Race: Lebensborn Children Break Silence," *Der Spiegel,* November 6, 2007, Spiegel online international edition, *www.spiegel.de/international/nazi-program-to-breed-master-race-lebensborn-children-break-silence-a-446978.html.*

105. Sybil Milton, "Non-Jewish Children in the Camps," Museum of Tolerance Multimedia Learning Center Online (annual 5, chapter 2), Simon Wiesenthal Center, accessed June 3, 2013, *motlc.wiesenthal.com.*

106. Lynn H. Nicholas, *Cruel World,* 242.

107. Melissa Eddy, "The Story of a Polish Child 'Germanized' by the Nazis…," Associated Press, May 8, 2007.

108. "The 'Lebensborn' Program (1935–1945)," Jewish Virtual Library, accessed June 3, 2013, *www.jewishvirtuallibrary.org/jsource/Holocaust/Lebensborn.html.*

109. Quoted in *Trials of War Criminals Before the Military Tribunal of Nuremberg*, vol. 4 (Washington, DC: US Gov. Printing Office, 1950), *www.loc.gov/rr/frd/Military_Law/pdf/NT_war-criminals_Vol-IV.pdf,* 677.

110. "The Kidnapping of Children by Nazi Germany," *Wikipedia,* last modified March 15, 2017, *en.wikipedia.org/wiki/Kidnapping_of_children_by_Nazi_Germany.*

111. Tadeusz Piotrowski, *Poland's Holocaust: Ethnic Strife, Collaboration with Occupying Forces and Genocide in the Second Republic, 1918–1947* (Jefferson, NC: McFarland and Co., 1998), 22 and Nicholas, *Cruel World.*

112. Linda Melvern, *Conspiracy to Murder: The Rwandan Genocide* (London: New Left Press, 2006), 5–6.

113. Bartholet, *Family Bonds,* 89.

114. Mary Ellen Fieweger, "Stolen Children and International Adoptions," *Child Welfare* 70, no. 2 (March/April 1991): 290.

115. Claudia Fonseca, "An Unexpected Reversal: The 'Demise' of International Adoption in Brazil," trans. Carolyn Brisset, *Dados-Revista de Ciências Sociais* 49, no. 1 (2007): 55.

116. Adriaan C. Van Oss, *Catholic Colonialism: A Parish History of Guatemala, 1524–1821*, Cambridge Latin American Studies (Cambridge: Cambridge University Press, 2004).

117. "Harry and Bertha Holt," Adoption History Project.

118. Sources for this story include Edward Orlebar, "Child Kidnapping Rumors Fuel Attacks on Americans," *Los Angeles Times,* April 2, 1994; Elizabeth Gleick, "Rumor and Rage," *People Magazine,* April 25, 1994; and "Foreigners Attacked in Guatemala," *New York Times*, April 5, 1994.

119. Ibon Villelabeitia, "Mayan Mob Kills Two 'Baby Stealers,'" *Guardian,* May 1, 2000.

120. "Foreigners Attacked in Guatemala," *New York Times.*

121. Claudia Fonseca, "An Unexpected Reversal: Charting the Course of International Adoption in Brazil," *Adoption and Fostering Journal* 26, no. 3 (2002).

122. Fonseca, "The 'Demise' of International Adoption," 58.

123. Todd Leventhal, *The Child Organ Trafficking Rumor: A Modern "Urban Legend,"* report submitted to the United Nations Special Rapporteur on the Sale of Children, Child Prostitution, and Child Pornography (Washington, DC: United States Information Agency, December 1994).

124. Ibid, 2.

125. Ibid.

126. Fonseca, "The 'Demise' of International Adoption," 57.

127. "Foreigners Attacked in Guatemala," *New York Times.*

128. Smolin, "Intercountry Adoption as Child Trafficking," 285.

129. See, for example, Jacobson, *Culture Keeping.*

CHAPTER 3

1. Pearl Buck, "I Am a Better Woman for Having My Two Black Children," *Today's Health*, January 1972, retrieved from Adoption History Project, *darkwing.uoregon. edu/~adoption/archive/BuckIBW.htm.*

2. The discussion of the case of Jenny Bell is drawn from Solangel Maldonado, "Race, Culture, and Adoption: Lessons from *Mississippi Band of Choctaw Indians v. Holyfield*," *Columbia Journal of Gender and Law* 17, no. 1 (2008).

3. Bartholet, *Family Bonds,* 86.

4. Ibid., 89.

5. Ibid., 89.

6. Maldonado, "Race, Culture, and Adoption," 2013.

7. Ellen Herman, *Kinship by Design* (Chicago: University of Chicago Press, 2008), 122.

8. Ibid., 124.

9. Ibid., 133.

10. Ibid., 131.

11. "Canadian Is Seized in Baby Sale Racket," *New York Times*, February 13, 1954.

12. Karen Balcom, *The Traffic in Babies: Cross-Border Adoption and Baby-Selling Between the United States and Canada, 1930–1972* (Toronto: University of Toronto Press, 2011), 63.

13. Fanshel, *Far from the Reservation*, 7.

14. Ibid., 17.

15. Quoted in Briggs, *Somebody's Children*, 73.

16. Fanshel, *Far from the Reservation*, 269.

17. Ibid., 281.

18. "Indian Adoption Project," Adoption History Project, University of Oregon, last updated Feb. 24, 2012. *pages.uoregon.edu/adoption/topics/IAP.html*.

19. Indian Child Welfare Act, 25 U.S.C. §1903 (4) (1978).

20. M. L. Meyer, "American Indian Blood Quantum Requirements: Blood Is Thicker than Family," in Matsumoto and Allmendinger, *Over the Edge*.

21. See, for example, Edward Drimmer, ed., *Captured by the Indians: 15 Firsthand Accounts 1750–1870* (New York: Dover Publications, 1985).

22. Jack D. Forbes, "Blood Quantum: A Relic of Racism and Termination," Native Intelligence (a column), Department of Native American Studies, University of California–Davis, November 27, 2000, *www.weyanoke.org/reading/jdf-BloodQuantum. html*.

23. Ibid.

24. The alternative for establishing membership in some larger tribes is lineal descent from a member included on the Dawes Rolls, a census of tribe members conducted by the federal government between 1898 and 1907.

25. "Indian Ancestry and How to Enroll or Register in a Federally Recognized Tribe," Native American Online, accessed August 12, 2016, *www.native-american-online.org/ blood-quantum.htm*.

26. Maldonado, "Race, Culture, and Adoption," 2013.

27. Briggs, *Somebody's Children*, 77.

28. Ibid., 79. Later, the figures one-quarter or one-third would be used incorrectly by some authors to specify the number of children *adopted* off the reservation rather than the number of children removed *either* to boarding schools *or* for adoption.

29. *Indian Child Welfare Program: Hearings Before the Subcommittee on Indian Affairs of the Committee on Interior and Insular Affairs*, 99th Cong. (April 8 and 9, 1974), 2.

30. Quoted in Pauline Strong, "What is an Indian Family? The Indian Child Welfare Act and the Renascence of Tribal Sovereignty," *American Studies* 46, no. 3 (Fall 2005/ Spring 2006): 209.

31. Indian Child Welfare Act of 1978, 25 U.S.C. § 1902 (1978).

32. Mississippi Choctaw Indian Band v. Holyfield, 490 U.S. 30 (1989).

33. "Indian Adoption Project," Adoption History Project.

34. To update coverage of the ICWA: Until 2013, *Holyfield* was the only Supreme Court decision on the ICWA and was strongly supportive of it. In 2013, the Court eroded the effects of ICWA in what became known as the Baby Veronica Case by ruling that the act does not apply to Indian fathers who never had custody of the children

they sired with non-Indian mothers. The Court also held that ICWA's preference for placement with an Indian family did not apply when only non-Indian families petitioned for custody. More recently, the Obama administration has sought to strengthen the ICWA. See Clint Bolick, "The Wrongs We are Doing Native American Children," *Newsweek*, November 2, 2015, *www.newsweek.com* and Marcia Yablon-Zug, "The Real Impact of Adoptive Couple v. Baby Girl," *Capital University Law Review* 42, no. 2 (2014).

35. "African-American Adoptions," Adoption History Project, University of Oregon, last updated Feb. 24, 2012. *pages.uoregon.edu/adoption/topics/AfricanAmerican.htm.*

36. Buck, "I Am a Better Woman," 64.

37. Peter Conn, *Pearl S. Buck: A Cultural Biography* (Cambridge: Cambridge University Press, 1996), 24.

38. Buck, "I Am a Better Woman," 64.

39. "Federal Court Voids a Law Prohibiting Biracial Adoption," *New York Times*, March 25, 1972.

40. Klemesrud, "Furor Over Whites Adopting Blacks."

41. Quoted in Rita J. Simon and Howard Alstein, *Adoption Across Borders: Serving the Children in Transracial and Intercountry Adoptions* (Lanham, Rowman & Littlefield, 2000), 38. Note that several other authors cite the original 1972 statement as containing the phrase regarding "this particular form of genocide." The 1972 statement as given on the NABSW website (which seems to be the original statement) does not contain it now, regardless of whether it originally did. National Association of Black Social Workers, "Position Statement on Transracial Adoption," September 1972, accessed July 18, 2013, *nabsw.org/?page=PositionStatements.* Simon and Altstein attribute the quote to the press announcement of the position statement given by Williams.

42. Quoted in Simon and Altstein, *Adoption Across Borders*, 38.

43. National Association of Black Social Workers, "Position Statement."

44. "National Association of Black Social Workers, 'Position Statement on Trans-Racial Adoption,' September 1972," Adoption History Project, University of Oregon, *pages. uoregon.edu/adoption/archive/NabswTRA.htm.* This website has a slightly different version of the 1972 statement (and includes this quote) than the NABSW website does.

45. Barbara Melosh, *Strangers and Kin* (Cambridge, MA: Harvard University Press, 2002), 176.

46. "National Association of Black Social Workers, 'Position Statement.'"

47. Klemesrud, "Furor Over Whites Adopting Blacks."

48. Alicia Howard, David D. Royse, and John A. Skerl, "Transracial Adoption: The Black Community Perspective," *Social Work* 22, no. 3 (May 1977).

49. "Transracial Adoptions," Adoption History Project, University of Oregon, last updated Feb. 24, 2012. *pages.uoregon.edu/adoption/topics/transracialadoption.htm.*

50. Elizabeth Bartholet, "Where Do Black Children Belong: The Politics of Race Matching in Adoption," *University of Pennsylvania Law Review* 139, no. 5 (May 1991): 1185.

51. Melosh, *Strangers and Kin*, 176.

52. Ibid.

53. Roland Fryer et al., "Measuring Crack Cocaine and Its Impact," *Economic Inquiry* 51, no. 3 (July 2013): 1655.

54. Steven D. Levitt and Stephen J. Dubner, *Freakonomics* (New York: William Morrow, 2005), 113.

55. Ibid., 114.

56. US General Accounting Office, *Drug Abuse: The Crack Cocaine Epidemic—Health Consequences and Treatment*, HRD-91-55FS (Washington, DC: US General Accounting Office, 1991), 17.

57. Peter Kerr, "Crack Addiction: The Tragic Toll on Women and Their Children," *New York Times*, February 9, 1987.

58. Peter Kerr, "Babies of Crack Users Fill Hospital Nurseries," *New York Times*, August 26, 1986.

59. Of course, there could be other explanations for the sharp increase in the per-capita number of children in foster care, especially children of color. One key explanation could be changes in the economy. But note that foster care rates increased only moderately during the Reagan era recession (early 1980s) and increased sharply during the upturn in the economy (late 1980s to early 1990s). Also, they had stopped increasing by the time of the Clinton-era welfare reforms of the late 1990s that presumably made it tougher for women to get welfare. Thus, neither the economy nor welfare reforms is likely an alternative explanation for the sharp increase in foster care rates in the "crack era." But also see Joe Kroll, "Testimony before United States Commission on Civil Rights" (testimony on behalf of the North American Council on Adoptable Children, September 21, 2007), *www.nacac.org/policy/Sept07CivilRightsTestimony.pdf*.

60. Fryer et al., "Measuring Crack Cocaine."

61. More recently, authors have begun to revise the analysis of the severity of the "crack epidemic." In particular, they argue that its effects were not as devastating as previously portrayed by the media. They also argue that a large part of the worsening situation for black children was a result of inequalities between the treatment of poor blacks and whites by the legal and welfare systems. We're still agnostic on this controversy. But we argue that foster care rates would increase as a result of the direct effects of crack using on women, or as a result of the indirect effects of crack using through the institutional racism of the treatment of blacks by the law and social welfare systems. The inequalities occur in the legal treatment of crack vs. cocaine in things like sentencing, as well as the possibility that the welfare system might be more likely to permanently remove children from crack-using women of color than Anglo alcoholic or cocaine-using women. See, for example, Briggs, *Somebody's Children* and Carl Hart, *High Price: A Neuroscientist's Journey of Self Discovery that Challenges Everything You Know about Drugs and Society* (New York: Harper Collins, 2013).

62. "Number of Executions by State and Region Since 1976," Death Penalty Information Center, accessed April 12, 2014, *www.deathpenaltyinfo.org/number-executions-state-and-region-1976*.

63.   Sarah Glazer, "Adoption: Do Current Policies Punish Kids Awaiting Adoption?" *CQ Researcher* 3, no. 44 (November 26, 1993), *library.cqpress.com/cqresearcher/ cqresrre1993112600.*

64.   Kroll, "Testimony before United States Commission on Civil Rights."

65.   It is unfortunate but not surprising that *60 Minutes* used the sensationalist example of black adoptive parents murdering their child, as it seems to imply that black parents murder their adopted children at a higher rate than white parents. There is no evidence to suggest this.

66.   MEPA (Pub. L. No. 103-82, October 20, 1994) was passed as a part of the *Improving America's Schools Act.*

67.   US Commission on Civil Rights. *The Multiethnic Placement Act: Minority Children in Foster Care in Adoption* (Washington, DC: USCCR, July 2010).

68.   Ibid., 37.

69.   But results were not as sanguine for American Indian children. Interviews with twenty Native American adoptees, thirteen women and seven men, found that six of the men and ten of the women "described very close, warm relationships with their adopted families and feeling very positive about their experiences growing up with non-Native parents and siblings." But the four remaining interviewees reported negative feelings toward their adoptive parents and had cut off ties. Interestingly all twenty respondents supported the Indian Child Welfare Act. US Commission on Civil Rights, *The Multiethnic Placement Act*, 80–81.

70.   Ibid., 78.

ISATA'S STORY, PART IV

1.   The information for this part of Isata's story is from an e-mail interview the authors conducted with Beckie Sibley on August 18, 2014.

2.   Shauna and Steven both wanted new first names when they joined the Sibley family.

CHAPTER 4

1.   Tinker had also created a poster of famous women, and we continued to read stories of famous women and women's literature. We made sure famous black women were included as well. We're not sure how much effect these and other efforts had, but, just as many parents do, we made them.

2.   We have the permission of Kurt and GB to discuss these issues in this book.

3.   Much of this discussion is based on Mark's essay, "How White Was My Prairie," in Marotte, Reynolds, and Savarese, *Papa, PhD.*

4.   Jacobson, *Culture Keeping.*

5.   Barbara Katz Rothman, *Weaving a Family: Untangling Race and Adoption* (Boston: Beacon Press, 2005).

6.   This information was revealed to us in an e-mail from Shaun M. on June 18, 2014.

7.   Obviously, our discussion with GB about how to behave toward the police had not yet occurred.

8. A good summary of the literature up to that time can be found in Arnold R. Silverman, "Outcomes of Transracial Adoption," *Adoption* 3, no. 1 (Spring 1993).

9. Fanshel, *Far from the Reservation*, 281.

10. Ruth G. McRoy and Louis A. Zurcher Jr., *Transracial and Inracial Adoptees: The Adolescent Years* (Springfield, IL: Charles C. Thomas, 1983).

11. In the category of "mixed," they include a number of responses: mixed, part-white, black-white, human, or American. But by far the most common response among these was "mixed." Most children in this category understood that society might see them differently than they saw themselves; 66 percent of those who said they were mixed thought society would view them as black.

12. Joan Shireman and Penny Johnson, "A Longitudinal Study of Black Adoptions: Single Parent, Transracial, and Traditional," *Social Work* (May 1, 1986).

13. At an earlier age, fewer of the children in either type of household self-identified as black: 73 percent for transracial, 80 percent for intraracial. By the time of the study cited, however, 100 percent of both groups self-identified as black.

14. Rita J. Simon and Howard Altstein, *Adoption, Race, and Identity: From Infancy Through Adolescence* (New York: Praeger, 1989).

15. The original sample in 1972 had 366 children. By the time of the 1989 study, there were 89 black transracial adoptees, 22 nonblack transracial adoptees, 22 white adoptees, and 85 birth children.

16. Simon and Altstein, *Adoption, Race, and Identity*, 155.

17. Femmie Juffer and Marinus H. van IJzenborn, "Adoptees Do Not Lack Self-Esteem: A Meta-Analysis of Studies on Self-Esteem of Transracial, International, and Domestic Adoptees," *Psychological Bulletin* 133, no. 6 (2007).

18. Ibid, 1067.

19. Femmie Juffer and Marinus H. van IJzenborn, "Behavior Problems and Mental Health Referrals of International Adoptees," *Journal of the American Medical Association* 293, no. 20 (May 25, 2005): 2501.

20. Hollee McGinnis et al., *Beyond Culture Camp: Promoting Healthy Identity Formation in Adoption* (New York: Evan B. Donaldson Adoption Institute), *www.adoptioninstitute.org/wp-content/uploads/2013/12/2009_11_BeyondCultureCamp.pdf*, 17.

21. Ibid., 17.

22. See, for example, Darron T. Smith, Brenda G. Juarez, and Cardell K. Jacobson, "White on Black: Can White Parents Teach Black Adoptive Children to Understand and Cope with Racism?" *Journal of Black Studies* 42, no. 8 (2011); Sara Dorow, *Transnational Adoption: A Cultural Economy of Race, Gender, and Kinship* (New York: New York University Press, 2006); Toby Alice Volkman, "Embodying Chinese Culture: Transnational Adoption in North America," in *Cultures of Transnational Adoption*, ed. T. A. Volkman (Durham, NC: Duke University Press, 2005). And for a deconstruction of the racial/ethnic identity of Korean adoptees, see Eleana Kim, *Adopted Territory: Transnational Korean Adoptees and the Politics of Belonging* (Durham, NC: Duke University Press, 2005).

23. Compton, *Adoption Beyond Borders*, 80.

24. Tobias Hubinette, "Post-Racial Utopianism, White Color-Blindness and 'the Elephant in the Room': Racial Issues for Transnational Adoptees of Color," in Gibbons and Rotabi, *Intercountry Adoption,* 225.

25. Ibid.

26. Ibid., 227.

27. Ibid.

28. Compton, *Adoption Beyond Borders,* 80–81.

ISATA'S STORY, PART V

1. Private letter from Beckie Sibley to the M. family, December 2012.

2. From an interview between the authors and Isata Sibley, August 2014.

3. Ibid.

4. The information and quotes in this section of Isata's story come from an e-mail interview with Beckie Sibley, August 14, 2014.

CHAPTER 5

1. Lola Adesioye, "Madonna Without Child," *Guardian,* April 3, 2009, *www. theguardian.com/commentisfree/2009/apr/03/madonna-adoption-malawi-court-refuse.*

2. Bartholet, "International Adoption: The Human Rights Position."

3. "Group to Block Madonna Adoption," *Metro,* October 12, 2006, *www.metro.co.uk/ 2006/group-to-block-madonna-adoption-282454.*

4. MSCA Adoption Appeal No. 28 of 2009, "In Re: The Adoption of Children Act CAP 26:01 and In Re: CJ A Female Infant of c/o P.O. Box 30871, Chichiri, Blantyre 3," Malawi Supreme Court of Appeal, June 12, 2009, *www.malawilii.org/mw/ judgment/supreme-court-appeal/2009/1,* 69.

5. Ibid.

6. *Trafficking in Persons Report,* 10th ed. (Washington, DC: US State Department, June 2010), *www.state.gov/documents/organization/142979.pdf.*

7. Graff, "Call It Trafficking."

8. Chad Turner, "Sometimes It Is Better Not to Be Unique: The U.S. Department of State View on Intercountry Adoption and Child Trafficking and Why It Should Change," *Duke Forum for Law and Social Change* 6, no. 91 (2014): 94.

9. *Child Trafficking in East and South-East Asia: Reversing the Trend* (Bangkok: UNICEF East Asia and Pacific Regional Office, August 2009), *www.unicef.org/eapro/Unicef_ EA_SEA_Trafficking_Report_Aug_2009_low_res.pdf.*

10. David M. Smolin, "Child Laundering: How the Intercountry Adoption System Legitimizes and Incentivizes the Practices of Buying, Trafficking, Kidnaping, and Stealing Children," *Wayne Law Review* 52, no. 1 (2006): 113–200.

11. Charlie Custer, "Kidnapped and Sold: Inside the Dark World of Child Trafficking in China," *Atlantic,* July 5, 2013. *www.theatlantic.com/china/archive/2013/07/ kidnapped-and-sold-inside-the-dark-world-of-child-trafficking-in-china/278107.*

12. Ibid.

13. Jack Chang, "Parents of Abducted Children in China Fight Against Authorities," *Denver Post*, December 28, 2014.

14. Kay Johnson, *Wanting a Daughter, Needing a Son* (St. Paul, MN: Yeong and Yeong Books, 2004). See chapters 3, 4, and 6, for example.

15. Jeffery Hayes, "One-Child Policy in China," *Facts and Details*, last modified June 2015, *factsanddetails.com/china/cat4/sub15/item128.html*.

16. Johnson, *Wanting a Daughter*, 36, 50, and 59.

17. "China Arrests Sixteen in Smuggling of Babies," *Washington Post*, December 4, 2005. While the gender of these children was unreported, as we shall see, most children sold to children welfare institutions are destined for international adoption and are therefore almost all girls.

18. Sharon LaFraniere, "Chinese Officials Seized and Sold Babies, Parents Say," *New York Times*, August 4, 2011.

19. Ibid.

20. Barbara Demick quoted in Brian H. Stuy, "Open Secret: Cash and Coercion in China's International Adoption Program," *Cumberland Law Review* 44, no. 3, (2013–2014): 387.

21. Stuy, "Open Secret," 391.

22. The Chinese government ended the one-child policy as of January 1, 2016. Families can now have two children. The stated reason was not the skewed sex ratio or the poor conditions and high mortality rates in orphanages overcrowded with girls, but the fact that too few young people support too many elderly family members. See "China's One-Child Policy Ends," BBC News, January 1, 2016, *www.bbc.com/news/av/world-asia-china-35208488/chinas-one-child-policy-ends*.

23. Siegal, *Finding Fernanda*.

24. Ibid., 13.

25. Ibid., 98.

26. Ibid., 61.

27. Ibid., 175.

28. Ibid., 180.

29. Ibid. 174. But Sue Hedberg was by no means out of the adoption game. In September of 2007, she opened up shop in Ethiopia, and also eventually in the Congo, neither of which were Hague compliant and where, therefore, adoption facilitators need not meet Hague criteria. It was not the end of her PR problems. In January of 2014, the CBS News show *48 Hours* did a story that featured Hedberg and documented the frustrations of parents trying to adopt two girls from the Congo through CCI. It also reviewed the *Finding Fernanda* story (and acknowledged that Hedberg had many, many families who were truly grateful to her for facilitating the adoption of their children.)

30. The numbers are reported by Guatemalan journalist Marta Yolanda Diaz-Duran, as quoted in John Stossel, "USA Makes Adoption Harder," opinion column, ABC News, February 6, 2008, *abcnews.go.com/2020/story?id=4246338*.

31. National Coalition for Child Protection Reform, *Spending So Much More, Getting So Much Less: The Numbers Tell the Story*, accessed April 17, 2014, *www.nccpr.org/reports/RIdataataglance95472ri19.pdf*.

32. Child removal is certainly not the same as child theft. The former allows the possibility of regaining custody. But given the differential removal rates for white and minority children, many critics find that taking kids from their families and placing them in foster care is uncomfortably closer to theft than we would like. See, for example, Dorothy Roberts, *Shattered Bonds: The Color of Child Welfare* (New York: Basic Books, 2002).

33. Erin Siegal, *The US Embassy Cables: Adoption Fraud in Guatemala 1987–2010*, (Oakland, CA: Cathexis Press, 2011), 32.

34. See, for example, Smolin, "Intercountry Adoption"; Graff, "Call It Trafficking"; and Kim, "International Adoption's Trafficking Problem."

35. E. J. Graff, "The Makeni Children," Slate.com, August 09, 2011, *www.slate.com/ articles/double_x/doublex/features/2011/the_makeni_children/how_flawed_is_the_ international_adoption_process.html*.

36. The facilitator of Mosley's Cambodian adoption, a certain Lauryn Galindo, became rather notorious, eventually pleading guilty to seventeen counts of visa fraud and money laundering. She was likely one of the key reasons that adoption shut down in Cambodia. See "US Families Learn Truth about Adopted Cambodian Children," ABC News, March 25, 2005, *abcnews.go.com/2020/International/story?id=611826*.

37. Her autobiography, written with her mother, Elaine DePrince, was published in 2014: *Taking Flight: From War Orphan to Star Ballerina* (New York: Alfred A. Knopf).

38. Graff, "The Makeni Children."

39. Yayah J. Koroma, "In Sierra Leone, HANCI Beneficiaries Beg President Koroma," *Awareness Times Newspaper*, April 17, 2012.

40. M. Lamin Kamara, "HANCI Adoption Case Goes High Court," *Concord Times* (Freetown), February 4, 2014.

41. The US embassy cables were released after the Schuster Institute for Investigative Journalism requested them under the Freedom of Information Act. See "US Government Documents, 2007–2008, Obtained via Freedom of Information Act," Schuster Institute for Investigative Journalism, Brandeis University, last modified February 28, 2011, *www.brandeis.edu/investigate/adoption/foias.html*.

42. Barbara Demick, "A Family in China Made Babies Their Business," *Los Angeles Times*, January 24, 2010.

43. Patricia J. Meier and Xiaole Zhang, "Sold into Adoption: The Hunan Baby Trafficking Scandal Exposes Vulnerabilities in Chinese Adoptions to the United States," *Cumberland Law Review* 39, no. 1, (2008/2009).

44. Stuy, "Open Secret," 372.

45. Ibid., 371.

46. Demick, "A Family in China."

47. Stuy, "Open Secret," 375.

48. Ibid., 380.

49. Ibid., 383.
50. Jacob Wheeler, *Between Light and Shadow: A Guatemalan Girl's Journey through Adoption* (Lincoln: University of Nebraska Press, 2011).
51. Ibid., 19.
52. Ibid., 24.
53. Ibid., 32.
54. Ibid., 126.
55. Ibid., 130.
56. Ibid., 131.
57. Ibid., 139.
58. Roby and Maskew report baby buying in Cambodia. Jini Roby and Trish Maskew, "Human Rights Considerations in Intercountry Adoption: The Children and Families of Cambodia and the Marshall Islands," in Gibbons and Rotabi, *Intercountry Adoption.* As we reported in Chapter 4, baby buying was common in Romania immediately after the fall of Ceauşescu.
59. China is the only one of these countries still placing children for foreign adoptions, and it only places older kids and those with disabilities. The US State Department announced a complete shutdown of IA from Ethiopia in May 2017. See "International Adoption Country Information," US State Department, *www.travel.state.gov/content/adoptionsabroad/en/country-information.html.*
60. Quoted in Demick, "A Family in China."
61. David Nassaw, "Vietnam Stops US Adoption Programme," *Guardian*, May 1, 2008.
62. See Siegal, *The US Embassy Cables.*
63. Some argue that international adoption should not occur in the aftermath of a crisis, such as a typhoon, earthquake, or war, to give time for displaced children to be reunited with their families. Others argue that it is precisely such times that orphaned children need to find new homes. However, here we are referring to war that lasts for years or decades, as some wars do. Often international adoption organizations don't operate while war continues, so adoption isn't an issue, but we would argue that if it can continue in a reasonable manner, it should continue. Some of the criticism, in the Haiti earthquake situation, for example, focuses on "pipeline" cases, children whose adoptions had already begun at the time of the crisis. These adoptions do not seem problematic to us. On the other hand, some of the criticism focuses on children taken out of the country without proper paperwork or parent permission, an action only possible as a result of the chaos existing in after a crisis. Such a case should not be allowed. With the help of receiving countries such cases should be avoidable.
64. "US Government Documents, 2007–2008," Schuster Institute for Investigative Journalism.
65. It is likely that the embassy would not have denied the visa on the strength of this single documentary glitch. But the birth mother was told, falsely, that the boy had a major health problem in order to pressure her to relinquish him. Essentially the baby was stolen. The immigrant visa was denied, and the baby was returned to his birth parents.
66. Roby and Maskew, "Human Rights Considerations," 61.

67. Ibid., 62.
68. This point is made by Mary Lyndon Stanley in *Making Babies, Making Families* (Boston: Beacon Press, 2001) and by Heather Jacobson in *Culture Keeping*.
69. Fiona Bowie, ed., *Cross-Cultural Practices in Adoption* (New York: Routledge, 2004), 3.
70. Erdmute Alber, "'The Real Parents are the Foster Parents': Social Parent Hood among the Baatombu in Northern Benin," in Bowie, *Cross-Cultural Practices in Adoption*, 33.
71. Esther Goody, *Parenthood and Social Reproduction: Fostering and Occupational Roles in West Africa* (Cambridge: Cambridge University Press, 1982).
72. Alber, "The Real Parents," 34.
73. Catrien Notermans, "Fosterage and the Politics of Marriage and Kinship in East Cameroon," in Bowie, *Cross-Cultural Practices in Adoption*.
74. Aud Talle, "Adoption Practices Among the Pastoral Maasai of East Africa," in Bowie, *Cross-Cultural Practices in Adoption*.
75. Gesue Gebrier Roberts, *Zammie Town to Zwedru: Memoir of a Village Childhood in Liberia* (Tamarac, FL: Llumina Press, 2011).
76. Roberts, *Zammie Town to Zwedru*, 91.
77. Bartholet, "International Adoption: Thoughts," 188.

ISATA'S STORY, PART VI

1. That story reveals something about how economists raise children. In 2006, Mary and a college companion were detained by the police in Freetown for snapping a picture of a mural "without a permit." She was told that she would experience all sorts or horrors *if* they took her to the main police station downtown. She noted that the "if" was repeated several times. That seemed to imply a legal loophole. Was it at all possible, she asked, that *these* policemen could sell her a permit, thus avoiding a trip downtown? Luckily, yes, they could! But there was still the issue of the fine, of course. These policemen informed Mary that the combined cost of the permit and the fine was 200,000 leones (about fifty dollars). No, said Mary, she thought the cost was more like 100,000 leones. Again, they vehemently threatened to take her downtown, recounting the horrors that would befall her there. Figuring that "downtown" these guys would not get any of the bribe, she told them to go ahead and take her downtown. They reluctantly reconsidered. Maybe the cost of the permit and fine was 150,000 leones. She paid, and they cheerfully released her with a "permit" scribbled on a piece of scrap paper. We would like to be able to report that upon hearing this story, two weeks later, we congratulated our daughter on her negotiating skills. But, in actuality, we screamed, "Are you crazy?"
2. Based on interviews directly from those who were taken in by the fabrications.

CHAPTER 6

1. E. J. Graff, "The Baby Business," *Democracy: A Journal of Ideas*, no. 17 (Summer 2010).
2. Bartholet, *Family Bonds*, 43.

3. Kimberly D. Krawiec, "Price and Pretense in the Baby Market," in Goodwin, *Baby Markets*, 41.

4. "Mabel Walker Willebrandt Dies; Lawyer for US in Prohibition," *New York Times*, April 9, 1963.

5. "Stevens County, Kansas," Kansas Historical Society, last modified April 2017, *www.kshs.org/kansapedia/stevens-county-kansas/15349*.

6. Mabel Walker Willebrandt, *The Inside of Prohibition* (Indianapolis, IN: Bobbs-Merrill Company, 1929), 300.

7. Ibid.

8. They were employed by the Treasury Department.

9. Willebrandt, *The Inside of Prohibition*, 143.

10. Quoted in Tom Feiling, *Cocaine Nation: How the White Trade Took Over the World* (New York: Pegasus Books, 2009), 217.

11. Daniel Okrent, *Last Call: The Rise and Fall of Prohibition* (New York: Scribner, 2010), 274.

12. Ibid.

13. Quoted in ibid.

14. See, for example, Gary S. Becker, Kevin M. Murphy, and Michael Grossman, "The Economic Theory of Illegal Goods: The Case of Drugs" (working paper 10976, National Bureau of Economic Research, 2004), *www.nber.org/papers/w10976*.

15. Eric Blumenson and Eva Nilsen, "No Rational Basis: The Pragmatic Case for Marijuana Law Reform," *Virginia Journal of Social Policy and the Law* 17, no. 1 (Fall 2009).

16. Jeffrey A. Miron, *The Budgetary Implications of Marijuana Prohibition*, report funded by the Marijuana Policy Project, June 2005, *www.cannabis-commerce.com/library/Miron_Report_2005.pdf*.

17. Jeffrey A. Miron and Jeffrey Zwiebel, "The Economic Case Against Drug Prohibition," *Journal of Economic Perspectives* 9, no. 4 (Fall 1995).

18. Interview with John Lowell, consular officer at the US embassy in Guatemala (2006–2007), November 27, 2012.

19. Ibid.

20. Remember: at this point, the US embassy was working hard, including using two DNA tests, to try to stop improper adoptions to the United States.

21. "Deciding Where to Adopt," US State Department, last modified March 23, 2017, *www.travel.state.gov/content/adoptionsabroad/en/adoption-process/deciding-where-to-adopt.html*.

22. A 2010 report by the Special Commission on the Practical Operation of the Hague Convention states, "Independent adoptions in which the adoptive family... locates a child without the intervention of a Central Authority or accredited body in the State of origin are also not compatible with the Convention." Quoted in Cantwell, *The Best Interests of the Child*, 43.

23. Personal interview, July 29, 2015.

24. Of course, some people would turn to substitutes for adoption such as reproductive technology or surrogacy. We thank an anonymous reviewer for this insight.

25. Richard A. Posner, "The Regulation of the Market in Adoptions," *Boston University Law Review* 67 (1987): 70.

26. Okrent, *Last Call*.

27. Unless she or the birth father is a member of a registered Indian tribe.

28. "The Laws Related to Adoption," US Department of Health and Human Services, Child Welfare Information Gateway, accessed June 12, 2015, *www.childwelfare.gov/topics/adoption/laws*.

29. Andrea B. Carroll, "Reregulating the Baby Market: A Call for a Ban on Payment of Birth-Mother Living Expenses," *University of Kansas Law Review* 59, no. 2 (January 2011): 325.

30. Adam Pertman, *Adoption Nation*, 2nd ed. (Boston: Harvard Common Press, 2011), 240.

31. Ibid.

32. We spoke with adoption lawyers who said they knew of colleagues who allowed payments that were technically illegal.

33. For an empirical analysis of adoptive parents' preferences over types of children, see Mariagiovanna Baccara, et al., "Child-Adoption Matching: Preferences for Gender and Race." *American Economic Journal: Applied Economics* 6, no. 3 (July 2014). For an analysis of race and kids in foster care, see Marian S. Harris, *Racial Disproportionality in Child Welfare* (New York: Columbia University Press, 2014) and Denneretee M. Derezotes, John Poertner, and Mark F. Testa, eds., *Race Matters in Child Welfare: The Overrepresentation of African American Children in the System* (Washington, DC: Child Welfare League of America Press, 2004). In recent years, the overrepresentation of black children has decreased somewhat. See Mary Ann Davis, *Children for Families or Families for Children: The Demography of Adoption Behavior in the US* (New York: Springer, 2011).

34. Kimberly D. Krawiec, "Altruism and Intermediation in the Market for Babies," *Washington and Lee Law Review* 66 (2009): 254.

35. Claudia Fonseca, "Inequality Near and Far: Adoption as Seen from the Brazilian Favelas," *Law and Society Review*, special issue, *Nonbiological Parenting* 36, no. 2 (2002): 425.

36. Pinderhughes, et al., *A Changing World*, 75. It must be admitted, however, that these are self-reports from a sample that may be nonrandom.

37. Carroll, "Reregulating the Baby Market," 288.

38. Ironically, this drug problem is not irrelevant to adoption because drug-related violence, and drug-law enforcement, fall disproportionately on blacks and Hispanics, exacerbating the racial imbalance in the foster care and adoption systems, though this racial imbalance is no doubt also due to some racial bias within the social welfare system, among other factors.

39. Robert Mackey, "Malawi Court Bars New Madonna Adoption," *New York Times*, April 3, 2009.

40. There are now postplacement contracts being used in adoptions in some states. They are enforceable in court in a couple of states.

41. We do think that post-adoption contact of children and birth families needs to be handled carefully and must be age appropriate. For example, we have told our older son, Kurt, several times that we will help him search for his birth parents whenever he wishes. While GB has not wanted anything to do with Sierra Leone, we have brought him along slowly until, most recently, he said that next time we go to Sierra Leone, he would go with us and see his birth mother. We think the more people who express love and caring for our children, the better off they will be. Their birth parents and we, their adoptive parents, play different roles in their lives, and that's OK. But the kids themselves have to be ready for the interaction.

42. Claudia Fonseca, "The Politics of Adoption: Child Rights in the Brazilian Setting," *Law & Policy* 24, no. 3 (September 2002): 207. See also Claudia Fonseca, "An Unexpected Reversal: Charting the Course."

43. Fonseca, "The Politics of Adoption," 207.

44. Fonseca, "An Unexpected Reversal: Charting the Course," 32.

45. Fonseca, "The Politics of Adoption," 205.

46. Ibid., 207.

47. Fonseca, "An Unexpected Reversal: Charting the Course," 35.

48. Domingos Abrue, "Baby-Bearing Storks," in *International Adoption: Global Inequalities and the Circulation of Children*, eds. Diana Marre and Laura Briggs (New York: New York University Press, 2009), 140.

49. Ibid.

50. Ibid., 143.

51. Ibid.

52. Ibid., 141.

53. Ibid., 147.

54. Ibid., 151.

55. Ibid.

56. Ibid., 146.

57. This is true in many countries. Foreigners are more likely to adopt Mayan children from Guatemala, Roma children from Bulgaria, and African American children from the US.

58. Adoption was possible during the Ceauşescu regime, but it was uncommon, as the dictator himself had to sign off on each case.

59. Hunt, "The Romanian Baby Bazaar."

60. Ibid.

61. The figure of 2,900 dollars for 100,000 lei is based on the December 1991 exchange rate of 34.9 lei per dollar, which is highly uncertain, as inflation was accelerating rapidly. The rate was taken from "Treasury Reporting Rates of Exchange as of March 31, 1991," US Treasury Department, last modified October 15, 2012, *www.gpo.gov/fdsys/search/searchresults.action?st=Rates+of+Exchange*. What we can be confident of is that the family relinquishing the child was receiving no more than one thousand dollars.

62. For information on Cambodia, see "Update on Status of Adoption from Cambodia," US State Department, last modified February 18, 2016, *www.travel.state.gov/content/*

adoptionsabroad/en/country-information/alerts-and-notices/cambodia16-02-16.html. Although in 2014 a "special adoption program" was developed for adoption from Vietnam to the US for special needs children and older children, only twenty-two adoptions occurred between 2010 and 2016. See "Operation of the US—Vietnam Special Adoption Program," US State Department, last modified January 2015, *travel.state.gov/content/adoptionsabroad/en/country-information/alerts-and-notices/ vietnam15-01-08.html* and "Vietnam," US State Department, last modified January 2016, *travel.state.gov/content/adoptionsabroad/en/country-information/learn-about-a- country/vietnam.html.*

63. Marijike Bruening and John Ishiyama, "The Politics of Intercountry Adoption: Explaining Variation in the Legal Requirements of Sub-Saharan African Countries," *Perspectives on Politics* 7, no. 1 (March 2009).

64. Pinderhughes, et al., *A Changing World*, 79.

65. Ibid.

66. Ibid., 80.

67. Ibid. We also heard this in interviews with directors of smaller adoption agencies.

68. Ibid., 81.

69. It is not always simple to determine whether a country is "Hague compliant." A country can ratify the convention long before meeting any of the conditions specified therein. When these are met, the convention is said to "Enter into Force" (EIF) in that country. For some poor countries, the period between ratification and compliance can be long. Even if the country is EIF, receiving countries may not approve adoptions. In 2015, three years after ratifying the convention (during which time the US and France were to help it comply), Vietnam announced its intention to resume adoption, only to have the US and France decide that its policies were not yet good enough. Germany and the Netherlands concurred. Adoption is still stalled in that country.

70. "Indian Couple Sells Newborn Baby Boy," *Daily Mail*, August 13, 2012.

71. Custer, "Kidnapped and Sold."

ISATA'S STORY, PART VII

1. Sierra Leone Adoption Act of 1989. Full text at *www.sierralii.org/sl/legislation/ act/1989/9.* Definition of orphan status at "Orphan," Department of Homeland Security, US Citizenship and Immigration Services, last modified July 15, 2015, *www.uscis.gov/tools/glossary/orphan.*

2. Diane X, email message to authors, August 30, 2014 (note: we identify her only by a pseudonym).

3. We should note that Diane and David, a Sierra Leone national, are now married.

CHAPTER 7

1. Pinderhughes, et al., *A Changing World*, 54–57.

2. *Roe v. Wade* and the advent of the Pill also helped end this type of fraud and mistreatment. See, for example, Anne Fessler, *The Girls Who Went Away: The Hidden History of Women Who Surrendered Children for Adoption in the Decades Before Roe v. Wade* (New York: Penguin Books, 2007).

3. Pinderhughes, et al., *A Changing World*, 14.

4. Lee Aitken, "The High Price of a Baby's Love," *Money* 21, no. 1 (January 1992): 98–113.

5. George Klein, *The Adventure: The Quest for my Romanian Babies* (Lanham, MD: University Press of America, 2007), 63.

6. Ibid., 65.

7. We also interviewed the director and country director of the orphanage and the adoptive family, and we met the son. The orphanage, at least at the time we interviewed its directors in January 2013, was not charging a fee for facilitating adoptions. Although it wasn't clear how long that practice could continue, it was unlikely any fee they charged would be large. And we're happy to report the family and son are doing well.

8. "Doctor Acts to Heal Romania's Wound Of Baby Trafficking," *New York Times*, October 31, 1991.

9. Oreskovic and Maskew, "Red Thread," 101.

10. Michael Sandel, *What Money Can't Buy: The Moral Limits of Markets* (New York: Farrar, Straus and Giroux, 2012), 111.

11. To deny a birth family the choice of releasing a child for compensation is to do what the Virginian Fitzhugh did in his defense of slavery. He decided what was in someone *else's* best interest. Slaves were intellectually incapable, he assumed, of surviving in a world where they must compete with whites. Thus, offering slaves their freedom was wrong because they might accept the offer—and be worse off.

12. Indrias Getachew, "In Ethiopia, Placing Institutions and Adoptive Practices Under Scrutiny—And Reuniting Children with Their Families," UNICEF.org, December 10, 2012, *www.unicef.org/protection/ethiopia_66598.html*.

13. Mark Riley, *Baseline Study: The State of Institutional Care in Uganda*, report for Uganda Ministry of Gender, Labour and Social Development, June 2012, *www.alternative-care-uganda.org/resources/moglsd-baseline-study-institutional-care-in-uganda-june-2012.pdf*, 6.

14. Ibid.

15. Ibid., 34.

16. Elsewhere, Mark Riley has been quite clear about having adopted internationally himself, and certainly not being opposed to it in all circumstances.

17. Riley, *Baseline Study*, 8.

18. Karen Dubinsky, *Babies without Borders: Adoption and Migration across the Americas* (Toronto: University of Toronto Press, 2010), 100.

19. Andrew Bainham, "International Adoption from Romania—Why the Moratorium Should Not be Ended," *Child & Family Law Quarterly* 15 (2003): 234.

20. Post, *Romania: For Export Only*, location 781. We caution the reader, however, that we could not find this statement in the published version of the report. A possible

explanation is that Post, as a staff member of the European Commission, got an early draft of the report from which the statement about abandonment was later redacted.

21. See, for example, Melissa Fay Greene, *There is No Me Without You* (New York: Bloomsbury USA, 2007). We also heard this from the director of a children's home in Rwanda.

22. "Adoption Cost and Timing 2015–2016," AdoptiveFamilies.com, last modified February 2017, *www.adoptivefamilies.com/resources/adoption-news/adoption-cost-and-timing-2015-2016.*

23. Getachew, "In Ethiopia, Placing Institutions and Adoptive Practices."

24. Interview with authors, March 12, 2013.

25. Interview with authors, January 8, 2013.

26. Interview with authors, December 27, 2012.

27. Quoted in Joyce, *The Child Catchers*, 261.

28. Requests for interviews were sent to a number of UNICEF officials. They were either ignored or denied.

29. "Statement by Anthony Lake, UNICEF Executive Director, on the Proposed Russian Adoption Ban," UNICEF.org, December 26, 2012, *www.unicef.org/media/media_66995.html.* It may or may not be significant that Lake was Clinton's national security advisor in the 1990s, but it is surely *in*significant that he was our colleague at Mount Holyoke College in the mid-1980s.

30. "The Child Without Family Care," UNICEF.org, last modified December 14, 2004, *www.unicef.org/childfamily/index_24511.html.*

31. Riley, *Baseline Study*, 23.

32. There was at least one occasion, however, when UNICEF took a stand in favor of adoption. According to US embassy cables, when the Ethiopian government was considering shutting down adoption, UNICEF and the State Department urged a compromise. Closing down adoption, they argued, would leave too many children in worse conditions. Moreover, UNICEF and the State Department wanted to avoid the pressure and bad publicity that followed the closing of adoption in Vietnam, Cambodia, and Guatemala. See Siegal, *The US Embassy Cables.*

33. He told us this during a second interview in 2013, when he had left the post of assistant to the minister and was a government translator.

34. Interview with Marijke Bruening, August 3, 2012.

35. Quoted in Joyce, *The Child Catchers*, 261.

36. We have seen, and read about, very good orphanages. For example, some have family houses with house parents and a smaller number of children that operate as a family; some pay for children's school fees, including for going away to school as they get older; some allow children to maintain contact after they "age out" so that they have a home base even as adults; some maintain their school for school children in the community in addition to orphanage children, or allow children in the community to stay at the orphanage for school and food but then allow them to return to their homes during school holidays (that is, the kids are neither institutionalized nor at home; they get the benefits of both when their family is too poor to fully care for them).

37. Some would argue that the popularity of newborns in America versus foster children is definite proof that babies would drive out older children in orphanages. But this ignores an important distinction between the adoption of children from abroad and the adoption of children from the American foster system. There are many reasons that a child in Africa might be placed for adoption, many of them factors that are beyond the parents' control, such as the family's extreme poverty or the death of a parent or, in the case of our son GB, atrocities in a civil war. But it is a sad aspect of the American system that a child enters foster care for primarily a single reason: problems with parenting. And the effects of these problems on the child's temperament and behavior often make the adoption of such a child a riskier enterprise.

38. Exceptions to the norm of institutionalized children being older and/or having higher rates of special needs might be China and Romania, where even healthy babies have sometimes been abandoned in large numbers.

39. Siegal, *The US Embassy Cables*, 37.

40. Ibid., 29.

41. DNA tests were routinely used in Guatemala. See Siegal, *The US Embassy Cables*.

42. We fully recognize that the overlap of these two groups, those who might be placed for adoption now and those who might end up in institutions in a few years, isn't exact.

43. Schoenmaker, et al., "Does Family Matter?" 2223.

44. In geek-speak we would say this as follows: For a given number of babies available for adoption, call it B, define $P = f(B)$ as the highest adoption price that would get them all placed in homes. In other words, at any price higher than P, some of these B babies would remain unadopted. P can be thought of as the "market value" of the *marginal* baby put up for adoption. (The function $f(B)$ is called the inverse demand curve.) The Law of Demand implies that the more babies that are available, the lower the P required to get them all adopted. Speaking mathematically—something you shouldn't do at a cocktail party—we say that $dP/dB = f'(B) < 0$. Assuming $f(B)$ has the technical properties of... yada, yada, yada... economists would measure the *monetary* value, which we call Willingness to Pay (WTP), of *all* the available babies, B, as $WTP(B) = \int_0^B F(B)dB$. In the market, we observe only P and B, the "price" and "quantity" of babies, not $f(B)$. So, we cannot infer from just observing P and B the monetary value (WTP) of *all* babies as a group. For that we need to know the inverse demand curve, which is not observable. This, incidentally, provides the resolution to the water-diamond paradox: water is so abundant that the last bucketful is nearly worthless, and diamonds are so scarce the last bucketful is worth a fortune. This does not mean, however, that society values *all* of its water less than *all* of its diamonds. In concluding this note we must caution the reader: if you care about, or (much worse) *understand* any of this you are seriously a nerd.

45. In addition to the open adoption movement, these were other changes that helped empower birth mothers placing their children for adoption.

46. Viviana A. Zelizer, *Pricing the Priceless Child* (New York: Basic Books, 1985), 169.

47. In *Pricing the Priceless Child*, Zelizer argues that various social and political forces during the nineteenth century altered the status of the child within the family from

useful resource (e.g. wage earner) to precious artifact. When child labor was out-lawed, for example, families had less incentive to have more children and tended to see them more as treasures than as means of production. Generally, we find her arguments persuasive. But they do leave an unanswered question: If children are now so much more precious, why do families produce fewer of them? Fertility, especially in industrialized countries, has plummeted since the nineteenth century. Demographers attribute much of this decline to the increasing cost of raising a child given mothers' hugely expanded employment opportunities. But when people have fewer children, we expect the value of the *marginal* child to be higher even if the total value of the family's children is lower. Thus, we get the same result that Zelizer attributes to social and political factors—that is, children are perceived as more valuable just because the cost of children is rising, and therefore fewer are being produced. This certainly does not discount Zelizer arguments, but it adds a supplemental explanation, we think.

48. For evidence that adopters respond to price differences, see Laura Argys and Brian Duncan, "Economic Incentives and Foster Child Placement," *Southern Economic Journal* 74, no. 1 (July 2007); Mary E. Hansen, "Using Subsidies to Promote the Adoption of Children from Foster Care," *Journal of Family Economic Issues* 28, no. 3 (September 2007); Mary E. Hansen and Bradley A. Hansen, "The Economics of Children from Foster Care," *Child Welfare* 85 no. 3 (May/June 2006); and P. A. Quiroz, *Adoption in a Color-Blind Society* (Lanham, MD: Rowman and Littlefield, 2007).

49. And we should think about what these costs of foster care and adoption subsidies mean for efforts to increase so-called permanent foster care and domestic adoption in poor sending countries as an alternative to IA.

50. Sometimes older children move from home to home or from home to institutions before "aging out" of the system. This is partly due to how long it takes to terminate parental rights for a child who has been removed from her family as well as the time required to find black or biracial families to adopt children of color. But it also implies that the subsidies are not high enough, as there are "excess" children within the system.

51. J. White quoted in Karen Smith Rotabi, "Fraud in Intercountry Adoption: Child Sales and Abduction in Vietnam, Guatemala and Cambodia," in Gibbons and Rotabi, *Intercountry Adoption*, 74.

CHAPTER 8

1. Stephen J. Dubner, "You Say Repugnant, I Say Let's Do It," Freako-nomics Radio, December 30, 2010, *freakonomics.com/podcast/freakonomics-radio-you-say-repugnant-i-say-lets-do-it*.

2. Jacob Riss quoted in Zelizer, *Pricing the Priceless Child*, 113.

3. Zelizer, *Pricing the Priceless Child*, 120.

4. Viviana A. Zelizer, "The Price and Value of Children: The Case of Children's Insurance," *American Journal of Sociology* 86, no. 5 (March 1981): 1041.

5. Ibid.

6.   "Child Life Insurance," *New York Times*, October 15, 1895.

7.   Benjamin Waugh, "Child-Life Insurance," *Contemporary Review*, 58 (July 1890): 53.

8.   Ibid., 43.

9.   "Graveyard Insurance," *Cambridge (MA) Tribune* XVIII, no. 2, March 16, 1895.

10.   As early as March 1894, a scientific inquest "failed to connect the prevalence of [child] neglect with any system of insurance." Hugh R. Jones, "The Perils and Protection of Infant Life," *Journal of the Royal Statistical Society* 57, no. 1 (March 1894): 60.

11.   Rev. O. R. Miller (East Boston, 1895) quoted in Zelizer, *Pricing the Priceless Child*, 113.

12.   Although it is not widely used. According to the American Council of Life Insurers, only 15 percent of Americans under eighteen have life insurance. "What is Child Term Life Insurance," BurialInsurance.com. *www.burialinsurance.com/Burial_Insurance_Child_Term_Life_Insurance.html.*

13.   Alvin, E. Roth, "Repugnance as a Constraint on Markets," *Journal of Economic Perspectives* 21, no. 3 (2007).

14.   Niall Ferguson, *The Ascent of Money* (New York: Penguin Books, 2008), 36.

15.   See, for example, Angus Maddison, *Growth and Interaction in the World Economy* (Cambridge, MA: AEI Press, 2004), 7.

16.   William Shakespeare, *The Merchant of Venice*, Act I, Scene 3.

17.   "Murder Act 1751," *Wikipedia*, last modified February 27, 2016, *en.wikisource.org/wiki/Murder_Act_1751.*

18.   A. W. Bates, *The Anatomy of Robert Knox* (Brighton, UK: Sussex Academic Press, 2010).

19.   Roth, "Repugnance as a Constraint" includes a discussion of this case also.

20.   Arthur Pigou, *The Economics of Welfare* (New York: Macmillan, 1920).

21.   John H. Dales, *Pollution, Property and Prices: An Essay in Policy Making and Economics* (Toronto: University of Toronto Press, 1968), 111.

22.   Robert E. Goodin, "Selling Environmental Indulgences," *Kyklos* 47, no. 4 (1994): 582.

23.   Sandel, *What Money Can't Buy*, 72.

24.   Johan Eyckmans and Snoore Kverndokk, "Moral Considerations in Trading Pollution Permits" (HUB research paper 2008/12, Hogeschool-Universitat Brussells, February 2008), 2. *citeseerx.ist.psu.edu/viewdoc/download?doi=10.1.1.582.9200&rep=rep1&type=pdf.*

25.   "How Cap and Trade Works," Environmental Defense Fund, accessed September 23, 2013, *www.edf.org/climate/how-cap-and-trade-works.*

26.   Elaine Landes and Richard Posner, "The Economics of the Baby Shortage," *Journal of Legal Studies* 7, no. 2 (June 1978).

27.   Robert S. Boynton, "Sounding Off," a review of *Public Intellectuals*, by Richard Posner, *Washington Post Book World*, January 20, 2002.

28.   Posner, "The Regulation of the Market in Adoptions," 59.

29.   Landes and Posner, "The Economics of the Baby Shortage," 344.

30.   Kapstein, "The Baby Trade," 115.

31. Margaret Jane Radin, "Market-Inalienability," *Harvard Law Review* 100 (June 1987): 29.

32. Sandel, *What Money Can't Buy*, 9.

33. Ironically, economists do tend to object to this aspect of baseball, not because it commodifies players, but because it effectively gives team owners a monopsonistic cartel over ball players' salaries.

34. Bartholet, *Family Bonds*, 43.

35. Ahad J. Ghods and Shekoufeh Savaj, "Iranian Model of Paid and Regulated Living-Unrelated Kidney Donation," *Clinical Journal of the American Society of Nephrology* 1, no. 6 (November 2006).

36. Dean Praetorius, "GoDaddy.com CEO Bob Parsons' Elephant Hunt Sparks Outrage," *Huffington Post*, March 31, 2011, *www.huffingtonpost.com.*

37. "GoDaddy CEO Elephant Shooting Video Spurs Competitor, Namecheap, to Raise $20,000 For Conservation Group," *Huffington Post*, April 7, 2011, *www.huffingtonpost.com.*

38. CITES stands for Convention on International Trade in Endangered Species.

39. This approach, called the Community Areas Management Programme for Indigenous Resources, was promoted by the US Agency for International Development.

40. Wayne M. Getz, et al., "Sustaining Natural and Human Capital: Villagers and Scientists," *Science, New Series* 283, no. 5409 (March 19, 1999).

41. Louisa Lombard, "Dying for Ivory," *New York Times*, September 20, 2012.

42. For example, according to the safari business African Sky, the 2017 trophy fee for an elephant in Zimbabwe was nineteen thousand US dollars. For 2018, it will be twenty-two thousand. "Price List Zimbabwe," African Sky, accessed August 28, 2017. *www.africanskyhunting.co.za/pricelist-zim.html.*

43. Quoted in Allan Richards, "The Elephant War," *UTNE Reader* (November–December 1996): 1.

44. In addition to reducing poaching, the CAMPFIRE system provides financial resources for some of the poorest people in the world. Haru Mutasa reports in Al Jazeera (March 24, 2010): "Daster Chisungo, the chief of a village in the Zambezi Valley near the Zambian border, says he has managed to build a local high school and clinic from the proceeds over the years. The hunters mainly want the head of the animal as a trophy—everything else goes to the community." Haru Mutasa, "Zimbabwe's Elephant Challenge," Al Jazeera, March 24, 2010, *www.aljazeera.com.*

45. We are not so naïve as to be unaware that some killing of elephants is required for herd management.

46. Quoted in Richards, "The Elephant War," 1.

47. Admittedly, we are speculating somewhat about the demography of elephant hunters, but surely we are not far from the mark. With permits costing tens of thousands of dollars, we can at least be confident that few of them are poor.

CHAPTER 9

1. Some of this discussion comes from Mark's article "How White Was My Prairie."

2. Michael Dorris, *The Broken Cord* (New York: Harper Perennial, 1990).

3. "Alcohol Effects on a Fetus—Topic Overview," WebMD, *www.webmd.com/baby/tc/ alcohol-effects-on-a-fetus-topic-overview#1*. Accessed August 8, 2017.

4. This is a point that Rickie Solinger makes in both *Wake Up Little Susie* (New York: Routledge), chapter 1 and elsewhere, and in *Beggars and Choosers* (New York: Hill and Wang, 2001), chapter 4 and elsewhere.

5. William Easterly, *The Elusive Quest for Growth: Economists' Adventures and Misadventures in the Tropics* (Cambridge, MA: MIT Press, 2001).

6. We are not saying what an ideal world would look like, nor even what the ideal set of complete family policies would be.

7. Save the Children, *International Adoption*, 1.

8. Romeo Dallaire, *Shake Hands with the Devil* (New York: Carol and Graff Publishers, 2003), 2.

9. Ibid., 4.

10. Ibid.

11. We should note, however, that after the genocide, a plea went out to Rwandans to take in genocide orphans, and some unknown number were informally adopted.

12. Dallaire, *Shake Hands with the Devil*, 4.

BIBLIOGRAPHY

Abrue, Domingos. "Baby-Bearing Storks." In *International Adoption: Global Inequalities and the Circulation of Children*, edited by Diana Marre and Laura Briggs, 134–153. New York: New York University Press, 2009.

Aitken, Lee. "The High Price of a Baby's Love." *Money* 21, no. 1 (January 1992): 98–113.

Alber, Erdmute. "'The Real Parents are the Foster Parents': Social Parent Hood among the Baatombu in Northern Benin." In Bowie, *Cross-Cultural Practices in Adoption*, 33–47.

Albertus, Latiefa, and Julia Sloth-Nielsen. "Relocation Decisions: Do Culture, Language and Religion Matter in the Rainbow Nation?" *Journal of Family Law and Practice* 1, no. 2 (Autumn 2010): 86–97.

Aleksander, Irina. "Cold War Kids: The International Dispute Over Russia's Orphans." *Harper's Magazine*, October 2013.

Ambrose, Michael W., and Anna Mary Coburn. *Report on Intercountry Adoption in Romania*. Prepared for the US Agency for International Development in Romania, January 22, 2001. *pdf.usaid.gov/pdf_docs/Pnacw989.pdf.*

Argys, Laura, and Brian Duncan. "Economic Incentives and Foster Child Placement." *Southern Economic Journal* 74, no. 1 (July 2007): 114–42.

Baccara, Mariagiovanna, Allan Collard-Wexler, Leonardo Felli, and Leeat Yariv. "Child-Adoption Matching: Preferences for Gender and Race." *American Economic Journal: Applied Economics* 6, no. 3 (July 2014): 133–58.

Bachman, Ronald D., ed. *Romania: A Country Study*. Washington, DC: Federal Research Division, Library of Congress, 1989. *www.loc.gov/item/90006449.*

Bainham, Andrew. "International Adoption from Romania—Why the Moratorium Should Not Be Ended." *Child and Family Law Quarterly* 15 (2003) 223–36.

Balcom, Karen. *The Traffic in Babies: Cross-Border Adoption and Baby-Selling Between the United States and Canada, 1930–1972*. Toronto: University of Toronto Press, 2011.

Bartholet, Elizabeth. *Family Bonds: Adoption, Infertility and the New World of Child Production* Boston: Beacon Press, 1999.

———. "Intergenerational Justice for Children: Restructuring Adoption, Reproduction and Child Welfare Policy." *Law, Ethics, and Human Rights* 8, no. 1 (2014): 103–30.

————. "International Adoption: The Human Rights Position." *Global Policy* 1, no. 1 (January 2010): 91–100.

————. "International Adoption: Thoughts on the Human Rights Issues." *Buffalo Human Rights Law Review* 13 (2007): 152–203.

————. "Where Do Black Children Belong: The Politics of Race Matching in Adoption." *University of Pennsylvania Law Review* 139, no. 5 (May 1991): 1163–256.

Bate, Robert. "Without DDT, Malaria Bites Back." *Spiked*, April 24, 2001. *www.spiked-online.com/newsite/article/11697#.WYI3mIgrJPY.*

Bates, A. W. *The Anatomy of Robert Knox.* Brighton, UK: Sussex Academic Press, 2010.

Becker, Gary S., Kevin M. Murphy, and Michael Grossman. "The Economic Theory of Illegal Goods: The Case of Drugs." Working Paper 10976, National Bureau of Economic Research, December 2004. *www.nber.org/papers/w10976.*

Belto, Danielle C. "3 Black Adoptees on Racial Identity After Growing Up in White Homes." *Root*, January 27, 2015. *www.theroot.com/3-black-adoptees-on-racial-identity-after-growing-up-in-1790858603.*

Black, David R., and Shona Bezanso. "The Olympic Games, Human Rights, and Democratization: Lessons from Seoul and Implications for Beijing." *Third World Quarterly* 25, no. 7 (2004): 1245–61.

Blumenson, Eric, and Eva Nilsen. "No Rational Basis: The Pragmatic Case for Marijuana Law Reform." *Virginia Journal of Social Policy and the Law* 17, no. 1 (Fall 2009): 43–82.

Bolick, Clint. "The Wrongs We Are Doing Native American Children." *Newsweek*, November 2, 2015. *www.newsweek.com.*

Bowie, Fiona, ed. *Cross-Cultural Practices in Adoption.* New York: Routledge, 2004.

Breslau, Karen. "Overplanned Parenthood: Ceausescu's Cruel Law." *Newsweek*, January 22, 1990.

Briggs, Laura. *Somebody's Children: The Politics of Transracial and Transnational Adoption.* Durham, NC: Duke University Press, 2012.

Bruening, Marijike, and John Ishiyama. "The Politics of Intercountry Adoption: Explaining Variation in the Legal Requirements of Sub-Saharan African Countries." *Perspectives on Politics* 7, no. 1 (March 2009): 89–101.

Buck, Pearl S. "I Am a Better Woman for Having My Two Black Children." *Today's Health*, January 1972. Retrieved from Adoption History Project, University of Oregon. *darkwing.uoregon.edu/~adoption/archive/BuckIBW.htm.*

Bunkers, Kelly McCreery, Victor Groza, and Daniel P. Lauer. "International Adoption and Child Protection in Guatemala: A Case of the Tail Wagging the Dog." *International Social Work* 52, no. 5 (2009): 649–60.

Burtless, Gary, ed. *Does Money Matter?* Washington, DC: Brookings Institution Press, 1996.

Cantwell, Nigel. *The Best Interests of the Child in Intercountry Adoption*. Innocenti Insight. Florence: UNICEF Office of Research, 2014. *www.unicef-irc.org/publications/712*.

Carroll, Andrea B. "Reregulating the Baby Market: A Call for a Ban on Payment of Birth-Mother Living Expenses." *University of Kansas Law Review* 59, no. 2 (January 2011): 285–329.

Chaudhary, Jeffrey, Michael Kremer, Karthik Muralidharan, and F. Halsey Rogers. "Missing in Action: Teacher and Health Worker Absence in Developing Countries." *Journal of Economic Perspectives* 20, no. 1 (Winter 2006): 91–116.

Cobett, Sara. "Where Do Babies Come From?" *New York Times Magazine*, June 16, 2002.

Compton, Rebecca J. *Adoption Beyond Borders: How International Adoption Benefits Children*. Oxford: Oxford University Press, 2016.

Conn, Peter. *Pearl S. Buck: A Cultural Biography*. Cambridge: Cambridge University Press, 1996.

Custer, Charlie. "Kidnapped and Sold: Inside the Dark World of Child Trafficking in China." *Atlantic*, July 5, 2013. *www.theatlantic.com/china/archive/2013/07/kidnapped-and-sold-inside-the-dark-world-of-child-trafficking-in-china/278107*.

Dales, John H. *Pollution, Property and Prices: An Essay in Policy Making and Economics*. Toronto: University of Toronto Press, 1968.

Dallaire, Romeo. *Shake Hands with the Devil*. New York: Carol and Graff Publishers, 2003.

Darcher, Jack. "Market Forces in Domestic Adoption: Advocating a Quantitative Limit on Private Agency Adoption Fees." *Journal for Social Justice* 8, no. 2 (Spring/Summer 2010): 729–72.

Davis, Mary Ann. *Children for Families or Families for Children: The Demography of Adoption Behavior in the US*. New York: Springer, 2011.

Denechere, Yves, and Beatrice Scutaru. "International Adoption of Romanian Children and Romania's Admission to the European Union." *Eastern Journal of European Studies* 1, no. 1 (June 2010): 135–51.

DePrince, Michaela, and Elaine DePrince. *Taking Flight: From War Orphan to Star Ballerina*. New York: Alfred A. Knopf, 2014.

Derezotes, Denneretee M., John Poertner, and Mark F. Testa, eds. *Race Matters in Child Welfare: The Overrepresentation of African American Children in the System*. Washington, DC: Child Welfare League of America Press, 2004.

Dillon, Sara. "Making Legal Regimes for Intercountry Adoption Reflect Human Rights Principles: Transforming the United Nations Convention on the Rights of the Child with the Hague Convention on Intercountry Adoption." *Boston University International Law Journal* 1 (Fall 2003): 179–259.

Dorow, Sara. *Transnational Adoption: A Cultural Economy of Race, Gender, and Kinship*. New York: New York University Press, 2006.

Dorris, Michael. *The Broken Cord.* New York: Harper Perennial, 1990.

Drimmer, Edward, ed. *Captured by the Indians: 15 Firsthand Accounts 1750–1870.* New York: Dover Publications, 1967.

Dubinsky, Karen. *Babies without Borders: Adoption and Migration across the Americas.* Toronto: University of Toronto Press, 2010.

Easterly, William. *The Elusive Quest for Growth: Economists' Adventures and Misadventures in the Tropics.* Cambridge, MA: MIT Press, 2001.

Eyckmans, Johan, and Snoore Kverndokk. "Moral Considerations in Trading Pollution Permits." HUB Research Paper 2008/12, Hogeschool-Universitat Brussells, February 2008.

Fanshel, David. *Far from the Reservation.* Lanham, MD: Scarecrow Press Inc., 1972.

Feiling, Tom. *Cocaine Nation: How the White Trade Took Over the World.* New York: Pegasus Books, 2009.

Ferguson, Niall. *The Ascent of Money.* New York: Penguin Books, 2008.

Fessler, Anne. *The Girls Who Went Away: The Hidden History of Women Who Surrendered Children for Adoption in the Decades Before Roe v. Wade.* New York: Penguin Books, 2007.

Fieweger, Mary Ellen. "Stolen Children and International Adoptions." *Child Welfare* 70, no. 2 (March/April 1991): 285–91.

Fitzhugh, George. *Cannibals All!; or, Slaves Without Masters.* Richmond, VA: A. Morris, 1857.

———. *Sociology of the South; or, The Failure of Free Society.* Richmond, VA: A. Morris, 1854. Accessed May 29, 2013 from University of North Carolina-Chapel Hill, Documenting the South: Library of Southern Literature. *docsouth.unc.edu/southlit/fitzhughsoc/menu.html.*

Fonseca, Claudia. "An Unexpected Reversal: Charting the Course of International Adoption in Brazil." *Adoption and Fostering Journal* 26, no. 3 (2002) 28–39.

———. "An Unexpected Reversal: The 'Demise' of International Adoption in Brazil." Translated by Carolyn Brisset. *Dados-Revista de Ciências Sociais* 49, no. 1 (2007): 41–66.

———. "Inequality Near and Far: Adoption as Seen from the Brazilian Favelas." *Law and Society Review.* Special Issue, *Nonbiological Parenting* 36, no. 2 (2002): 397–432.

———. "The Politics of Adoption: Child Rights in the Brazilian Setting." *Law and Policy* 24, no. 3 (September 2002): 199–227.

Forbes, Jack D. "Blood Quantum: A Relic of Racism and Termination." Native Intelligence. A Column from the Department of Native American Studies, University of California–Davis, November 27, 2000. Accessed March 29, 2014. *www.weyanoke.org/reading/jdf-BloodQuantum.html.*

Freeman, Michael. "Culture, Childhood and Rights." *Family in Law Review* 5, no. 15 (2011): 16–33.

Fruendlich, Madelyn. *The Market Forces in Adoption*. Vol. 2 of *Adoption and Ethics*. New York: Donaldson Adoption Institute, 2000.

Fryer, Roland, Paul Heaton, Steven Levitt, and Kevin Murphy. "Measuring Crack Cocaine and Its Impact." *Economic Inquiry* 51, no. 3 (July 2013): 1651–81.

Getz, Wayne M., Louise Fortmann, David Cumming, Johan du Toit, Jodi Hilty, Rowan Martin, Michael Murphree, Norman Owen-Smith, Anthony M. Starfield, and Michael I. Westphal. "Sustaining Natural and Human Capital: Villagers and Scientists." *Science, New Series* 283, no. 5409 (March 19, 1999):1855–6.

Ghods, Ahad, and Shekoufeh Savaj. "Iranian Model of Paid and Regulated Living-Unrelated Kidney Donation." *Clinical Journal of the American Society of Nephrology* 1, no. 6 (November 2006): 1136–45.

Gibbons, Judith L., and Karen Smith Rotabi, eds. *Intercountry Adoption: Practices, Policies and Outcomes*. Burlington, VT: Ashgate, 2012.

Glazer, Sarah. "Adoption: Do Current Policies Punish Kids Awaiting Adoption?" *CQ Researcher* 3, no. 44 (November 26, 1993). *library.cqpress.com/cqresearcher/cqresrre1993112600.*

Goodin, Robert E. "Selling Environmental Indulgences." *Kyklos* 47, no. 4 (1994): 573–96.

Goodwin, Michele Bratcher, ed. *Baby Markets: Money and the New Politics of Creating Families*. Cambridge: Cambridge University Press, 2010.

Goody, Esther. *Parenthood and Social Reproduction: Fostering and Occupational Roles in West Africa*. Cambridge: Cambridge University Press, 1982.

Graff, E. J. "The Baby Business." *Democracy: A Journal of Ideas*, no. 17 (Summer 2010). *democracyjournal.org/magazine/17/the-baby-business.*

———. "Call It Trafficking," *American Prospect*, January 3, 2013.

Greene, Melissa Fay. *There Is No Me Without You*. New York: Bloomsbury USA, 2007.

Hague Conference on Private International Law. *Convention on Protection of Children and Co-operation in Respect of Intercountry Adoption, Concluded 29 May 1993*. The Hague: HCCH, 1993. *www.hcch.net/en/instruments/conventions/full-text/?cid=69.*

Hansen, Mary E. "Using Subsidies to Promote the Adoption of Children from Foster Care." *Journal of Family Economic Issues* 28, no. 3 (September 2007): 377–93.

Hansen, Mary E., and Bradley A. Hansen. "The Economics of Children from Foster Care." *Child Welfare* 85 no. 3 (May/June 2006): 559–83.

Harris, Marian S. *Racial Disproportionality in Child Welfare*. New York: Columbia University Press, 2014.

Hart, Carl. *High Price: A Neuroscientist's Journey of Self Discovery that Challenges Everything You Know about Drugs and Society*. New York: Harper Collins, 2013.

Hatzfield, Jean. *The Killers of Rwanda Speak*. Translated by Linda Coverdale. New York: Farrar, Straus and Giroux, 2006.

——. *Life Laid Bare: The Survivors of Rwanda Speak*. Translated by Linda Coverdale. New York: Farrar, Straus and Giroux, 2006.

Herman, Ellen. *Kinship by Design*. Chicago: University of Chicago Press, 2008.

Holmlund, Helena, Sandra McNally, and Martina Viarengo. "Does Money Matter for Schools?" *Economics of Education Review* 29, no. 6 (December 2010): 1154–64.

Howard, Alicia, David D. Royse, and John A. Skerl. "Transracial Adoption: The Black Community Perspective." *Social Work* 22, no. 3 (May 1977): 184–9.

Hubinette, Tobias. "The Adoption Issue in Korea: Diaspora in the Age of Globalization." *Stockholm Journal of East Asian Studies* 12 (2000): 141–53.

———. *Comforting an Orphan Nation: Representations of International Adoption and Adopted Koreans in Korean Popular Culture*. Stockholm: Stockholm University, Department of Oriental Languages, 2005.

———. "From Orphan Trains to Babylifts." In Trenka, Oparah, and Shin, *Outsiders Within*, 139–50.

———. "Post-Racial Utopianism, White Color-Blindness and 'the Elephant in the Room': Racial Issues for Transnational Adoptees of Color." In Gibbons and Rotabi, *Intercountry Adoption*, 231–2.

Hughes, Virginia. "Detachment: Can Research on Romanian Orphans be Ethical?" *Aeon Magazine*, May 12, 2014.

Independent Group for International Adoption Analysis. *Final Report: Re-Organizing the International Adoption System and Child Protection System*. Bucharest: IGIAA, March 2002.

Inglehart, Ronald, and Hans-Dieter Klingemann. "Genes, Culture, Democracy and Happiness." In *Culture and Subjective Well-Being*, edited by Edward Diener and Eunkook M. Suh, 165–83. Cambridge, MA: MIT Press, 2000.

Jacobson, Heather. *Culture Keeping: White Mothers, International Adoption, and the Negotiation of Family Difference*. Nashville, TN: Vanderbilt University Press, 2008.

Johnson, Dana E. "Thirty Years of International Adoption: Lessons Learned." Presentation to the Putting Family First Conference, Sponsored by the Joint Council on International Children's Services and the Adoption Council, Arlington, VA, June 22–24, 2015.

Johnson, Kay. *Wanting a Daughter, Needing a Son*. St. Paul, MN: Yeong and Yeong Books, 2004.

Jones, Hugh R. "The Perils and Protection of Infant Life." *Journal of the Royal Statistical Society* 57, no. 1 (March 1894): 1–103.

Joyce, Kathryn. *The Child Catchers: Rescue, Trafficking, and the New Gospel of Adoption*. New York: Public Affairs, 2013.

Juffer, Femmie, and Marinus H. van IJzenborn. "Adoptees Do Not Lack Self-Esteem: A Meta-Analysis of Studies on Self-Esteem of Transracial, International, and Domestic Adoptees." *Psychological Bulletin* 133, no. 6 (2007): 1067–83.

———. "Behavior Problems and Mental Health Referrals of International Adoptees." *Journal of the American Medical Association* 293, no. 20 (May 25, 2005): 2501–15.

Kapstein, Ethan B. "The Baby Trade." *Foreign Affairs* 82, no. 6 (Nov–Dec 2003): 115–25.

Kim, Eleana. *Adopted Territory: Transnational Korean Adoptees and the Politics of Belonging*. Durham, NC: Duke University Press, 2005.

Kim, Gina. "International Adoption's Trafficking Problem." *Harvard Political Review*, June 20, 2012. *harvardpolitics.com/world/international-adoptions-trafficking-problem*.

Klein, George. *The Adventure: The Quest for My Romanian Babies*. Lanham, MD: University Press of America, 2007.

Krawiec, Kimberley D. "Altruism and Intermediation in the Market for Babies." *Washington and Lee Law Review* 66 (2009): 203–57.

———. "Price and Pretense in Baby Markets." In Goodwin, *Baby Markets*, 41–55.

Kroll, Joe. "Testimony before United States Commission on Civil Rights." Testimony on behalf of the North American Council on Adoptable Children, September 21, 2007. *www.nacac.org/policy/Sept07CivilRightsTestimony.pdf*.

Landes, Elaine, and Richard Posner. "The Economics of the Baby Shortage." *Journal of Legal Studies* 7, no. 2 (June 1978): 323–48.

Lataianu, Camelia Manuela. "Social Protection of Children in Public Care in Romania from the Perspective of EU Integration." *International Journal of Law Policy and the Family* 17, no. 1 (April 2003): 99–120.

Layard, Richard. "Has Social Science a Clue?: What is Happiness? Are We Getting Happier?" Lionel Robbins Memorial Lecture Series, London, March 3–5, 2003.

Leventhal, Todd. *The Child Organ Trafficking Rumor: A Modern "Urban Legend."* Report Submitted to the United Nations Special Rapporteur on the Sale of Children, Child Prostitution, and Child Pornography. Washington, DC: United States Information Agency, December 1994.

Levitt, Steven D., and Stephen J. Dubner. *Freakonomics*. New York: William Morrow, 2005.

Lyslo, Arnold. "Background on Indian Adoption Project." In Briggs, *Somebody's Children*, 36–7.

Maddison, Angus. *Growth and Interaction in the World Economy*. Cambridge, MA: AEI Press, 2004.

Maldonado, Solangel. "Race, Culture, and Adoption: Lessons from *Mississippi Band of Choctaw Indians v. Holyfield.*" *Columbia Journal of Gender and Law* 17, no. 1 (2008): 2010–30.

Marotte, Mary Ruth, Paige Reynolds, and Ralph Savarese, eds. *Papa, PhD: Essays on Fatherhood in the Academy*. New Brunswick, NJ: Rutgers University Press, 2010.

Maskew, Trish. "Child Trafficking and Intercountry Adoption: The Cambodian Experience." *Cumberland Law Review* 35, no. 3 (2004/2005): 619–38.

Matsumoto, Valerie J., and Blake Allmendinger, eds. *Over the Edge: Remapping the American West*. Berkeley: University of California Press, 1999.

McGinnis, Hollee, Susan Livingston Smith, Scott D. Ryan, and Jeanne A. Howard. *Beyond Culture Camp: Promoting Healthy Identity Formation in Adoption*. New York: Evan B. Donaldson Adoption Institute, November 2009. *www.adoptioninstitute.org/wp-content/uploads/2013/12/2009_11_BeyondCultureCamp.pdf*.

McRoy, Ruth G., and Louis A. Zurcher Jr. *Transracial and Inracial Adoptees: The Adolescent Years*. Springfield, IL: Charles C. Thomas, 1983.

Meier, Patricia J., and Xiaole Zhang. "Sold into Adoption: The Hunan Baby Trafficking Scandal Exposes Vulnerabilities in Chinese Adoptions to the United States." *Cumberland Law Review* 39, no. 1 (2008/2009): 87–130.

Melosh, Barbara. *Strangers and Kin*. Cambridge, MA: Harvard University Press, 2002.

Melvern, Linda. *Conspiracy to Murder: The Rwandan Genocide*. London: New Left Press, 2006.

Meyer, Melissa L. "American Indian Blood Quantum Requirements: Blood Is Thicker than Family." In Matsumoto and Allmendinger, *Over the Edge*, 231–49.

Miguel, Edward, and Michael Kremer. "Worms: Identifying Impacts on Education and Health in the Presence of Treatment Externalities." *Econometrica* 72, no. 1 (January 2004): 159–217.

Milton, Sybil. "Non-Jewish Children in the Camps." Museum of Tolerance Multimedia Learning Center Online (annual 5, chapter 2), Simon Wiesenthal Center. Accessed June 3, 2013. *motlc.wiesenthal.com*.

Miron, Jeffrey A. *The Budgetary Implications of Marijuana Prohibition*. Report Funded by the Marijuana Policy Project, June 2005. *www.cannabis-commerce.com/library/Miron_Report_2005.pdf*.

Miron, Jeffrey A., and Jeffrey Zwiebel. "The Economic Case against Drug Prohibition." *Journal of Economic Perspectives* 9, no. 4 (Fall 1995): 175–92.

Montgomery, Mark. "How White Was My Prairie." In Marotte, Reynold, and Savarese, *Papa, PhD*, 88–94.

Nadeau, Robert L. "The Economist Has No Clothes." *Scientific American*, May 2008.

National Coalition for Child Protection Reform. *Spending So Much More, Getting So Much Less: The Numbers Tell the Story*. Accessed April 17, 2014. *www.nccpr.org/reports/RIdataataglance95472ri19.pdf*.

Naughton, Dana. "Exiting or Going Forth? An Overview of USA Outgoing Adoptions." In Gibbons and Rotabi, *Intercountry Adoption*, 161–71.

Nedclu, Christina, and Victor Groza. "Child Welfare in Romania: Contexts and Processes." In Gibbons and Rotabi, *Intercountry Adoption*, 91–102.

Nersessian, David. "Rethinking Cultural Genocide under International Law." *Human Rights Dialogue: Cultural Rights* (Spring 2005), Carnegie Council for Ethics in International Affairs.

Nicholas, Lynn H. *Cruel World: The Children of Europe in the Nazi Web.* New York: Alfred A. Knopf, 2005.

Nicholson, Emma. *The Secret Society: Inside and Outside the Conservative Party.* London: Indigo, 1996.

Notermans, Catrien. "Fosterage and the Politics of Marriage and Kinship in East Cameroon." In Bowie, *Cross-Cultural Practices in Adoption*, 48–63.

Okrent, Daniel. *Last Call: The Rise and Fall of Prohibition.* New York: Scribner, 2010.

Oreskovic, Johanna, and Trish Maskew. "Red Thread or Slender Reed: Deconstructing Prof. Bartholet's Mythology of International Adoption." *Buffalo Human Rights Lew Review* 147 (2008): 71–128.

Pelton, Robert Young. *The Hunter, the Hammer, and Heaven.* Guilford, CT: Lyons Press, 2002.

Pertman, Adam. *Adoption Nation.* 2nd ed. Boston: Harvard Common Press, 2011.

Peterson, Scott. *Me Against My Brother: At War in Somalia, Sudan and Rwanda.* New York: Routledge, 2001.

Philips, Sloan. "The Indian Child Welfare Act in the Face of Extinction." *American Indian Law Review* 21, no. 2 (1997): 351–64.

Pigou, Arthur. *The Economics of Welfare.* New York: Macmillan, 1920.

Piotrowski, Tadeusz. *Poland's Holocaust: Ethnic Strife, Collaboration with Occupying Forces and Genocide in the Second Republic, 1918–1947.* Jefferson, NC: McFarland and Co., 1998.

Pinderhughes, Ellen, Jessica Matthews, Georgia Deoudes, and Adam Pertman. *A Changing World: Shaping Practices through Understanding of the New Realities of Intercountry Adoption.* New York: Donaldson Adoption Institute, October 2013. *www.adoptioninstitute.org/old/publications/2013_10_AChangingWorld.pdf.*

Posner, Richard A. "The Regulation of the Market in Adoptions." *Boston University Law Review* 67 (1987): 59–72.

Post, Roelie. *Romania For Export Only: The Untold Story of Romanian "Orphans."* Hoekstra Drukkerij: Sint Annaparochie, Netherlands, 2007. Kindle edition.

POV. "First Person Plural." Written and directed by Deann Borshay Liem. PBS (Dec. 18, 2000, (premiere broadcast). *www.pbs.org/pov/firstpersonplural.*

Quiroz, Pamela Anne. *Adoption in a Color-Blind Society.* Lanham, MD: Rowman and Littlefield, 2007.

Radin, Margaret Jane. "Market-Inalienability." *Harvard Law Review* 100 (June 1987): 174–94.

Richards, Allan. "The Elephant War." *UTNE Reader,* November–December 1996.

Riley, Mark. *Baseline Study: The State of Institutional Care in Uganda*. Report for Uganda Ministry of Gender, Labour and Social Development, June 2012. *www.alternative-care-uganda.org/resources/moglsd-baseline-study-institutional-care-in-uganda-june-2012.pdf.*

Roberts, Dorothy. *Shattered Bonds: The Color of Child Welfare*. New York: Basic Books, 2001.

Roberts, Gesue Gebrier. *Zammie Town to Zwedru: A Memoir of Village Childhood in Liberia*. Tamarc, FL: Llumina Press, 2011.

Roberts, Ryan, Gordon Hanson, Derek Cornwell, and Scott Borger. "An Analysis of Migrant Smuggling Costs along the Southwest Border." Working Paper, Office of Immigration Statistics, Department of Homeland Security, Washington, DC, November 2010. *www.dhs.gov/xlibrary/assets/statistics/publications/ois-smuggling-wp.pdf.*

Roby, Jin, and Trish Maskew. "Human Rights Considerations in Intercountry Adoption: The Children and Families of Cambodia and the Marshall Islands." In Gibbons and Rotabi, *Intercountry Adoption,* 55–66.

Roby, Jini L., and Stacey A. Shaw. "The African Orphan Crisis and International Adoption." *Social Work* 51, no. 3 (2006): 199–210.

Root, Veronica S. "Angelina and Madonna: Why All the Fuss? An Exploration of the Rights of the Child and Intercountry Adoption within African Nations." *Chicago Journal of International Law* 8, no. 1 (Summer 2007): 323–54.

Rotabi, Karen Smith. "Fraud in Intercountry Adoption: Child Sales and Abduction in Vietnam, Guatemala and Cambodia." In Gibbons and Rotabi, *Intercountry Adoption,* 67–76.

Roth, Alvin E. "Repugnance as a Constraint on Markets." *Journal of Economic Perspectives* 21, no. 3 (2007): 37–58.

Rothman, Barbara Katz. "Motherhood under Capitalism." In *Consuming Motherhood,* edited by Janelle Taylor and Linda Layne, 19–30. New Brunswick, NJ: Rutgers University Press, 2014.

———. *Weaving a Family: Untangling Race and Adoption*. Boston: Beacon Press, 2005.

Rothschild, Matthew. "Babies for Sale: South Koreans Make Them, Americans Buy Them." *Progressive,* January 1988.

Sachs, Jeffrey, and Pia Malaney. "The Economic and Social Burden of Malaria." *Nature* 145 (February 7, 2002): 680–5.

Sandel, Michael. *What Money Can't Buy: The Moral Limits of Markets*. New York: Farrar, Straus and Giroux, 2012.

Save the Children, Child Protection Initiative. *International Adoption*. Policy Brief, June 2012. *resourcecentre.savethechildren.net/node/6250/pdf/6250.pdf.*

Schoenmaker, Christie, Femmie Juffer, Marinus H. van IJzendorn, and Marian J. Bakermans-Kranenberg. "Does Family Matter? The Well-Being of Children Growing

Up in Institutions, Foster Care and Adoption." In *The Handbook of Child Well-Being: Theories, Methods and Policies in Global Perspective*, edited by Asher Ben-Arieh, Ferran Casas, Ivar Frønes, and Jill E. Corbin, 2197–228. New York: Springer Science and Business Media, 2014.

Selman, Peter. "Global Trends in Intercountry Adoption: 2001–2010." *Adoption Advocate* (A Publication of the National Council for Adoption) no. 44 (February 1, 2012). *www.adoptioncouncil.org/images/stories/documents/NCFA_ADOPTION_ADVOCATE_ NO44.pdf.*

———. *Key Tables for Intercountry Adoption: Receiving States 2003–2012; States of Origin 2003–2011*, March 26, 2014. *www.hcch.net/upload/selmanstats33.pdf.*

Shireman, Joan, and Penny Johnson. "A Longitudinal Study of Black Adoptions: Single Parent, Transracial, and Traditional." *Social Work* (May 1, 1986): 172–6.

Siegal, Erin. *Finding Fernanda*. Boston: Beacon Press Books, 2011.

———. *The US Embassy Cables: Adoption Fraud in Guatemala 1987–2010*. Oakland, CA: Cathexis Press, 2011.

Silverman, Arnold R. "Outcomes of Transracial Adoption." *Adoption* 3, no. 1 (Spring 1993): 104–18.

Simon, Rita J., Howard Altstein, and Marygold S. Melli. *The Case for Transracial Adoption*. Washington, DC: American University Press, 1994.

Simon, Rita J., and Howard Altstein. *Adoption Across Borders: Serving the Children in Transracial and Intercountry Adoptions*. Lanham, MD: Rowman and Littlefield, 2000.

———. *Adoption, Race, and Identity: From Infancy Through Adolescence*. New York: Praeger, 1989.

———. *Transracial Adoption*. Hoboken, NJ: John Wiley and Sons, 1977.

Smith, Darron T., Brenda G. Juarez, and Cardell K. Jacobson. "White on Black: Can White Parents Teach Black Adoptive Children to Understand and Cope with Racism?" *Journal of Black Studies* 42, no. 8 (2011): 1195–230.

Smolin, David M. "Child Laundering: How the Intercountry Adoption System Legitimizes and Incentivizes the Practices of Buying, Trafficking, Kidnaping, and Stealing Children." *Wayne Law Review* 52, no. 1 (2006): 113–200.

———. "Intercountry Adoption as Child Trafficking." *Valparaiso Law Review* 39, no. 2 (2004/2005): 281–325.

Solinger, Rickie. *Beggars and Choosers: How the Politics of Choice Shapes Adoption, Abortion, and Welfare*. New York: Hill and Wang, 2001.

———. *Wake Up Little Susie: Single Pregnancy and Race before Roe v. Wade*. New York: Routledge, 1991.

Spar, Deborah. *The Baby Business: How Money, Science, and Politics Drive the Commerce of Conception*. Cambridge, MA: Harvard Business School Press, 2006.

Stanley, Mary Lyndon. *Making Babies, Making Families*. Boston: Beacon Press, 2001.

Straus, Scott. *The Order of Genocide: Race, Power, and War in Rwanda*. Ithaca, NY: Cornell University Press, 2008. Kindle edition.

Strong, Pauline. "What is an Indian Family? The Indian Child Welfare Act and the Renascence of Tribal Sovereignty." *American Studies* 46, no. 3 (Fall 2005/Spring 2006): 205–31.

Stuy, Brian H. "Open Secret: Cash and Coercion in China's International Adoption Program." *Cumberland Law Review* 44, no. 3 (October 2014) 315–416.

Talle, Aud. "Adoption Practices Among the Pastoral Maasai of East Africa." In Bowie, *Cross-Cultural Practices in Adoption*, 64–78.

Thomas, Jeffrey. "Congressional Resolution Urges Romania to Amend Adoption Ban." *Washington File* (April 11, 2006). *news.findlaw.com/wash/s/20060411/200604111238591.html*.

Trenka, Jans Jeong, Julia Chinyere Oparah, and Sun Yung Sin, eds. *Outsiders Within: Writing on Transracial Adoption*. Cambridge, MA: South End Press, 2006.

Trials of War Criminals Before the Nuremberg Military Tribunal, Vol. 4. Washington, DC: US Government Printing Office, 1950. *www.loc.gov/rr/frd/Military_Law/pdf/NT_war-criminals_Vol-IV.pdf*.

Turner, Chad. "Sometimes It Is Better Not to Be Unique: The U.S. Department of State View on Intercountry Adoption and Child Trafficking and Why It Should Change." *Duke Forum for Law and Social Change* 6, no. 91 (2014): 91–112.

UNICEF. *Africa's Orphaned Generations*. New York: UNICEF, November 2003. *www.unicef.org/sowc06/pdfs/africas_orphans.pdf*.

———. *Child Trafficking in East and South-East Asia: Reversing the Trend*. Bangkok: UNICEF East Asia and Pacific Regional Office, August 2009. *www.unicef.org/eapro/Unicef_EA_SEA_Trafficking_Report_Aug_2009_low_res.pdf*.

US Commission on Civil Rights. *The Multiethnic Placement Act: Minority Children in Foster Care and Adoption*. Washington, DC: USCCR, July 2010.

US General Accounting Office. *Drug Abuse: The Crack Cocaine Epidemic—Health Consequences and Treatment*, HRD-91-55FS. Washington, DC: US General Accounting Office, 1991.

US State Department. *Trafficking in Persons Report*. 10th ed. Washington, DC: US State Department, June 2010. *www.state.gov/documents/organization/142979.pdf*.

Van Oss, Adriaan C. *Catholic Colonialism: A Parish History of Guatemala, 1524–1821*. Cambridge Latin American Studies. Cambridge: Cambridge University Press, 2004.

Voigt, Kevin. "International Adoption: Saving Orphans or Child Trafficking?" *CNN* US Edition (September 18, 2013). *www.cnn.com/2013/09/16/world/international-adoption-saving-orphans-child-trafficking/index.html*.

Volkman, Toby Alice. "Embodying Chinese Culture: Transnational Adoption in North America." In *Cultures of Transnational Adoption*, edited by Toby Alice Volkman, 81–114. Durham, NC: Duke University Press, 2005.

Waugh, Benjamin. "Child-Life Insurance." *Contemporary Review* 58 (July 1890): 40–63.

Wheeler, Jacob. *Between Light and Shadow: A Guatemalan Girl's Journey through Adoption*. Lincoln: University of Nebraska Press, 2011.

Willebrandt, Mabel Walker. *The Inside of Prohibition*. Indianapolis, IN: Bobbs-Merrill Company, 1929.

World Health Organization. *World Malaria Report 2014*. Geneva: WHO Press, 2014. *www.who.int/malaria/publications/world_malaria_report-2014/en*.

Yablon-Zug, Marcia. "The Real Impact of Adoptive Couple v. Baby Girl." *Capital University Law Review* 42, no. 2 (2014): 327–60.

Zelizer, Viviana A. "The Price and Value of Children: The Case of Children's Insurance." *American Journal of Sociology* 86, no. 5 (March 1981): 1036–56.

———. *Pricing the Priceless Child*. New York: Basic Books, 1985.

Zugravescu, Alexandra, and Ana Iacovescu. "The Adoption of Children in Romania." In *Intercountry Adoptions: Laws and Perspectives of "Sending" Countries*, edited by Eliezer D. Jaffe, 42–54. Leiden: Martinus Nijoff Publishers, 1995.

INDEX